Chronicle
of the year 1995

A DORLING KINDERSLEY BOOK

Managing Editor Jane Laing
Senior Editor Lee Stacy
Editor Christina Bankes
Managing Art Editor Ruth Shane
Designers Sue Caws, Jamie Hanson, Luke Herriott, Tony Limerick,
Rebecca Willis
Production Manager Ian Paton

Editorial and design by Brown Packaging Ltd
255-257 Liverpool Road, London N1 1LX
Authors Steve Adamson, Alison Ali, Nigel Cawthorne,
John Collis, Graham McColl
Design Steve Wilson

First published in Great Britain in 1996
by Dorling Kindersley Limited,
9 Henrietta Street, London WC2E 8PS

A CIP catalogue record for this book is available from the British Library.

ISBN 0 7513 3012 4

Reproduced by Kestrel Digital Colour Ltd., Chelmsford, Essex
Printed and bound in Great Britain by The Bath Press

How to use this book

Chronicle of the Year 1995 reports the events of the year as though they had just happened. The weekly chronology summaries do not aim to cover all the most important events since these are reported in greater detail in the reports adjoining the summaries. The summaries include less important events and those leading up to the main events reported elsewhere or their consequences. These chains of development can be tracked through a system of cross-references that complements the index by pointing to the next link in the chain. Arrows indicating the next link appear at the end of the reports or summaries. They point only forward in time, but can lead to either an entry in the weekly summaries or to one of the fuller reports. They look like this: (→Feb 17).

Chronicle
of the year 1995

DORLING KINDERSLEY
LONDON · NEW YORK · STUTTGART

S	M	T	W	T	F	S
1	2	3	4	5	6	7
8	9	10	11	12	13	14
15	16	17	18	19	20	21
22	23	24	25	26	27	28
29	30	31				

Brasília, 1
Fernando Henrique Cardoso inaugurated as the president of Brazil.

Bosnia, 1
A cease-fire officially begins, amid widespread fears that it will be no more durable than its predecessors. (→ January 9)

Cairo, 2
Twelve people killed in gun battles between police and Islamic militants in the Nile Valley town of Mallawi.

Mexico City, 2
International financial markets are bracing themselves for a shock as the peso continues to totter. The crisis threatens trade links established between Mexico and the US.

Jerusalem, 3
Israeli troops shoot dead three Palestinian policemen in an accidental exchange of fire.

Colombo, 3
The Tamil Tigers, the Sri Lankan separatist guerrillas, agree a cease-fire with government forces.

Fort Lauderdale, 4
Prisoners in Florida dig a 20-m (60-ft) tunnel in an attempt to break out of gaol.

Rome, 4
The Vatican announces that the Pope will not be deterred from visiting the Philippines later this month despite death threats. (→ January 14)

Hamburg, 5
Günther Parche, the man who stabbed top women's tennis player Monica Seles, goes on trial.

London, 5
Author Martin Amis hires US literary agent Andrew Wylie, in an attempt to get $750,000 for the publishing rights to his next novel, *The Information*. (→ January 11)

Deaths
Siad Barre, former president of Somalia, aged 80, January 1.

Joe Slovo, leader of South Africa's Communist Party and long-time opponent of apartheid, January 5. (→ January 15)

Comedian Larry Grayson, aged 71, January 7.

Russians pound Grozny in new offensive

A Chechen resistance fighter darts across open ground near the Presidential Palace, the focus of Russian assaults on Grozny.

Russian forces have redoubled their efforts to take the city of Grozny, the capital of the breakaway republic of Chechnya, where Chechen rebels are holding out despite the superiority of the Russian army. Fierce hand-to-hand fighting now rages in the streets, but the situation is too chaotic to judge who has the advantage.

The Russian offensive began on December 11 amidst optimism that President Yeltsin's troops would make light work of retaking the city. Facing the superbly equipped Russian army is, effectively, only a group of lightly armed guerrillas, but they are making the Russians fight every inch of the way. The conscripts who form the bulk of the Russian army proved to have little stomach for the early fighting, and their wrecked tanks still litter the streets. Artillery bombardment also failed to subdue the rebels. Today's offensive was preceded by a massive artillery and air assault, after which tanks and special forces went in. Russian snipers took up vantage points in the centre of the city.

The objective of the russians is to capture the former Presidential Palace, symbol of Chechen resistance and site of the underground bunker that is the headquarters of separatist leader Dzhokhar Dudayev. Unconfirmed reports say he has been forced out to the suburbs of the city. In Moscow, President Yeltsin said that a main aim for 1995 was to bring peace to the republic. (→ January 19)

Breakout from Parkhurst

Three dangerous prisoners broke out of Parkhurst maximum security prison on the Isle of Wight using a forged key. They had been gone for an hour before the escape was discovered this evening.

Matthew Williams, 25, Keith Rose, 45, and Andrew Rodger, 44, copied a master key that gave them access to the exercise yard. Then, using bolt cutters taken from the prison's Vocational Training Centre, they cut through the perimeter fence. Finally, they scaled the outer wall using a ladder they had made in the prison workshop. (→ January 8)

Massachusetts, Sunday 1. Flowers on the pavement outside the abortion clinic in Brookline, where "pro-life" campaigner John Salvi shot dead two women receptionists. Salvi also sprayed bullets into an abortion clinic in Virginia before being arrested.

Astronomers stretch the universe

Scientists operating the Keck telescope situated here on Mauna Kea mountain have found a galaxy more distant than any previously known. They have prosaically named their discovery 8C 1435+63.

The new galaxy is reckoned to be 15 billion light years away. This is more than a billion light years further than anything seen before, and places it at the outer edge of the universe.

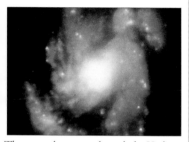

The new galaxy, seen through the Keck.

Frederick West hangs himself

Alleged serial killer Frederick West, accused of killing 12 young women, was found hanged in his maximum security cell at Winson Green prison, a month before he was due to be committed for trial. The 53-year-old builder had been arrested last February after the discovery of the body of his missing daughter in the garden of his home at 25 Cromwell Street, Gloucester.

Eight more bodies were unearthed there, and then the bodies of his first wife, Catherine, and former nanny Anne McFall, 18, were found in a field outside Gloucester. Later, the body of his daughter from his first marriage, Charmaine, who was eight when last seen in 1972, was found under the kitchen floor in the Wests' former home at Midland Street, Gloucester.

West was alone in his cell during lunchtime and took advantage of light security to hang himself. His body was found at 12.55 p.m. Prison staff tried to revive him, but he was declared dead at 1.22 p.m. He leaves his second wife, Rosemary, 41, to face several murder charges. (→ October 3)

New Congress has a different hue

The new US Congress assembles outside the Capitol building in Washington DC.

The new Congress that is to be sworn in today is very different from its predecessors. For the first time in 40 years it will be dominated by Republicans. The leader in the Senate will be Robert Dole, one of the party's best-known politicians. In the House of Representatives the new majority leader is Newton "Newt" Gingrich, whose flair for publicity and determination to stick to a clear and simple policy were key factors in the Republicans' election victories last autumn.

Gingrich now has the task of steering through the ten-point "Contract with America" that he persuaded all Republican candidates for the House to subscribe to, and which laid out a highly popular set of measures that, supposedly, everyone could understand. The Republicans are now committed to excising what they see as waste in the welfare system, to balancing the budget, to cutting taxes, and to a fierce drive against crime. Their measures may bring them into conflict with President Clinton, but Dole has no qualms about this: "We control the Congress now and we're going to set the agenda," he stated. Or, as some car stickers proclaim: "Have a Happy Newt Year!"

Marion Barry comes back from the political dead

Mayor Barry makes his inaugural speech.

Marion Barry, the former mayor of Washington DC whose political career seemed indisputably ruined after he was convicted of drugs use in 1990, returned once again to his old office. Barry has made no secret of the problems of his past, but toughness, honesty, and massive sympathy from the city's black population have enabled him to stage an amazing political comeback.

In his inauguration speech, the new mayor pledged to "bring integrity back into government", and also said that he would restore Washington's position "from the ground up". He realizes the size of the task: "We have difficult days ahead of us…And we have some difficult decisions to make."

Saatchi forced out of his agency

Maurice Saatchi today stormed out of the advertising agency he founded with his brother, sending an open letter to the staff in which he gave full vent to his feelings. "Saatchi & Saatchi has been taken over," he wrote. "No shareholder vote has been taken. But make no mistake – Saatchi & Saatchi is under new control." His anger is directed particularly at David Herro, 34-year-old American fund manager, who wanted Maurice replaced as Chairman (offering him the honorary post of Company President), and who urged the board to abandon Saatchi's share option package. The questions gripping the City are, will Saatchi set up a new company? And can he take his blue-chip clients with him?

January

S	M	T	W	T	F	S
1	2	3	4	5	6	7
8	9	10	11	12	13	14
15	16	17	18	19	20	21
22	23	24	25	26	27	28
29	30	31				

New York, 9
The trial opens of 12 Muslims, including a blind religious leader, charged with planning to blow up the World Trade Center.

Washington DC, 9
The new Senate majority leader, Robert Dole, wants the President to have to get Congressional assent before forces can be committed to any UN peace-keeping operation.

Johannesburg, 10
South Africa's top police chief is to stand down as the country's police force is overhauled because of its role in supporting apartheid.

La Jolla, California, 10
Scientists at the Scripps Research Institute have discovered a way of destroying cancers by cutting off the blood supply to them.

London, 11
Martin Amis signs a deal with publishers HarperCollins worth $700,000 for a novel and a book of short stories.

Minneapolis, 12
Malcolm X's daughter is arrested for arranging a hitman to murder Islamic separatist Louis Farrakhan, who she contends was responsible for the death of her father.

Beijing, 12
Deng Xiaoping's daughter admits that her father's health has now gone into decline.

Rome, 13
Former treasury minister, Lamberto Dini, agrees to become Italy's prime minister. Silvio Berlusconi resigned before Christmas.

Mexico City, 13
Middle-class demonstrators clash with police in protests against the country's financial crisis. (→ January 21)

Warsaw, 13
The Polish government is rocked by the resignation of foreign minister Andrzej Olechowski, who claims that the ideals of the ruling coalition are against the interests of the people.

Death
Prince Souphanouvong, the "Red Prince" of Laos, who fought against the USA with the Vietcong and Pathet Lao, January 10.

No pull-back from Sarajevo warns Mladic

PALE, BOSNIA, MONDAY 9

General Mladic, flanked by a translator and other Serb officers, at the press conference.

In the Bosnian Serb capital of Pale tonight, Ratko Mladic, commander of the Bosnian Serb forces, said that he would not withdraw his forces from around the beleaguered city of Sarajevo unless the Muslim government troops abandon territory they hold on Mount Ignam, south of the city. This the government is unlikely to do as it would mean losing all the ground they gained in their assault last autumn. The defiant stance by the Serbs threatens an already fragile cease-fire, which after only a week now appears even closer to collapse.

UN commander, General Rose, has assured General Mladic that the Muslims appear to have withdrawn from the demilitarized zone established on Mount Ignam, as was demanded by the Serbs as one of their conditions for releasing their stranglehold on access to the city. However, Mladic is now demanding complete Muslim withdrawal from all parts of the mountain, and says that until this happens his Serb forces will maintain their blockade of Bosnia's isolated capital.

Fighting also continues around Bihac in the north of Bosnia where the Bosnian government is confronting rebel Muslims who have joined nationalist Serbs from Croatia who did not agree to the earlier cease-fire. (→ January 15)

Flood devastation in California

LOS ANGELES, WEDNESDAY 11

Over $61 million dollars' worth of damage has been caused across California in the last three days by storms blowing in from the Pacific. The storms have caused floods throughout the state, affecting areas stretching from the border with Oregon down to the desert around San Bernadino.

So far the death toll has reached eight, including an 11-year-old boy who drowned while crossing a creek in Orange County, and a marine officer who was swept out to sea while on exercises.

End of daylight patrols in Belfast

BELFAST, THURSDAY 12

In a move that is seen as proof of the strength of the peace process in Northern Ireland, it was announced today that troops will be withdrawn from the streets of Belfast during daylight hours for the first time in 25 years. RUC chief constable, Sir Hugh Annesley, said that he hoped that night-time patrols could also be dropped eventually.

Soldiers will continue to be seen in daytime in some of the more volatile areas of the province such as the border areas of South Armagh. But even here it is hoped to be able to reduce the military presence in time.

"Dirty war" allegations in Spain

MADRID, TUESDAY 10

Spain's opposition parties today called for the resignation of Prime Minister Felipe González after his appearance on television last night. In a half-hour broadcast, González angrily rebuffed allegations that he and his party were involved in a "dirty war" against Basque separatists. However, he has failed to convince his critics that the government was not behind death squads that killed 28 people in attacks on Basque separatists in southwestern France in the mid-1980s.

London, Monday 9. Satirist and comedian Peter Cook, 57, dies in hospital. He rose to fame in 1959 with the revue *Beyond the Fringe*. His partner in the 1960s TV series *Not Only...But Also*, Dudley Moore, described Cook as a "creative genius".

LONDON, TUESDAY 10

Parker Bowles to divorce

Camilla Parker Bowles attempts to escape the attentions of the world's press.

The woman held to be Prince Charles' mistress, Camilla Parker Bowles, 47, is to divorce. The decision had been made by "mutual consent" after she had lived apart from her husband, Andrew, for two years.

Public speculation about her relationship with the Prince of Wales peaked last summer when Prince Charles admitted publicly that he had had an adulterous affair after his marriage had irretrievably broken down. Mrs Parker Bowles, who first met the Prince in 1970, was named as "the other woman" in Andrew Morton's bestselling biography of Princess Diana in 1992. News of the Parker Bowles divorce fuelled renewed speculation about the future of Prince Charles' own marriage. An official spokesman said: "The situation remains as it was in October 1994, when solicitors for both the Prince and Princess said jointly that there were no plans for divorce." The Church of England does not marry a divorced person during the lifetime of the former partner.

The moves for a divorce were led by Brigadier Parker Bowles, following the publication of a transcript of intimate phone calls between Mrs. Parker Bowles and the Prince in January 1993. The Parker Bowleses have been married for 21 years and have two children.

ISLE OF WIGHT, SUNDAY 8

Parkhurst jailbreakers caught

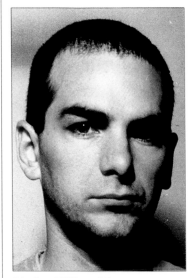

Matthew Williams, 25.

Three prisoners who escaped from Parkhurst maximum security prison were recaptured after their meticulously planned breakout failed. Having got out of the prison using a forged key and a home-made ladder, they had planned to steal a light aircraft and fly off the Isle of Wight. But although one of the escapers, Keith Rose, 45, holds a pilot's licence, he could not start a Cessna at Sandown airport. The men also failed to break into another plane.

The three men slept rough for five nights, afraid to force their way into a house or steal a car during the intense manhunt. Eventually, they were spotted walking down a country road by an off-duty warder only a few miles from the prison.

Keith Rose, 45.

Andrew Rodger, 44.

MANILA, SATURDAY 14

Pope's success in Philippines

Even the arrest of two Arabs with bomb-making equipment and police fears that a 20-man hit squad is stalking him has not checked Pope John Paul II in his triumphant passage through the Philippines. The first leg of his four-nation Asian and Pacific tour opened here to massive crowds.

The Pope has made a special point of delivering a message to the young on his visit. The accent on the young culminates today, the last full day of his three-day tour, when he addresses a three-hour open-air mass being held in Manila to mark World Youth Day. A congregation of at least 3 million people is anticipated. The tour is the first time that the Pope has ventured far from the Vatican for 16 months, and his first major overseas trip for three years. Security problems forced him to cancel planned visits to Beirut and Sarajevo, and a broken leg those to Belgium and the US. He arrived in the Philippines supported by a walking stick, but he looked well and was in good humour.

The 11-day tour is to go on from here to areas that no pope has visited before: Papua New Guinea, Australia, and Sri Lanka. The Pope is also using the tour to appeal to the Chinese authorities to relax restrictions on Catholic worship in China.

The Pope is greeted by enthusiastic crowds as he arrives at Manila airport.

S	M	T	W	T	F	S
1	2	3	4	5	6	7
8	9	10	11	12	13	14
15	16	17	18	19	20	21
22	23	24	25	26	27	28
29	30	31				

Sarajevo, 15
Two teenage girls in Bihac killed by Serb shelling in response to a Bosnian attack on Serb positions.

Baghdad, 15
Fourteen senior Iraqi air force officers are executed for attempting to assassinate Saddam Hussein.

Los Angeles, 16
A long-running dispute between Faye Dunaway and Andrew Lloyd Webber over her dismissal as star of the Los Angeles production of *Sunset Boulevard* is settled out of court.

Washington DC, 18
Democrats attack Speaker Newt Gingrich, a Republican, for agreeing a book deal with a company owned by Rupert Murdoch.

Chechnya, 19
Russian forces capture the Presidential Palace in Grozny.

Brightlingsea, 19
Twenty-one animal-rights protesters are arrested during an attempt to halt live exports of sheep.

London, 19
Private Lee Clegg, the paratrooper who shot a joyrider at an Ulster checkpoint, has his appeal rejected by five Law Lords. (→ July 3)

London, 19
The Royal Astronomical Society announces that there is a 13th sign of the Zodiac called Ophiuschus, which should govern those born between November 30 and December 17.

Washington, 20
US agrees trade pact with North Korea and lifts sanctions that have been in place since the Korean War.

Frankfurt, 21
A key Lockerbie bombing suspect is freed by Germany and returned to Syria in a secret deal with Iran.

Mexico, 21
Mexican financial markets go into a further fall after US Congress refuses to back Clinton's plan to support the peso. (→ January 31)

Deaths
Conductor Sir Alexander Gibson, founder of the Scottish Opera Company, aged 68, January 15.

Raincoat magnate Lord Kagan, aged 79, January 18.

UNION, SOUTH CAROLINA, MONDAY 16

Mother accused of drowning her two young sons

Susan Smith entering the courtroom in Union at the start of her trial.

A 23-year-old woman appeared in court today accused of the murder of her two sons, aged 14 months and three years. Mrs. Susan V. Smith, who did not enter a plea, broke down in tears several times during the hearing.

The story of the disappearance of the children caused alarm throughout American when it broke last October. Mrs. Smith claimed that an unidentified black man had stolen her car and kidnapped the boys. The prosecution claims that when after nine days the searches proved fruitless, Mrs. Smith admitted to investigating police officers that she had let her car roll into a lake near Union with the two boys strapped into their seats inside.

Susan Smith was going through a divorce from her husband at the time of the deaths of the two boys. If she is found guilty of murder she could face the electric chair, in which case she would become the first woman to be executed in America for over ten years. (→ July 10)

SOWETO, SUNDAY 15

Joe Slovo given hero's funeral

There were tears in the eyes of South African president, Nelson Mandela, as he gave the main address at the state funeral of Joe Slovo, his old friend and ally in the battle against apartheid. Slovo died of cancer ten days ago.

Under the old regime, Slovo, the Lithuanian-born leader of South Africa's Communist Party, had been regarded as Public Enemy Number One. The fact that Nationalist Party leaders attended his funeral is a measure of the extent of recent changes in South Africa. Meanwhile, the people of Soweto celebrated the life of the man who championed freedom and justice with dawn-to-dusk dancing in the streets.

South African communist Joe Slovo.

PARIS, WEDNESDAY 18

20,000-year-old paintings found

Ancient cave paintings similar to those at Lascaux have been discovered in the Ardèche region of southern France. They were found a week before Christmas, but were kept secret while the caves were made secure from intruders.

"We have a selection of animals infinitely more varied than at the other sites and with exceptional features and purity," said Geneviève Martin, of the Rhônes-Alpes archaeological service. The animals depicted are thought to include woolly-haired rhinos, bears, oxen, and mammoths.

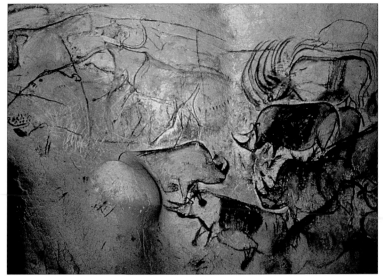

Cave paintings discovered in the Ardèche, after being undisturbed for thousands of years.

TOKYO, TUESDAY 17

Earthquake devastates Kobe

Fires fuelled by ruptured gas pipes rage out of control and destroy earthquake-shattered buildings in the Japanese city of Kobe.

A truck toppled from a freeway buckled by the force of this morning's earthquake.

A huge earthquake hit western Japan this morning, causing massive damage in the city of Kobe. A busy port near Osaka with a population of 1.4 million people, Kobe is in the heart of one of Japan's most important industrial areas.

The early reports of 300 dead have been constantly revised upwards during the day to 2,700. Over 1,100 buildings collapsed, as did overhead freeways, sending motorists plunging to their deaths. Fires raged across the city, fed by fractured gas lines, as firemen struggled to reach them through blocked roads and over rubble. Fires also broke out in various other towns and cities across the region, including Osaka itself.

The earthquake hit at 5.46 a.m. local time, when most of the population was in bed. Measuring 7.2 on the Richter scale, it is Japan's worst earthquake since 1923, when Tokyo was devastated and more than 142,000 people were killed. Near-freezing temperatures have made matters worse for thousands of homeless people and hundreds of thousands of others whose homes are without power and heating. (→ March 15)

BRUSSELS, TUESDAY 17

Delors steps down from Europe

Jacques Delors formally stepped down today, after ten years as president of the European Commission. He will be replaced by Jacques Santer.

Delors' achievements include the establishment of the single market, which is now 90 per cent complete. He has also made a single currency inevitable, though under the Maastricht treaty the timetable has yet to be finalized.

However, he had been much criticized for his drive towards federalism, which nearly led to disaster when the Danes rejected Maastricht and a referendum in France ratified it by a tiny majority.

Taking over, Luxembourg politician Santer told the European Parliament that a "giant leap forward" was required to integrate Europe. He also called for Britain to drop its opt-out from the Social Chapter.

This immediately brought a swingeing attack by Prime Minister John Major in the House of Commons. He maintained that the "high tide" of federalism in Europe had passed and vowed to resist any further erosion of sovereignty.

This speech failed to appease Conservative Euro-rebel MPs who renewed their attack on Major. They did so by voting against two crucial European Union rulings giving Spanish fishing boats access to British waters and by making public their own Euro-sceptic agenda.

Idaho, Sunday 15. The first four of 30 Canadian grey wolves are reintroduced into the wild near the Salmon River. Local farmers oppose the move.

	S	M	T	W	T	F	S
	1	2	3	4	5	6	7
	8	9	10	11	12	13	14
	15	16	17	18	19	20	21
	22	23	24	25	26	27	28
	29	30	31				

Los Angeles, 22
Hugh Grant takes the Golden Globe award for Best Actor in a Comedy, while Tom Hanks picks up Best Actor, and *Forrest Gump* Best Picture.

London, 22
The Prince of Wales plans to sue his former housekeeper over a book about her years in his service.

Washington DC, 23
US intelligence reports that Iran paid $10 million for Lockerbie bombing.

Sarajevo, 23
The US embassy shows dissent from its government's new policy of direct talks with the Bosnian Serbs.

Rangoon, 23
Burmese opposition leader Aung San Suu Kyi pledges no deal with the ruling junta to end her house arrest.

Washington DC, 24
President Clinton today delivered the longest-ever State of the Union address, pleasing Congress with talk of welfare reform and tax cuts.

Dublin, 25
A five-man gang steals over £3 million from a security depot in the Republic's biggest-ever cash robbery.

Miami, 29
The San Francisco 49ers overwhelm the San Diego Chargers 49-26 in the Super Bowl.

Melbourne, 29
Andre Agassi beats Pete Sampras in the final of the Australian Open Tennis Championship.

Washington DC, 31
Failing to get Congressional backing for his $40 billion rescue plan for the Mexican economy, Clinton instead pledges $20 billion on his own emergency authority.

London, 31
The leakage of plans for a joint North-South Irish authority causes alarm amongst Ulster Unionists.

Amsterdam, 31
Over 200,000 people are evacuated from their homes in eastern and central Holland as rising rivers burst their protective dykes.

Death
Zoo pioneer and animal writer Gerald Durrell, aged 70, January 30.

CANBERRA, THURSDAY 26

Opposition leader resigns in Australia

Alexander Downer, leader of the Federal Liberal Party, resigned today after just eight months in office. His resignation is widely seen as a sacrifice in order to try to keep his warring party together.

Downer is the sixth leader the Liberals have had since 1983, when Bob Hawke formed the first in what has since been an unbroken series of Labour Party administrations. John Howard, 55, is expected to take over as leader of the Federal Liberals. He is one of the party's most respected figures, having previously held the post of Leader of the Opposition between 1985 and 1989.

LIMA, SUNDAY 29

Peru launches new attack on Ecuador

Four days of border clashes between Peru and Ecuador escalated today when the Peruvians launched a major offensive against their western neighbour. The fighting is along a 48-mile stretch of border in the Andes that has been in dispute since 1960. An earlier demarcation agreement determined the countries' mutual borders but in the last 30 years Ecuador has chafed against being cut off from the Amazon. (→ February 6)

Massachussetts, Tuesday 24. Rose Kennedy, who died at the age of 104, is buried in the presence of her son Ted Kennedy and other relatives.

TEL AVIV, SUNDAY 22

Suicide bomb attacks in Israel

An Israeli soldier mourns his murdered comrades after the suicide bombing.

Nineteen people, mostly soldiers, were killed this morning and 61 injured in a double suicide bomb attack at Nordiya near the seaside town of Netanya. Islamic Jihad claimed responsibility, and said that two of its members blew themselves up in the attacks. The killings took place at 9.30 a.m. at a bus stop outside an army base. Rabbis wearing surgical gloves were still sorting through the remains several hours later trying to identify the victims.

The Israeli government responded immediately by sealing off the occupied territories tonight, preventing Palestinians from entering the rest of the country.

VIENNA, MONDAY 30

BAe entangled in corruption deal

Following a string of denials, the British Aerospace company has finally admitted that for five years it tried to sell its BAe 146-1000 jet transport aircraft in Austria. The admission could link the company to a political bribery scandal.

Two politicians in the ruling coalition – Peter Marizzi of the Social Democrats and Hermann Kraft of the People's Party – have resigned over the proposed disposal of an estimated £4.1 million "commission" on the £222.3 million deal. Taped conversations indicated that the money was going to be used to bribe the Defence Ministry or go straight into the coffers of the political parties that make up the coalition.

There is nothing to suggest that British Aerospace knew where the "commission" was going to go. However, a top-secret contract was drawn up as part of the deal and some of those involved were required to sign confidentiality agreements.

LOS ANGELES, TUESDAY 24

O.J. Simpson trial starts

O.J. Simpson confers with one of his defence attorneys.

The trial of O.J. Simpson, accused of murdering his ex-wife, Nicole, and her friend Ronald Goldman, opened in a packed courtroom here today. Chief Prosecutor Marcia Clark said that a trail of blood led directly from the house where Nicole Simpson was murdered to the former football star's bedroom. The prosecution alleges that Simpson is a deeply jealous man with a history of wife abuse who reg-

ularly beat Nicole in the 15 years that they had known each other.

The trial had been scheduled to start yesterday, but arguments over evidence meant that opening statements were held over to this morning. In a critical ruling, Judge Lance A. Ito yesterday gave the defence permission to cross-examine a key prosecution witness, detective Mark Fuhrman, for racial prejudice. (→ February 15)

WASHINGTON DC, MONDAY 23

US intelligence report that Iran paid £6.5 million for Lockerbie

A document newly released under the US Freedom of Information Act casts doubt on the American and British government assertions that only Libyan nationals were responsible for the Lockerbie bombing which killed 270 people when a Pan Am airliner exploded over southern Scotland in 1988.

The document, a report compiled during the Gulf War by the US Air Force Signals Intelligence Unit, alleges that a minister in the Iranian government paid $10 million for the attack. The report accuses the minister of giving the same amount to the terrorist groups Abu Abbas and the

PFLP-GC, led by Abu Nidal, for other terrorist activities. The document was obtained by the makers of a forthcoming television documentary about the Lockerbie bombing.

The governments of both the US and the UK have maintained that Colonel Gaddafi, president of Libya, ordered the attack, and that it was carried out by two Libyans for whom American and Scottish courts have issued arrest warrants. The response of the British Foreign Office to the report is that there is still a case for the Libyans to answer and that it will continue to press for the extradition of the two men. (→ February 4)

MANCHESTER, FRIDAY 27

Cantona banned for the rest of the season

Eric Cantona has been banned from football for the rest of the 1994-95 season by his club Manchester United. The ban follows Cantona's two-footed leap into the crowd to assault a Crystal Palace fan in South London on Wednesday night.

The punishment was announced by club chairman Martin Edwards, who said that the action had been taken for the good of the game. The loss of their star forward will hurt United almost as much as the player himself and is bound to hinder their attempt to win the FA Premiership for a third successive season.

It is not, however, likely to be the only punishment meted out to the Frenchman, whose enormous skills

are matched by his temper. He has also been stripped of the captaincy of his national team by the French Football Association. The police are investigating the incident and criminal charges could follow for Cantona while the English FA have charged him with bringing the game into disrepute. The player has also been fined two weeks' wages by United, approximately £15,000.

Cantona's is the longest suspension in English football since 1964 but his assault was unprecedented. United's swift application of their punishment has been seen in some quarters as a bid to pre-empt the possibility of even more severe measures by the English FA. (→ February 21)

London, Wednesday 25. Eric Cantona, Manchester United's French star, stunned the soccer world by launching a kung-fu-style kick at a fan on the terraces. He had just been sent off at Crystal Palace. The ensuing mêlée was broken up by police. (→ January 27)

Ceremonies commemorate the liberation of Auschwitz

Fifty years ago today, advancing Soviet troops entered Auschwitz, in Poland, and liberated the survivors of the Nazis' largest factory of death. Both an extermination camp and a slave labour camp, Auschwitz has become the most potent symbol of the Holocaust.

Thirteen presidents, three kings, Nobel Peace Prize winners, camp survivors, and more than 10,000 mourners gathered at Auschwitz to commemorate the fiftieth anniversary of the liberation and the death of 1.5 million inmates, the majority of them Jews. A minute's silence was observed and prayers were offered in a moving ceremony for the dead.

The organization of the ceremony had provoked bitter controversy between Jewish groups and Polish Catholics. The Jews had feared that the commemorations, hosted by Polish president Lech Walesa, a committed Catholic, would downplay the specifically Jewish tragedy of the Holocaust. To Poles the camp is also a symbol of national suffering. But many Jews feel that the anti-semitism prevalent in Poland contributed to the Holocaust.

Two days before the ceremony, Jewish activist and Nobel laureate Elie Wiesel, himself a camp survivor, made an impassioned attack on what he saw as complacent calls for a general spirit of reconciliation. Addressing a crowd of Auschwitz mourners, he said: "God, do not have mercy on those who have created this place. God of forgiveness, do not forgive those murderers of Jewish children here."

But in the event, the ceremony, which was attended by the German president, Helmut Kohl, was conducted with dignity and without dissent. As the world leaders toured Auschwitz's "bathhouses" for gassing prisoners, its corpse cellars, and its cremating ovens, none could remain unmoved by the evidence of what an agreed statement called "the biggest crime of the century".

Political and religious leaders attend the 50th anniversary commemoration service.

Memorial candles burn as a survivor mourns those who died in the camp.

Grim interior of an Auschwitz dormitory.

Faces and uniforms of some of the millions of victims displayed in the Auschwitz museum.

Concrete, barbed wire, and electrified fencing encircled the camp.

The anniversary was a time for solidarity.

Liberation 50 years ago

Joyous prisoners greet the Soviet army in 1945.

A funeral procession of prisoners after the liberation.

The children of Auschwitz look forward to freedom.

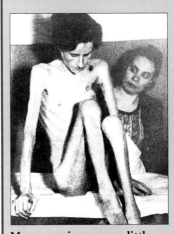

Many survivors were little more than skin and bone.

February

Washington DC, 1
A US State Department report condemns human rights abuses in Russia and China. Moscow is accused of massive cruelty in Chechnya while Beijing is criticized for its crackdown in Tibet.

Shepperton, 1
Two of Britain's most famous film directors, the brothers Ridley and Tony Scott, lead a £12-million take-over of Shepperton Studios.

Rome, 1
The Vatican removes all blocks on married Anglican clergy becoming Catholic priests.

London, 2
Fourteen police officers traumatized by the Hillsborough soccer disaster are each to receive up to £250,000 in compensation.

Rome, 2
A third of the estate of Italian composer Giacomo Puccini is awarded to his son's illegitimate daughter after a wrangle with the family butler.

Oxford, 2
Oxford University drops its entrance exam, which is thought to favour pupils from independent schools.

Paris, 2
Road deaths in France fell by 5.7% last year, due to new drink-driving and seat-belt regulations.

Chechnya, 4
Chechen rebels shoot down a Russian jet fighter, but the Chechens' fate is sealed as Russian shelling seals off the last roads into Grozny. (→ March 23)

Washington DC, 4
Trade war looms as US puts 100% tariff on Chinese goods.

Twickenham, 4
England beat France 31-10 in rugby's Five Nations Championship.

Lockerbie, 4
Mystery concerning a missing body from the Pan Am disaster over the Scottish town: the police surgeon issued 59 death certificates, but the police have details of only 58 bodies.

Death
Broadway producer, director, and writer George Abbott, aged 107, February 1.

John Major makes TV plea to people of Ulster

John Major tried to reassure Unionist MPs today that his government had their best interests at heart. This followed furious reactions to the news leaked yesterday that the British and Irish were planning a joint body to have wide powers in the province.

In only the third special TV broadcast on Ulster of his four years in office, Major implored the people of Ulster not to throw away the prospect of peace for another 25 years of bombings and murder. The Prime Minister re-affirmed his earlier pledge that no settlement would be forced on them by Dublin and London. "After five months of peace," he said,

"surely it is time to look ahead. Judge our proposals as a whole. There is nothing you need to fear."

However, his pleas did little to alleviate the fears of many Unionist politicians, some of whom immediately threatened to withdraw their support from the government. Given the Conservatives' slender majority, such a move could precipitate an early general election.

Meanwhile, the Irish premier, John Bruton, rallied to Major's support, praising his "commitment to the peace process" and reiterating the two countries' common purpose in seeking a just peace. (→February 22)

London, Thursday 2. Actor Donald Pleasence, well known for playing villains, dies aged 75. He first came to prominence in Pinter's *The Caretaker* (1960).

Europe and US split on peso crisis

Britain and five other European countries have refused to endorse President Clinton's plans to bail out the Mexican peso, in the face of what Alan Greenspan, the head of the US Federal Reserve, has described as the worst international currency crisis for 30 years.

Following Clinton's controversial personal commitment of US funds from the Exchange Stabilization Fund on Tuesday, the President today sought a package of $17.8 billion in loans for Mexico from the International Monetary Fund (IMF).

Although the IMF agreed, Britain, Germany, Denmark, Switzerland, Belgium, and the Netherlands all abstained – an almost unprecedented public lack of support for US policy. Given only one hour to study the proposal, the Europeans objected to being rushed into the IMF's largest-ever currency rescue operation. They feared the action would deplete funds needed for other purposes.

Many Americans are also unhappy with the bailout of Mexico. Congress rejected Clinton's original request for a $40-billion loan. (→ March 10)

Jiang calls for talks with Taiwan

Chinese president, Jiang Zemin, has made a bid to become Deng Xiaoping's successor as Communist Party chairman by calling for re-unification with Taiwan. His appeal – which was run in all official Chinese newspapers – calls for both sides to drop adversarial positions and for China to listen to the opinions of the Taiwanese. However, he refused to renounce the threat of force against the island.

Deng Xiaoping, aged 90, is thought to be close to death.

Worst floods for seventy years

Tonight, as flood waters continue to rise across the Netherlands, Belgium, northwest Germany, and northeast France, more people have been forced to leave their homes than at any time since the Second World War. Flooding has already left 27 dead and caused hundreds of millions of pounds' worth of damage. The rainfall is now starting to ease, but Dutch dykes have suffered extensive damage and a state of emergency has been declared in the Netherlands.

London, Thursday 2. Britain's last winner of the Wimbledon Men's Singles, Fred Perry, 85, died today, after slipping in his hotel shower. He was champion for three consecutive years from 1934 to 1936.

Jill Phipps killed by lorry carrying calves

Animal rights campaigners try to stop a lorry carrying animals for export. Protesters say the conditions are inhumane.

Animal rights protester Jill Phipps, 31, died today after she flung herself in front of a lorry carrying veal calves into Coventry airport for export. She had broken through a police cordon and slipped under the wheels of the lorry. Phipps was a regular protester at the airport. She was there today with her mother and about 40 others.

"As the cattle lorry came into view, the protesters moved towards it," a police spokesman said. "Repeated requests were made for them to move back." When the lorry slowed down, one protester climbed on to it. Two others ran in front of the lorry. Phipps seized the front of the cab, but she lost her grip. "Police yelled for the lorry driver to stop and it did, but with the wheels right on her body," a witness said. "She was obviously in immense agony."

The Police Complaints Authority has announced that it will investigate the incident. Phoenix Aviation, which flies veal calves out of Coventry airport, said that they would suspend livestock flights for the "forseeable future".

The tragedy occurred only a day after the airline had resumed commercial flights from Coventry airport to Holland and France. Their traffic

Jill Phipps (left), who was killed during yesterday's protest at Coventry airport.

had previously been suspended since December 1994, when a Boeing 737 leased to them from Air Algérie crashed killing all five members of the crew.

As soon as flights resumed, so did the protests against the veal trade. Earlier demonstrations had sometimes resulted in violence and only the previous day Jill Phipps herself had told a local television station, "I think it's very probable that someone will get hurt soon."

Jill Phipps, a divorcée, leaves a nine-year-old son. She had been a lifelong campaigner for numerous causes and was a founder member of the "Coventry Animal Alliance". Her mother, Nancy Phipps, also an animal rights activist, later said: "I am proud of her. She did not deserve to die. She was a beautiful, kind, and loving daughter and mother." A fellow animal rights protester said: "Animals were her life. Now she has died for them." (→ February 14)

Moscow politician in "Mafia" shooting

MP Sergei Skorochkin, 33, who took on the Moscow "Mafia", has been found murdered. He had been handcuffed and shot in the head.

As a businessman he refused to pay off local gangsters, and in May he shot dead a Georgian bandit who was threatening him. To ordinary Russians, he had become a hero.

The influence of the Russian so-called "Mafia" has been growing rapidly in recent years. However, in a country with endemic bureaucratic corruption that is still unused to entrepreneurial methods, it is often hard to distinguish between aggressive business methods and organized crime. In such a climate, Russian gang wars have spread far and wide.

Sino-US trade war looms

Pirated US goods on sale in Asia.

President Bill Clinton has imposed punitive duties on Chinese imports worth hundreds of millions of dollars. The move comes in response to the failure of the Chinese to deal with alleged piracy of US software, movie, and music copyrights.

Republicans have applauded the move, but, despite claims that millions of dollars are being lost in royalties, US businessmen are nervous about the prospect of a trade war with such a major economy.

February

S	M	T	W	T	F	S
			1	2	3	4
5	6	7	8	9	10	11
12	13	14	15	16	17	18
19	20	21	22	23	24	25
26	27	28				

Sicily, 5
The Mafia's first "godmother" is arrested by the Italian police. Her husband, a clan chief, was jailed two years ago for murder.

Lima, 6
Fighting flares again along the Peru-Ecuador border. (→ February 14)

Washington DC, 6
Four Catholic priests have been sacked after admitting sexual abuse of an altar boy.

Washington DC, 6
President Clinton's new $1.61 trillion budget is criticized by Republicans for lacking the courage to make deeper cuts.

New York, 6
In the World Trade Center terrorist trial, a defendant pleads guilty of plotting to kill President Mubarak of Egypt and turns state's evidence.

London, 7
The captain of Chelsea football club, Dennis Wise, is found guilty of assaulting a taxi driver.

Johannesburg, 7
ANC leader Dr. Allan Boesak embezzled funds during the apartheid years, an inquiry finds.

London, 7
The electrical goods chain Rumbelows closes its 311 shops with the loss of some 3,000 jobs.

Colombia, 8
At least 23 people are killed and 200 injured in an earthquake. Worst hit is the city of Pereira.

India, 8
India's ruling Congress (I) party faces defeat at poll in the crucial western state of Maharastra.

Washington DC, 9
Former vice-president, Dan Quayle, drops out of the 1996 Presidential race, stating his campaign is starved of funds.

Krajina, 11
The fragile Bosnian truce breaks down as Croatians and Bosnian Serbs face each other over disputed border.

Death
Novelist Patricia Highsmith, creator of the psychopathic protagonist Tom Ripley, February 5.

Mir and Discovery rendezvous in space

The US space shuttle *Discovery* flew within 10 m (33 ft) of Russia's *Mir* space station in a rehearsal for the docking of the two craft in June.

Earlier the Russians had banned the Shuttle from coming within 300 m (1,000 ft) of *Mir*, because they were concerned about a leaking thruster and feared that chunks of frozen nitrogen might damage the space station's solar panels. But American scientists convinced them that the danger was non-existent.

Russian and American crews agreed that the fly-by – at a speed of 28,000 km/h (17,500 mph), 500 km (315 miles) above South America – was one of the most beautiful things they had ever seen. This was the first rendezvous between Russian and US spacecraft for 20 years.

Right: Mir *seen from* Discovery.

Below: The crew of the US space shuttle Discovery *pose for publicity photographs before taking off on their latest mission.*

Los Angeles, Monday 6. American actor Doug McClure, dies aged 59. He first achieved fame as Trampas in TV's *The Virginian* and went on to star in B-movies such as *The Land that Time Forgot*.

"Coal first used 74,000 years ago"

Cave men came home to real coal fires, according to a report published this week in the prestigious British science journal *Nature*. An article supplied by French researchers claims that Stone Age man was burning coal nearly 74,000 years ago. Previously, the use of coal as a fuel had been traced back only 18,000 years.

Isabelle Thery and a team of researchers from the University of Montpellier unearthed evidence from fossils found in hearths at Les Canalettes and Les Usclades in the southern Massif Central in France. These showed that early man collected coal from local outcrops, presumably when firewood was scarce.

Coal outcrops are not confined to a single area and the use of coal as a fuel is now thought to have been widespread from the earliest times. The advantages of this to early humans would have been manifold. Coal generates higher temperatures than wood and provides a more constant heat for cooking.

The discovery indicates that early humans were more sophisticated than had previously been believed. They may have found other technological uses for the greater heat obtained from coal fires, and it may now become necessary to revise previous notions about the approximate date of the start of the Bronze Age.

BOSNIA, SATURDAY 11
Bosnian cease-fire violations threaten latest peace plan

The designated safe havens are under increasing pressure from Bosnian Serbs.

The recent cease-fire in Bosnia seems to be going the way of all the others as tension mounts on five fronts. Heavy fighting has taken place throughout the last week in the so-called safe haven of Bihac, while there have also been hostilities in the enclaves at Srebenica and Gorazde. Government troops are massing by the Posavina Corridor in the northeast, where Serb positions are vulnerable. Most ominously, President Tudjman of Croatia has asked the UN to remove its troops from his country, implying that he is about to attack Krajina, the region lost to the Serbs in 1991.

The UN has recorded 62 helicopter flights in five days as Serbia moves military supplies to Bosnia in violation of Serbian president Milosevic's purported blockade of the Bosnian Serbs. (→ February 12)

CHICHESTER, MONDAY 6
Virginia Bottomley to go to court

Health Secretary Virginia Bottomley has been summoned by Judge Anthony Thorpe to appear at Chichester Crown Court on February 10 to answer questions about the case of Sharon Towes. Accommodation was not found for Towes, 24, a seriously disturbed mental patient, despite repeated court orders that she should be held in a secure institution.

The fact that Towes has since been found a reasonably secure bed does not mean that the summons lapses. And as it has been issued in Mrs. Bottomley's name it means that the minister cannot simply send a representative, but must appear in court in person. One possible solution, however, would be for the Health Secretary to write to Judge Thorpe: this would then make it a matter of the Judge's discretion whether she appeared or not.

Health Secretary Virginia Bottomley.

Paris, Tuesday 7. Work began on a much-needed new coat of paint for the 106-year-old Eiffel Tower. It is expected that the job will take three years to complete.

LONDON, MONDAY 6
PowerGen bosses make £5.3m

Boardroom pay for the privatized electricity generating company PowerGen has rocketed from an average £646,000 per director when it was under public ownership to over £5.3 million in the last financial year. Directors have made a further £5 million in share options and will make another £18 million if and when they cash in their shares.

According to Labour's shadow Chancellor of the Exchequer, Gordon Brown, six PowerGen directors and senior executives made £3.4 million between them in one day in April 1994. He blames the government, who put a price tag of £4 million on their generating shares, for selling too cheap.

PowerGen refused to comment on the controversy. But company sources pointed out that if directors were to cash in their shares they would face a massive tax bill. Nevertheless, Brown accused them of "corporate greed".

John Baker, chief executive of National Power, claims that the remuneration of board members is not something that has ever bothered the company's shareholders. But the row over "fat cats" seems set to continue here and in the other newly privatized utilities.

GERMANY, MONDAY 6
German metal workers decide to go on strike

A German metal worker demonstrates outside his factory against the latest wage offer.

The massive German engineering union, IG Metall, is preparing for a nationwide strike. The 3 million members of the union are threatening to withdraw their labour if employers do not accede to their demands for a 6 per cent pay increase. The union has warned that employees' patience is wearing thin.

Some 247,000 union members have made one-day stoppages during the past few weeks. Employers want cost-cutting included in all wage talks. The union, however, is adamant that employers have not made a suitable response to their claims. They say the talks are over and that they will now call a strike ballot.

S	M	T	W	T	F	S
			1	2	3	4
5	6	7	8	9	10	11
12	13	14	15	16	17	18
19	20	21	22	23	24	25
26	27	28				

Wales, 12
A 39-year-old woman is charged with abducting six-day-old Lydia Owens in Prestatyn last Friday. Police found the child 21 hours later.

Bosnia, 12
Heavy fighting breaks out around the Muslim enclave of Bihac, as Serbs begin a spring offensive.(→ March 6)

Washington DC, 12
Controversy erupts over President Clinton's choice of surgeon general, Dr. Henry Foster, who once sterilized mentally retarded women.

Angola, 12
Unita rebels accept peace treaty to end 19 years of war in Angola.

Coventry, 14
Brigitte Bardot attends the funeral of animal rights protester Jill Phipps, killed beneath the wheels of a lorry exporting livestock.

Pakistan, 14
Sectarian fighting in Karachi leaves 20 dead, bringing the death toll in the city this month to 83.

Italian Tyrol, 14
The 5,300-year-old mummified man found in the Alps is to go on display in an Italian museum.

London, 14
A plaque to Oscar Wilde is unveiled in Westminster Abbey, 100 years after the first performance of *The Importance of Being Earnest.*

London, 16
Nurses belonging to the union UNISON reject a 1 % pay offer and demand 3 % instead.

Thailand, 16
Thai forces are on full alert after incursion by Burmese forces.

Los Angeles, 16
Key witness in the O.J. Simpson trial, Rosa Lopez, quits the country and returns to El Salvador. (→ March 13)

London, 17
The UK modifies the ban excluding Irish Republicans from the mainland.

Mineola, New York, 17
Colin Ferguson is found guilty of the Long Island Railroad shootings.

Death
Maverick Conservative MP, Sir Nicholas Fairburn, February 18.

DUBLIN, WEDNESDAY 15

Riot halts soccer match

A friendly soccer international between England and the Republic of Ireland was stopped tonight when English fans hurled wood and other debris down from an upper terrace at Lansdowne Road stadium on to Irish fans below. Forty English fans and three Irish were arrested and at least 20 people were taken to hospital with serious injuries. The Garda, the Irish police, are inexperienced at handling large-scale crowd trouble, but they controlled the violence using riot shields and truncheons.

Trouble began before the game, when English fans sang "God Save the Queen" and shouted "IRA bastards". It continued later when 500 English fans boarded ferries from Dublin to Holyhead. Some shouted "Rule Britannia" and "No surrender to the IRA" and scuffles broke out.

At the time play was abandoned, Ireland were leading 1-0.

Off-field violence continues to bring English soccer into disrepute at home and abroad.

New York, Wednesday 15. O.J. Simpson's book, *I Want To Tell You,* goes straight to the top of the *New York Times* bestsellers.

SOUTH AFRICA, SUNDAY 12

Mandela tells Winnie to resign

President Nelson Mandela told his estranged wife, Winnie, to apologize or resign today after she criticized his government, of which she is a member. The government had failed to redress "apartheid imbalances" and quash racism in the workplace, she said. And in a personal attack on her husband, she maintained that his emphasis on reconciliation was a weakness.

Mrs. Mandela also lost the support of the ANC Women's League, which she heads, when 11 executive members quit. (→ March 1)

ZAIRE, MONDAY 13

Aid workers forced to pull out of Rwandan camps

International medical organization Médecins Sans Frontières (MSF) is pulling out of the refugee camps around Rwanda. They believe that their continued presence will only strengthen the Hutu militia who were responsible for last year's enormous massacres in this war-torn African nation.

Hutu leaders in the camps made no secret of their plans to launch a new offensive back in Rwanda. Aid is being stockpiled for the campaign or sold off to buy arms. MSF says it is unacceptable that aid should "strengthen and legitimize the power of leaders of a regime which organized and perpetrated genocide."

Rwandan refugees set off hopefully in search of safe havens away from the killing.

Peru and Ecuador end border fighting

Ecuadorian troops at a staging post on their way to the disputed border region.

The governments of Peru and Ecuador have both claimed victory in their long-running border dispute today and have ordered a cease-fire. Peru claims that it has expelled Ecuadorian troops from the last three jungle bases in the disputed area, while Ecuador maintains that it has held on to the three outposts. Whatever the truth, the two sides have finally agreed to end hostilities.

The cease-fire will be verified and monitored by an international team of independent observers who will be flown in by helicopter, the only means by which the remote border area can be reached. Argentina, Brazil, Chile, and the US, who have brokered the settlement, are now confident that they can find a permanent solution to this long-running source of friction between the nations. However, two previous cease-fires have broken down and a Peruvian officer claims that mortar rounds exploded near one of the jungle outposts only hours after the latest armistice had been announced.

The recent fighting has claimed the lives of 38 Peruvians and ten Ecuadorians, according to official sources. A further 60 Peruvians and 37 Ecuadorians have been wounded.

London, Friday 17. It was announced that the new Rover MG sportscar – the MGF – will make its debut in Geneva next month. But its designation will disappoint enthusiasts who ordered special "MGD" number plates (following on from the MGC model), unaware that the D and E models never reached the showroom.

Reconciliation speech in Dresden

President Roman Herzog of Germany made a speech of reconciliation in Dresden today, on the fiftieth anniversary of the Allied destruction of the city.

"We must guard against our mourning being seen as an attempt to square the suffering of the victims of crimes committed by Germans with the suffering of German victims," he said.

He also acknowledged Germany's responsibility for the Second World War, but pointed out that the bombing of Dresden killed refugees, resistance fighters, and Nazis alike.

The candlelit ceremony of reconciliation was attended by German, American, and British officials. However, there was a scuffle between demonstrators and police, and six people were arrested.

Indianapolis, Tuesday 14. Former world heavyweight boxing champion Mike Tyson's release date has been set. He is to be freed from the Indiana Youth Center on March 25, after serving half of a six-year sentence for rape. (→ March 25)

February

S	M	T	W	T	F	S
			1	2	3	4
5	6	7	8	9	10	11
12	13	14	15	16	17	18
19	20	21	22	23	24	25
26	27	28				

California, 19
A professor claims that between 5% and 10% of the world's 6,000 languages will die out in the next century, due to the spread of English.

Brussels, 19
NATO chief, Willy Claes, denies receiving bribes for an Italian helicopter contract in 1988.

London, 19
Social Services Secretary Peter Lilley admits that crime may be linked to poverty and unemployment.

Paris, 20
A senior French policeman, Jacques Franquet, resigns over the wire-tapping of a politician ordered by Prime Minister Edouard Balladur.

Hong Kong, 20
Five companies suspend trading on the Hong Kong Stock Exchange after their chairman, an associate of Deng Xiaoping's family, is arrested.

Scotland, 21
After three days trapped in a snow hole, Andrew Wilson is rescued. His is the longest sub-zero survival on record, outside military exercises.

San Francisco, 21
AIDS patients are to be injected with bone marrow cells from baboons immune to the virus.

London, 21
Eric Cantona, Manchester United's French star, is charged with assault after he kicked an abusive fan after being sent off. (→ March 23)

London, 22
The House of Commons approves a new Northern Ireland framework peace document. (→ March 16))

Mississippi, 22
A judge rejects tobacco companies' traditional "free will" plea that smokers knew the risks of smoking.

London, 26
Boxer Gerald McClellan undergoes an operation to remove a blood clot from his brain after losing to WBC super-middleweight Nigel Benn.

Death
Oscar-winning playwright Robert Bolt, aged 70, February 22.

US Marines land in Somalia

US forces landing at Mogadishu at the start of their bid to reach colleagues embroiled in the Somali civil war.

The US Marines stormed the beach at Mogadishu once again today, in a rerun of their landing there two years ago. But this time their aim was not to aid the Somali people. The task force of 2,500 US Marines, 500 Italian Marines – backed by helicopters, gunships and a fleet of 18 vessels – is there to oversee the withdrawal of the remaining 2,500 UN troops beleaguered in the midst of the civil war in Somalia.

The beach-head is a tiny spit of land where both the city's port and airport are located. It is now ringed with razor wire with warning notices telling the Somalis not to cross it.

Eighty armoured vehicles are being brought ashore, along with a force of 14,000 American, British, Italian, French, and Malaysian troops. They will form a rearguard as the remains of the failed UN peace-keeping force – mainly Pakistanis and Bangladeshis – are withdrawn.

Two years ago 28,000 US troops landed in the same spot to try to restore order and end the famine in the lawless country. Now Somalia has been given up as a lost cause.

14-year-old who went to Malaysia on father's credit card is returned

Runaway 14-year-old Peter Kerry.

Fourteen-year-old Peter Kerry, who ran away from his family's north London home after a row, has been found near the Thai border. The teenager stole his father's passport and two credit cards and boarded a plane for the Far East. He was detained as he tried to cash travellers' cheques in northern Malaysia.

Foreign Office officials report that after his adventure Peter was "well but tired". And once he has slept, he will be returned to London. Previously, Peter has run away to Edinburgh and Paris. This time, enquiries are being made as to how a 14-year-old could travel halfway round the world on the passport of his 59-year-old father.

Beijing, Sunday 19. Swedish group Roxette become the first big western band to play here since Wham! offended Chinese sensibilities ten years ago.

Barings Bank collapses: Leeson on the run

Nick Leeson, at centre right, on the dealing floor in Singapore before his disappearance.

Frantic attempts are being made here tonight to find a buyer for Barings, one of the City's oldest and most respected merchant banks. The bank faces losses of more than £800 million after trader Nick Leeson, 28, lost £17 billion on the Japanese futures market. Leeson is now on the run.

If the bank cannot find a buyer, it will go into administration. Some 4,000 jobs are at risk and deposits, including £1 million belonging to the Prince's Trust, are frozen.

The UK stock market fell sharply and the pound plunged more than two pfennigs against the German mark. Meanwhile, regulatory authorities are seeking ways to prevent other banks from being similarly exposed by derivatives trading. (→ March 3)

London, Wednesday 22. Concern grows for the safety of Stephen Fry who disappeared after the West End opening of the play *Cell Mates*. (→ March 21)

George Graham sacked over "bung"

Arsenal manager George Graham, 50, was sacked today by the north London football club for allegedly taking a "bung". A Premier League inquiry is already investigating reports that Graham accepted cash payments for the transfer of foreign players to the club. Among the allegations is that he received £285,000 from the £1.1 million deal that brought Denmark's John Jensen to Arsenal in 1992.

Graham, who earns a reported £300,000 a year, says that the money was a gift, although he later handed it over to the club. He intends to fight his sacking, claiming that he has been treated shabbily after 15 years' commitment to the club – eight as manager and seven as a player.

Five US citizens expelled from France for spying

An American woman, said to be working undercover in Paris, and four US embassy officials, including the CIA's Paris bureau chief, are being expelled from France for industrial espionage. Two other US embassy officials accused of spying have already left the country. The latest incident marks the lowest point in Franco-US relations for 20 years.

US ambassador, Pamela Harriman, has twice been summoned before French Interior Minister, Charles Pasqua, and she has also been seen by Prime Minister Edouard Balladur.

The CIA's intelligence activity centres on the General Agreement on Tariff and Trade (GATT). The US and France have been at loggerheads over GATT for some time. According to the French, the CIA tried to recruit a senior adviser to Balladur and a Cultural Ministry official with access to key communications. Both turned out to be members of the French counterespionage services, the DST.

Large sums of money were also said to have been offered to a senior French official in exchange for precise information about the French negotiating position. The French claim to have photographic evidence, signatures in hotel registers, and credit card receipts in false names to substantiate their allegations.

On three occasions in recent years, French diplomats have been accused of spying in the US, and Washington is expected soon to announce the expulsion of five French embassy officials in retaliation.

Last rebel stronghold falls in Burma

Burmese government forces display captured armaments used by Karen rebels.

Hundreds of Karen guerrillas are pouring across the border into Thailand after Kawmoora, their last outpost in Burma, fell to government troops. The Karen have been fighting for over 50 years for their independence. They first split from Burma during the Second World War, when they were allies of the British against the Japanese.

The writing has been on the wall for the Karen separatists since other Burmese ethnic minorities signed a ceasefire with the government in 1992. Then, last December, 500 Buddhist Karen mutinied against the Christian leadership of the 4,000-strong Karen army.

Rebel spokesmen say that some Karen soldiers were rendered unconscious when shells containing foul-smelling substances exploded. The Burmese government denies using chemical weapons. It also denies allegations that Burmese troops executed wounded prisoners.

S	M	T	W	T	F	S
			1	2	3	4
5	6	7	8	9	10	11
12	13	14	15	16	17	18
19	20	21	22	23	24	25
26	27	28	29	30	31	

London, 1
The Dillons bookshop chain goes into receivership after failing to extend its £55-million overdraft to £75 million. Thorn EMI, owner of the HMV record shop chain, is poised to take over.

Soweto, 1
South African police raid the home of Arts Minister Winnie Mandela, on the orders of her estranged husband, President Nelson Mandela, looking for evidence of fraud and corruption. (→ March 27)

Batavia, Illinois, 2
Physicists find the "top quark", a vital sub-proton particle predicted by theory but never before observed.

London, 2
Tiny Rowland is forced out of Lonhro after 34 years with the company. He threatens to sue.

Palermo, 3
Italian former prime minister Giulio Andreotti, 76, is charged with being a member of the Mafia. He headed six governments between 1972 and 1992.

Mogadishu, 3
The 2,500 US Marines, who covered the UN withdrawal from Somalia, themselves withdrew today.

Singapore, 3
Barings' Singapore office reveals it warned the bank's headquarters in London three years ago of the potentially disastrous consequences of Nick Leeson's futures trading. (→March 5)

Washington DC, 4
Cheyenne Ben Nighthorse Campbell, the first Native American to serve as a senator in 60 years, switches from Democrat to Republican.

Moscow, 4
The streets of Moscow are lined with mourners for the funeral of Vladislav Listyev, a TV journalist murdered by the Mafia.

Manchester, 4
Manchester United trounce Ipswich Town 9-0 in the club's most decisive victory since beating Wolverhampton Wanderers 10-1 in 1892.

LONDON, FRIDAY 3
Mohammed Fayed refused UK citizenship

Harrods, Britain's leading department store and part of the Fayed empire.

The owner of Harrods and of the Paris Ritz hotel, Egyptian-born Mohammad Fayed, is considering legal action after his application for British citizenship was turned down. His brother Ali Fayed also had his application for citizenship rejected after Mohammad Fayed told the *Guardian* newspaper that Treasury Minister Jonathan Aitken had not paid for his stay at the Paris Ritz.

Prime Minister John Major told the House of Commons that he had reported Mohammad Fayed to the Director of Public Prosecutions for "attempted blackmail". But the Crown Prosecution Service had decided to take no action.

LONDON, WEDNESDAY 1
Lamont supports Labour in Commons vote

The former Chancellor of the Exchequer, Norman Lamont, voted with Labour over Europe in a move that could have brought the government down. Since he was sacked two years ago, Lamont has become increasingly critical of the government's policy on the European Union. At the time, it was widely thought that Lamont was carrying the can for the government's failure to keep the pound in the European exchange-rate mechanism – a policy put in place by Prime Minister John Major himself, during his time as Chancellor.

But Labour's attempt to embarrass the government failed when four of the nine Conservative Euro-rebels who had been denied the Tory whip voted with the government. The nine Ulster Unionists and three Democratic Unionists voted against the government as a protest over the agreement with the Irish government for the future of the province.

The government won by five votes. If it had lost, it would have faced an embarrassing vote of no confidence. As it was, Labour leader Tony Blair exploited divisions over Europe in the cabinet in what is acknowledged to be his best Commons performance yet. When asked why he voted against his party, Lamont said: "I listened to the speeches. I didn't believe what I heard. I asked various questions, but I didn't believe the answers."

WASHINGTON, THURSDAY 2
Democrats halt budget measure

Senate Democrats are celebrating tonight after inflicting their first reverse on the Republicans' Contract with America, having defeated by a single vote a constitutional amendment to enforce a balanced federal budget by the year 2002. Bob Dole, the Republican leader in the Senate, had been trying for three days to get the two-thirds majority necessary to pass a constitutional amendment, but with Republican Senator Mark Hatfield of Oregon intransigent in his opposition to the measure Dole eventually had to give up. Fourteen Democrats supported the amendment, but no others could be found to vote with them.

The amendment would probably have been passed if the Republicans had added a clause barring the use of the Social Security trust fund to help reduce the deficit. An opinion poll last week showed wide support among the population for balancing the budget, but only if it was not at the cost of cutting Social Security.

Los Angeles, Thursday 2. Sheryl Crow wins three Grammys: the Record of the Year for "All I Wanna Do", Best Female Pop Vocal Peformance, and Best New Artist. Also among the winners are Bruce Springsteen, as the writer of the Best Song, "Streets of Philadelphia", and the Rolling Stones for Best

BICESTER, WEDNESDAY 1

Racing driver Damon Hill banned for speeding

The ban will not cramp Damon Hill's style on the race track.

The Formula One championship contender Damon Hill, 34, was banned from driving for seven days after he admitted having driven at 102.7 mph (165 kmph) on the M40 last December.

The extraordinary brevity of the ban will allow Hill to obtain his RAC competitor's licence, and hence his Formula One licence, in time for the Brazilian Grand Prix on March 26.

It was Hill's first driving offence since he passed his driving test at the age of 17. At the time he was stopped by the police, he had been running late for a live TV appearance at BBC's Pebble Mill studio. He was planning to promote his book on the 1994 Grand Prix season in which Hill finished as runner-up in the Formula 1 World Championship to his bitter rival Michael Schumacher.

Hill was fined £350 and ordered to pay £25 costs. The racing driver promised that he would never drive at that speed on a public road again. (→ March 26)

London, Friday 3. *Red Dwarf* **star Craig Charles, 30, walks free from Southwark Crown Court after being cleared of rape. The TV actor and his co-defendant John Peploe, 36, expressed relief at the verdict. His counsel, Stephen Solley QC, said the case should never have been brought.**

LOS ANGELES, FRIDAY 3

Man gets 25 years for stealing pizza

California's "three strikes and you're out" law exacted a tough punishment on Jerry Dewayne Williams, 27, today. He was sentenced to 25 years-to-life for stealing a slice of pizza.

Williams had stolen the pizza from four children. With five previous convictions for drug possession and robbery, he met the law's requirement for a lengthy sentence for anyone convicted of two previous felonies. The case has reopened the controversy about the law. Allan Parachini, of the American Civil Liberties Union, said, "No matter how many pizza thieves it sends to prison this law is not going to make our streets safer." Prosecutor Bill Gravlin defended the law: "The people of California are sick of revolving-door justice and they're sick of judges who are soft on crime."

Ironically, Williams threw the pizza into the sea because it contained pepperoni, which he does not like.

MIDLAND, MICHIGAN, FRIDAY 3

Neo-Nazis charged with murder of parents in Pennsylvania

Bryan and David Freeman in police custody on suspicion of murdering their parents.

Two teenage skinheads have been charged with murdering their parents and their younger brother at their home in Salisbury Township, Pennsylvania. Following a traced call, the FBI were waiting for them when they arrived at a house in Hope, Michigan, two days after the bodies were found.

Bryan Freeman, 17, and David Freeman, 15, both weighing over 101 kg (16 stones), are covered with neo-Nazi tattoos. Both are followers of the Pennsylvania-based Christian Identity Movement cult, which preaches that God will instruct whites to kill all non-Aryans at the Apocalypse, starting in the US.

March

S	M	T	W	T	F	S
			1	2	3	4
5	6	7	8	9	10	11
12	13	14	15	16	17	18
19	20	21	22	23	24	25
26	27	28	29	30	31	

London, 5
The Dutch Bank ING is to buy Barings for just £1 – but will inject £660 million new capital. (→ April 3)

Beijing, 5
The Chinese premier, Li Peng, admits that the country's economic boom has brought in its wake high inflation, corruption, and increased crime.

Tokyo, 5
Arguments rage among members of the Japanese parliament over whether the country should apologize to other Asian nations for World War II.

San Diego, 5
Australia's America's Cup contender, a favourite for the finals, sinks.

Copenhagen, 6
UN World Summit on Social Development opens. About 100 world leaders will discuss poverty, unemployment, civil unrest, and uncontrolled migration.

Zagreb, 6
Croatia and Bosnia sign a pact establishing a common military front against the Serbs. (→ March 27)

Washington DC, 8
President Clinton announces that he will not be attending the VE celebrations in London. He will celebrate in Moscow.

Washington DC, 8
A CIA report says that 90% of "ethnic cleansing" in the former Yugoslavia was carried out by Serbs, and that leading politicians were certainly involved.

Karachi, 10
Eleven people are killed and 24 injured by a car bomb in continued fighting between Shiite and Sunni Muslims.

London, 10
Lloyd's names win the right to £500 million from the underwriting agencies that acted for them.

Death
Vivian Stanshall, of the Bonzo Dog Doo-Dah Band, aged 52, March 6.

Los Angeles, Thursday 9
Hamburgers cause more pollution than buses in Los Angeles

A McDonalds in the Los Angeles suburbs. Are such fast food outlets major polluters?

Researchers at the University of California have found that fast foods such as hamburgers produce nine times more pollution in Los Angeles than the city's buses and could be a major contributor to poor health.

The leader of the research team said that pollution was mainly created by the grilling, in which fat drips out of the hamburgers and is burned off at high temperatures. The researchers estimate that fast-food restaurants account for 13.7 tons of smoke every day, and 19 tons of organic compounds. These reflect sunlight, adding to the smog which has become synonymous with the city. They could also increase the risk of cancer and respiratory problems.

Environmental officials in California are now pressing for legislation to force fast-food restaurants to change the fare they serve, or else to install pollution control devices. Restauranteurs are challenging the experiment's findings.

The researchers cooked thousands of hamburgers and hundreds of fish, beef, and chicken products every day during the research period.

Glencoe, Thursday 9
Three climbers dead in Highlands

The bodies of three climbers who went missing at the weekend were found today. They had been hit by an avalanche and buried by snow.

Gregory Taylor, 30, Simon Blundell, 34, and Kevin Ashurst, 29, were all from the Manchester area. They had planned to spend a week climbing in Scotland, but failed to report at a checkpoint on Sunday. On Tuesday, their tent and equipment were found.

Ten people have died so far this year in the Scottish highlands. Rescuers are currently searching for two more missing parties, who are feared dead.

London, Monday 6
Tory minister resigns over affair

Robert Hughes has resigned as junior minister for the Office of Public Service and Science after admitting an extra-marital affair. The affair ended six months ago, he said, but he could not carry out his ministerial responsibilities at the same time as trying to put his marriage back together again.

John Major has lost nine ministers since forming the present government in 1992. Five have resigned over personal indiscretions.

London, Wednesday 8
Illingworth to be England manager

The Test and County Cricket Board have sacked team manager Keith Fletcher. Ray Illingworth, who is already chairman of the selectors, is to replace Fletcher by taking on the manager's job as well.

Former England test captain Illingworth is to do the job until the end of next year's World Cup, when the position will be reviewed. Alan Smith, the board's chief executive, says Illingworth is "a motivator, someone who will raise team spirit and get the best out of individual players and the team as a whole."

San Francisco, Sunday 5. The top two men's tennis players in the world, Pete Sampras and Andre Agassi, surprise passers-by in San Francisco by playing a game of tennis in the street. The stunt is a fund-raising ploy for charity.

MADRID, FRIDAY 10

Spain sends gunboat to confront Canada

A week of conflict in the north Atlantic came to a head today as Spain sent a gunboat to protect its trawlers fishing in international waters off Newfoundland.

Canadian coastguards are patrolling the area on the look-out for Spanish fishing vessels. The owners of one Spanish trawler have already been arrested and the ship escorted to Canada, following a four-hour chase by three Canadian ships.

The argument is over Greenland halibut. A meeting last month of the North Atlantic Fisheries Organization ruled that Europe's share should be only 3,400 tonnes, compared with last year's catch of 40,000. Canada's permitted amount increased more than four times. The European Commission lodged an objection but, citing the need to protect fish stocks, Canada ordered all EU trawlers out of the area. (→March 14)

MEXICO CITY, FRIDAY 10

New austerity measures from Mexican government

Guillermo Ortiz fighting for the peso.

As the peso fell to another new low on international exchanges Mexico's treasury secretary, Guillermo Ortiz, announced a package of emergency measures. Increases in the minimum wage will not exceed 10 per cent, while sales tax will rise 5 per cent to 10 per cent, and electricity and petrol prices will rise by 35 per cent. Other wage rises will not be restricted. Subsidies of basic foodstuffs will increase in an attempt to protect the poor. Inflation is expected to level out, according to Señor Ortiz, at 42 per cent by the end of the year.

Scotland, Thursday 9. Far from being gentle and peaceful, dolphins are shown in a BBC Television Scotland programme to attack and kill porpoises in the Moray Firth. They do not eat them, but batter them and toy with them for up to 45 minutes before the porpoises die.

New York, Tuesday 7. Carol Shaya-Castro is dismissed from her job as a New York policewoman for posing both nude and in her uniform in *Playboy* who paid her $100,000.

LEEDS, WEDNESDAY 10

Injured man is flown from London to Leeds

A man who was critically injured after being deliberately knocked down by a car after a fight outside a pub, was flown 200 miles to Leeds when no hospital bed could be found for him in London.

After a seven-hour operation to remove a potentially fatal blood clot from the brain of victim Malcolm Murray, surgeon Phil van Hille said that the patient would have been better served if he had been given more immediate attention. His condition remains critical.

The Department of Health has asked the regional health authority to investigate the shortage of beds in London hospitals.

KABUL, MONDAY 6

Afghan government attacks last rebel stronghold in Kabul

Government forces loading artillery in Afghanistan's three-year-long civil war.

Government forces in the Afghan capital launched an all-out attack today on the last rebel stronghold in the city. After rocket attacks, air strikes, and artillery shelling, ground forces captured positions in the rebel enclave of Karte Se.

Rebel forces have responded with rocket attacks on the government-held sectors of the city. Hospitals on both sides of the fighting have been hit, and the Red Cross in the city reports numerous civilian casualties. Many foreign aid workers are trapped in the battle zone.

The civil war has lasted for three years but the UN is attempting to arrange a peaceful transfer of power on March 21. A UN delegation was to have landed in Kabul today, but was prevented from doing so by the fighting. It is unclear what effect the government attack will have on the prospects for peace. (→March 19)

S	M	T	W	T	F	S
			1	2	3	4
5	6	7	8	9	10	11
12	13	14	15	16	17	18
19	20 · 21	22	23	24	25
26	27	28	29	30	31	

Las Vegas, 12
Riddick Bowe is to discuss a possible bout with Mike Tyson, having taken the WBO heavyweight title from Briton Herbie Hide.

Copenhagen, 12
After talks with US officials, the Croatian president, Franjo Tudjman, withdraws his demand that UN forces leave his country.

London, 13
England footballer and Chelsea captain Dennis Wise is sentenced to three months in jail for an assault on a taxi driver. He is bailed pending his appeal against the sentence.

New York, 13
The UN Security Council votes to maintain sanctions against Iraq, imposed at the time of the invasion of Kuwait.

New York, 14
Ex-president of Mexico, Carlos Salinas, appears in Manhattan denying that he has been exiled from his country.

Newfoundland, 14
Spanish trawlers return to contested fishing grounds, watched by Canadian planes. (→April 16)

Washington DC, 14
Conoco pulls out of an agreement to develop two off-shore oilfields for Iran, following a threat from the White House to block the deal.

Istanbul, 15
Three days of rioting by the moderate Islamic Alawite sect end when four people are killed and 25 injured.

Twickenham, 18
England beat Scotland 24-12 to win the rugby Grand Slam.

Philippines, 16
Vietnamese boat people facing deportation are threatening to kill themselves rather than be returned.

Deaths
Carlos Facundo Menem, 26-year-old son of the Argentinian president, when his helicopter crashes into power cables, March 16.

War heroine Odette Hallowes, aged 83, March 16.

WASHINGTON DC, THURSDAY 16

Adams visits White House

Gerry Adams speaking at a press conference during his week-long American visit.

This year's St. Patrick's Day celebrations have been given a special significance with an historic handshake between President Clinton and Gerry Adams, leader of Sinn Fein, the political wing of the IRA. Although he had invited Mr. Adams to the White House luncheon it was doubtful that the President would actually embrace the Irish Republican in any way, and he did avoid contact with the Sinn Fein leader while there were photographers present.

However, those at the luncheon – mainly Irish-American members of Congress – said that the private handshake was warm and enthusiastic. The two men spoke freely with each other for five minutes.

President Clinton has been under pressure from the British government, which is openly unhappy about the visit and the official reception that has been accorded to Mr. Adams. John Major is refusing to enter into further talks with Sinn Fein until the IRA have handed in their arms.

Mr. Adams is on a week-long visit to the US, which started on Sunday with Sinn Fein's first-ever legal fundraising event in the US, held in Queens, New York. Mr. Adams announced at the event that Sinn Fein would be opening an office in Washington DC. During his visit he has met Governor Pataki of New York, and will be at the White House again on Friday for a reception in honour of the Prime Minister of Ireland, John Bruton.

The President is reported as having told Mr. Adams that he is committed to the peace process, and insisted that it would be successful. (→April 4)

LONDON, THURSDAY 16

Clarke makes gaffe on radio

Kenneth Clarke, the Chancellor of the Exchequer, is in hot water again with the people of Consett, County Durham, after referring in a Radio 5 Live breakfast interview to a thriving disposable nappy factory that, in fact, closed down four years ago.

The gaffe follows a similar blunder only two weeks ago when Mr. Clarke cited Consett's steel industry as a northeast success story – unaware that the town's steel factory had closed down 15 years ago with the loss of 3,000 jobs.

NEW YORK, WEDNESDAY 15

New song from surviving Beatles

Paul McCartney announced that he, Ringo Starr, and George Harrison have been working together to record new songs for release later this year. The three have been meeting in secret in a studio in London to record what McCartney called "a couple of tracks" to be included on *The Beatles Anthology*, which will be released in November. It was discovered last year that the three surviving Beatles had been adding to the vocals of a John Lennon song that his widow, Yoko Ono, had on tape. (→November 20)

LOS ANGELES, MONDAY 13

O.J. cop quizzed

Lawyers in confrontation at the O.J. trial.

Defence lawyers in the O.J. Simpson trial have been given the go-ahead to quiz Detective Mark Fuhrman on alleged racism. They claim that Fuhrman tampered with evidence and that racism could supply the motive for his actions. (→March 27)

HAMPSHIRE, TUESDAY 14

Grobbelaar, Segers, and Fashanu arrested on match-fixing allegations

Three top footballers are languishing in gaol today after being arrested by Hampshire police officers investigating bribery charges.

Bruce Grobbelaar, Hans Segers, and John Fashanu are being held along with Fashanu's girlfriend Melissa Kassa-Mapsi and London-based Malaysian businessman Heng Suan Lim, following a tip off that the footballers were being paid to fix matches by a Far Eastern betting syndicate. Grobbelaar, the current Southampton and former Liverpool goalkeeper, has been under investigation for four months now, after allegations of match fixing were made by his former business partner Chris Vincent. According to his solicitor, Grobbelaar has co-operated with the police investigation while strongly denying all the charges.

Twenty police officers were involved in the raid, which also yielded a haul of papers and property. Detective Chief Inspector Rod Davis said that all five people arrested were linked to the same conspiracy.

John Fashanu arrives at Fareham police station to answer questions on match fixing.

Madrid, Saturday 18. Spain comes to a halt for three hours as almost the entire population watches on television the wedding of King Juan Carlos' daughter Elena to Jaime de Marichalar Saez de Tejada. In Seville hundreds of thousands of people line the route to the cathedral, where the wedding is taking place.

Slough, Friday 17. Gangster Ronnie Kray (above, left, with his twin Reggie) died today, aged 61, after a heart attack. He had been in prison since 1969.

TOKYO, WEDNESDAY 15

Eleven Japanese gangsters arrested for profiteering from Kobe earthquake

Eleven gangsters were arrested earlier today on charges of profiteering from the recent earthquake in Kobe. The January quake not only claimed 5,500 lives, but also caused massive devastation and made hundreds of thousands homeless. Relief operations are still going on. The police claim that the gangsters pretended to be victims of the quake in order to be awarded relief loans of 4.6 million yen (£34,000) from a social welfare office in the city.

One of the 11 arrested is believed to be the head of a gang that is affiliated to the largest of Japan's crime syndicates, *Yamaguchi-gumi*, which is estimated to have a membership of 30,000. In a country which has an enviably low crime rate, members of organized gangs, or *yakuza*, are responsible for a large proportion of the crimes that are committed. Indeed, *yakuza* members account for about two out of three prisoners in the country's jails.

Frauds such as the alleged one at Kobe are favourite ploys of Japanese gangsters. They rarely target individuals, and attacks on the general public, especially those involving physical assault, are rare in Japan. Fighting between opposing gangs is, however, more common.

Bonn, Friday 17. Fashion designer Karl Lagerfeld's injunction stops the showing of Robert Altman's film *Prêt à Porter* on grounds of libel.

S	M	T	W	T	F	S
			1	2	3	4
5	6	7	8	9	10	11
12	13	14	15	16	17	18
19	20	21	22	23	24	25
26	27	28	29	30	31	

Kabul, 19
The Afghan army re-enters the capital, having driven out the rebel Taliban Islamic movement.

Ankara, 20
Thirty-five thousand Turkish troops enter northern Iraq looking for Kurdish separatists. (→ May 4)

London, 21
Actor Stephen Fry, who unexpectedly withdrew from a West End play last month, returns and checks into hospital.

St. Andrews, 22
University professor states that the spread of flowering plants in the Arctic proves global warming.

Washington DC, 22
Record US trade deficit is posted for January, soaring to $12.23 billion.

Mineola, New York, 22
Colin Ferguson, the Long Island Rail Road murderer, is sentenced to 200 years.

London, 23
Eric Cantona, Manchester United's French star, is sentenced to two weeks' jail for assaulting a specator, but freed on bail. (→ April 18)

Washington DC, 23
Veterans are told that the "VJ" Day designation will not be replaced by "VP Day", despite Japanese protests.

Moscow, 23
The Russian commander forecasts a long war in Chechnya, while the Chechen leader states that only discussion can end the conflict. (→ April 19)

Washington DC, 23
A Senate committee proposes outlawing Internet pornography. (→ September 12)

Nigeria, 24
Human Rights Watch reports that the Nigerian military government is deliberately persecuting and killing the Ogoni people. (→ November 11)

Baghdad, 25
Two Americans who strayed into Iraq are sentenced to eight years for spying.

Death
BBC newsreader Peter Woods, aged 64, Wednesday 22.

TOKYO, MONDAY 20

Nerve gas attack on Tokyo subway

Rescuers help victims of the nerve gas attack outside a subway station in Tokyo.

A guerrilla-style attack paralyzed Tokyo this morning at the height of the rush hour as a deadly nerve gas was released in the subway system. Ten people have died, and 5,500 others have been injured, many of them critically. It appears that up to 15 canisters were left at important stations on three of the subway system's lines and were timed to release the gas more or less simultaneously.

First tests indicate that the gas was sarin, a poison developed by the Nazis during the World War 2 though never used by them. Passengers reported seeing a liquid oozing from lunch boxes wrapped in newspapers. "I saw no gas, but I saw a transparent liquid spreading on the floor, and people falling on the ground one by one," reported one woman.

Passengers staggered onto the platforms from the trains, and many collapsed. Several had bubbles coming from their mouths, and others were bleeding from the nose. A similar incident, but without fatalities, took place on the Yokohama subway earlier this month, while last June seven people died mysteriously from gas poisoning in Matsumoto in central Japan. Sarin was also suspected then. No group has claimed responsibility for today's attack, but police attention has focused on the Aum Supreme Truth cult. (→ March 30)

LONDON, SUNDAY 19

Conservative party split widens

Chancellor of the Exchequer Kenneth Clarke is the victim of a blistering attack by the Thatcherite Conservative Way Forward group. A leader in the group's *Forward* magazine accuses him of undermining Prime Minister John Major by trying to push Britain into a single European currency.

The darling of the right wing, Employment Secretary Michael Portillo, is trying to limit the damage. On BBC Radio 4's *The World This Weekend,* he stated: "Personal attacks can't help our party at all. We are too close to the next election for factional struggle."

New York, Sunday 19. Breeders are petitioning for official status for the Munchkin cat after its appearance at the International Cat Show. The cat, named after the characters in *The Wizard of Oz*, has exceptionally short legs and can turn quickly and run backwards.

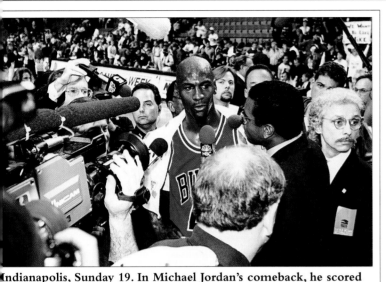

Indianapolis, Sunday 19. In Michael Jordan's comeback, he scored 19 points as his Chicago Bulls lost 103–96 to Indianapolis. After his first game for 21 months he criticized some of the other basketball players: "The younger guys aren't taking responsibility."

Mike Tyson released from jail

After serving three years of his ten-year sentence for the rape in 1991 of a teenage beauty queen, Mike Tyson was released from the Indiana Youth Correction Center this morning into a cold dawn. Four years of his sentence were suspended and he was excused three years for good behaviour. Wearing a white Islamic skullcap and surrounded by Black Muslim bodyguards, Tyson refused to talk to the waiting reporters. However, a written statement was handed out in which he said, "I'm very happy to be out and on my way home." He was also met by boxing promoter Don King and it is expected that the fit-looking boxer will shortly be back in the ring. (→ August 19)

Mike Tyson, with Don King, leaving jail.

BONN, SATURDAY 25

Border controls removed in EU

French customs man: a thing of the past?

At midnight tonight seven of the 15 members of the European Union offically remove the border controls between themselves. The move, hailed by Foreign Minister Klaus Kinkel of Germany as the "precursor to complete freedom of movement in all of Europe", is highly symbolic for those who want closer European integration. The seven countries, known as the "Schengen group", include Germany, France, Holland, and Spain. It excludes Great Britain, which is opposed to the arrangement on the grounds that laxer border controls will encourage terrorists and drug smugglers.

LONDON, FRIDAY 24

Teenage girls found guilty of mugging Elizabeth Hurley

The three teenage girls who held actress and model Elizabeth Hurley at knifepoint and robbed her of £10 were found guilty today. The jury took less than an hour to reach a unanimous verdict. The girls were then returned to Holloway prison, where they have been held since their arrest on November 23 last year. They each face a gaol term. Hurley flew in from New York to give evidence in the three-day trial. Round-trip air fares are thought to have cost her £4,000.

The attack took place in Kensington as Hurley was walking home to the house she shares with her boyfriend Hugh Grant, star of the blockbuster film *Four Weddings and a Funeral*. The girls' families claim that they have been treated unfairly because Hurley is a celebrity.

LONDON, TUESDAY 21

Deputy governor of Bank of England resigns over affair

Rupert Pennant-Rea, deputy governor of the Bank of England, gave up his fight to hold on to his job today. His position has been in doubt since Mary Ellen Synon, 44, revealed to the *Sunday Mirror* that she had been his lover for three years. She said they had made love in his office and in his official car.

As the story was breaking last Saturday, Pennant-Rea, 47, issued a statement saying he had the full backing of the Bank's governor, Eddie George. But it transpired that this had amounted to a conversation they had had last April when Pennant-Rea told George of the affair. Pennant-Rea eventually tendered his resignation to "avoid the possibility of the Bank being damaged by some foolish mistake I made".

Pennant-Rea's third wife Helen, 49, said: "I support and respect my husband's decision to resign from the Bank. His relationship with Ms. Synon ended over a year ago and Rupert told me about it then. Over the last year, despite her threat to publicize the affair, we have endeavoured to rebuild our marriage and protect our children."

Mr. Pennant-Rea is a former editor of *The Economist* magazine, which is where he first met Ms. Synon.

TORONTO, SUNDAY 19

Cancer supergun unveiled

Some 6,000 attendees at the American Association for Cancer Research have been told of a new treatment for cancer that has halted tumor growth in tests on mice. The secret is a hand-held gun that shoots microscopic gold bullets into the patient. The bullets are coated with genetic material that enters the cancers and stimulates the body's immune system to fight them.

Cape Town, Monday 20. The Queen arrives here for the first royal visit to South Africa for nearly 50 years.

S	M	T	W	T	F	S
			1	2	3	4
5	6	7	8	9	10	11
12	13	14	15	16	17	18
19	20 · 21		22	23	24	25
26	27	28	29	30	31	

Beijing, 26
The Chinese government introduces a five-day working week for government employees in an attempt to reduce unemployment.

Sarajevo, 27
The United Nations threatens air strikes against the Bosnian Serbs unless they stop shelling the UN "safe areas". (→ May 2)

Algiers, 27
Between 300 and 600 Islamic militants have been killed in six days as Algerian government forces step up their campaign against the rebels.

Los Angeles, 27
An important prosecution witness in the O.J. Simpson trial is ruled "hostile", allowing the prosecution to cross-examine him. (→ May 1)

London, 27
Martin Amis's *The Information* is published by HarperCollins, which paid the author a £500,000 advance.

Tokyo, 28
The world's largest bank is to be created by the merger of the Bank of Tokyo and the Mitsubishi Bank. It will have assets of $819 billion.

Washington DC, 28
Lobbying Congress in person, the King of Jordan gets a cool reception to his request for the US to honour its pledge to write off his country's national debt.

New York, 29
The baseball players' union says they will return to work if a judge forces owners to restore salary arbitration.

Paris, 30
A 24-hour strike by transport unions in support of a pay claim brings chaos to France.

Tokyo, 30
Japan's top policeman is shot outside his home, following warnings from the Aum Supreme Truth cult. (→ April 14)

London, 30
National Aids Trusts says a boy aged five, born with the Aids virus, cured himself, giving hope for a vaccine.

Burundi, 31
An estimated 20,000 Hutu refugees flee for Tanzania after several of them are attacked and killed.

MANILA, SUNDAY 26
Imelda Marcos campaigns to be elected to Filipino Congress

Imelda Marcos addressing a crowd on her home island of Leyte, where she is still sure of finding faithful supporters.

Despite being on bail as she appeals against the corruption conviction that sentenced her to life imprisonment, Imelda Marcos, widow of the deposed president of the Philippines, is not easily giving up her fight to re-enter Filipino politics.

She is currently campaigning in the villages on the island of Leyte in order to drum up support for her candidacy in the elections to the country's Congress this May. Leyte is Mrs. Marcos's home island, and she is treated like royalty there.

Mrs. Marcos, who came fifth of the seven candidates in the 1992 presidential election, is campaigning on a platform of restoring the Philippines to what she still sees as an international respectability enjoyed during her husband's tenure of office.

SÃO PAULO, SUNDAY 26
Schumacher stripped of victory

Formula One World Champion Michael Schumacher was disqualified after finishing first in the Brazilian Grand Prix when Stewards found that his Benetton team had been using illegal fuel.

David Coulthard, who came second in a Williams, was also stripped of his place. Both Benetton and Williams were fined £20,000. Gerhard Berger, who finished third in a Ferrari, was declared the winner. Only eight of the 26 starters finished the race. Damon Hill spun off after 31 of the 71 laps.

Schumacher won the drivers' championship last year after having been banned from two races and being penalized by having points deducted in two more.

HOLLYWOOD, MONDAY 27
Forrest Gump sweeps board at Oscars

The feel-good factor triumphed at the Academy Awards as *Forrest Gump*, the tale of a simple man caught up in national events, garnered six Oscars. Its star, Tom Hanks, won Best Actor, Robert Zemeckis won Best Director, and the film was judged Best Picture. It also won the the awards for Best Editing, Best Visual Effects, and Best Adapted Screenplay. Star Tom Hanks let his emotions show as he collected his second Best-Actor award in successive years.

Jessica Lange gained the Best-Actress award for her performance in *Blue Sky*. Dianne Wiest won Best Supporting Actress in *Bullets Over Broadway*, and Martin Landau won Best Supporting Actor for his portrayal of Bela Lugosi in *Ed Wood*. Quentin Tarantino was awarded Best Screenplay for *Pulp Fiction*.

Tom Hanks with his Oscar for Best Actor.

PORT-AU-PRINCE, TUESDAY 28

Aristide opponent shot and killed

President Jean-Bertrand Aristide of Haiti.

A prominent opponent of Haitian president Jean-Bertrand Aristide has been assassinated. Ms. Mireille Durocher Bertin, a 33-year-old lawyer and head of a leading opposition party, was shot in her car by gunmen who fired from a taxi. The assassination follows three weeks of political violence in which more than 30 have died and comes only one day before President Clinton is due to visit the island. President Aristide has condemned the killing.

LONDON, TUESDAY 28

Plans for 14-lane M25 scrapped

Transport Secretary Dr. Brian Mawhinney has abandoned plans to turn sections of the M25 into a 14-lane American-style superhighway after protests by local councils and Conservative MPs in Surrey. The £165-million plan would have added three-lane link roads either side of the motorway between the intersections with the M3 and M4. This section of the M25 is the busiest motorway in Britain. It carries 165,000 vehicles a day, and is expected to carry 260,000 a day by the year 2000.

Instead, there will be limited widening of the road and vehicles will be restricted to a speed of 50 mph when the road is busy. The "green" lobby is jubilant. Friends of the Earth transport campaigner Roger Higman said: "This a victory for democracy, but our fight continues."

More crucially, ministers feared that local protests might hurt the Conservative party in the local elections in May. It marks a significant shift in government policy away from building more roads to accommodate increasing levels of traffic.

British Airways say no road widening is needed to cope with traffic to the new Terminal 5 opening in 2010.

BUCHAREST, FRIDAY 31

59 die in Romanian airbus crash

Wreckage from the plane operated by Romanian airline Tarom in a field near Bucharest.

An Airbus operated by the Romanian national airline, Tarom, crashed into a field only three minutes after taking off from Bucharest airport today. All of the 59 people who were on board, 32 of them Belgian, are believed to have died.

The Brussels-bound plane, an A310-300 Airbus, was found 28 km (17 miles) from Bucharest airport, shattered into tiny pieces, of which the largest is only 2 m (6.5 ft) long. The cause of the crash is not known.

Weather conditions today were good and sabotage has not been ruled out. Witnesses reported hearing an explosion before the plane hit the ground. Two weeks ago a similar Tarom flight to Brussels made an emergency landing after a caller rang the airline saying there was a bomb on board. None was found. Another Tarom Airbus nearly crashed recently over Paris when it nose-dived after the automatic pilot suddenly malfunctioned.

Johannesburg, Monday 27. Winnie Mandela remains defiant after her dismissal from government by President Mandela for repeated attacks on the government.

LONDON, WEDNESDAY 29

Aitken "arms to Iran" affair

In a desperate attempt to save his political skin, Treasury Chief Secretary Jonathan Aitken issued a blunt denial of breaching the government's embargo on arms sales to the belligerents in the Iran-Iraq war. He was a non-executive director of a company that shipped naval guns to Iran in the 1980s.

Aitken says that he neither knew about nor was involved in that contract, and complains that he is the victim of a witch-hunt. But Gerald James, former chairman of Astra Holdings which owned British Manufacturer and Research Company, the firm involved, dismisses Aitken's denials as "rubbish". Labour's trade and industry spokesman Jack Cunningham says it was inconceivable that "a director recruited specifically to promote contracts in the Middle East should not have been told of existing contracts in the area". He called for an immediate enquiry to clarify the "manifest inconsistencies" in Aitken's account.

Aitken is supported in his denials by Major-General Donald Isles, who was in charge of the naval gun project at BMARC, and by William McNaughton, another director.

The Prime Minister is said to be satisfied with Aitken's statement. But Aitken is still politically beleaguered. Last October, he was embroiled in a row over who paid his bill at the Ritz Hotel in Paris. Aitken denied that it had been settled by a Saudi Arabian businessman. More recently, he has attacked the BBC for bias.

Milan, Tuesday 28. Maurizio Gucci, 45, grandson of the founder of the luxury leather goods company and himself head of the company until 1993, has been shot dead by a gunman outside his office in central Milan.

S	M	T	W	T	F	S
						1
2	3	4	5	6	7	8
9	10	11	12	13	14	15
16	17	18	19	20	21	22
23	24	25	26	27	28	29
30						

Gaza Strip, 2
Eight people are killed by a bomb explosion in an area renowned as a stronghold of the Palestinian separatist group Hamas. A spokesman for the PLO said they believed it was an accident as Hamas members were preparing a bomb. (→ April 9)

Wembley, 2
Liverpool win the Coca-Cola Cup, beating Bolton 2-1.

Dorset, 2
An 1,100 lb (500 kg) unexploded bomb dropped by a German aircraft during World War II is defused. Over 4,000 people can now return to their homes.

London, 3
The former chairman and deputy chairman of Barings Bank both resign because of the financial devastation caused by its rogue trader Nick Leeson. (→ November 24)

Burundi, 3
Robert Krueger, US ambassador to Burundi, reports that hundreds of Hutus have been massacred over the past weeks.

Bosnia, 4
As the weather improves, heavy fighting breaks out near the town of Tuzla in northern Bosnia, as Bosnian government forces attack Serb positions. (→ April 24)

Washington DC, 4
President Clinton backs John Major in calling for the IRA to give up their arms.(→ May 3)

Madrid, 4
Spanish premier, Felipe Gonzalez, claims that Britain should show solidarity with Spain in the fishing dispute with Canada. (→ April 11)

London, 5
Law Lords rule that Home Secretary Michael Howard acted illegally in imposing a fixed rate of compensation for victims of violence.

Bristol, 5
Bristol Royal Infirmary admits that it should have informed parents that an artery operation performed on their children was known to be dangerous. Nine out of 13 babies operated on died within 18 months.

BERLIN, WEDNESDAY 5

Kohl attacks US over pollution at global environment conference

Britain and Germany set the tone on the first day of the Ministerial Summit on Climate Change today, by accusing America, the world's largest polluter, of not doing enough to cut down emissions of greenhouse gases.

Chancellor Helmut Kohl urged industrialized nations with high energy consumption to face up to their "special responsibility" to prevent environmental disasters. In a pointed reference to the difficulty the Clinton administration has had in committing itself to cuts in emissions after the year 2000, he said: "There must be no shirking. We must not destroy the soil on which our children's food must grow."

UK environment secretary, John Gummer, reinforced Kohl's stance, saying that computer models run by the Met Office's Hadley Centre forecast change within the lifetime of our children. "If that is the case," he added, "you cannot put short-term political needs ahead of that."

Gummer said that cuts in carbon dioxide emissions of up to 10 per cent by 2010, as promised by Britain, were the only kind of commitment acceptable from industrial countries, while Kohl reiterated Germany's commitment to cutting emissions by 25 per cent by 2005.

Kohl's speech was well received by environmentalists and developing countries. Atiq Raman of Climate Action Network for Southeast Asia said: "He has put reductions back as central to debate. No nation, however big, should hold hostage the future of the planet."

LONDON, TUESDAY 4

Kenny Everett dies of AIDS

The comedian Kenny Everett, who revealed he was HIV positive two years ago, has died of AIDS, aged 50. Everett's career was turbulent – he was sacked twice by the BBC because of his outrageous style on Radio 1 – but his television shows, particularly *The Kenny Everett Video Show*, were highly successful.

Kenny Everett, comedian and DJ.

MANILA, MONDAY 3

World Trade Center bombing suspects arrested

Six Arabs, said to be linked to the man accused of carrying out the 1993 bombing of the World Trade Center in New York, were arrested yesterday in the Philippine capital, Manila.

Police seized guns, explosives, timing devices, and computer disks in the raid on a suburban flat. They believe that the arrested men have ties to Ramzi Ahmed Yousef, who has been extradited from Pakistan to the US to face charges that he masterminded the 1993 bombing.

A wrecked car after the 1993 bombing.

WASHINGTON DC, SUNDAY 2

Water in liquid form found on Mars

Scientists claim that meteorite debris shows humans can create a second world on Mars.

One of the greatest obstacles to establishing life on Mars has been removed, with the crucial discovery that water in liquid form exists on the planet's surface. The finding also increases the probability that primitive life already exists there, although it does not represent definitive proof.

Last week, Professor Thomas Donahue of the University of Michigan explained how studies of meteorites that have fallen to Earth from Mars show that the air in the thin Martian atmosphere is interacting with water at its surface.

"If water was spread on the surface uniformly," said Donahue, "it would cover Mars to a depth of 24 m (78 ft). All that colonists on Mars will need to do is sink wells to get it out. This will make establishing settlements easier and cheaper than was previously thought."

LONDON, TUESDAY 4

Blandford held on drugs charges

The Marquess of Blandford, 39, was last night charged with forging drug prescriptions and stealing drugs from a chemist near his home in Chelsea. He was arrested at an Earl's Court hotel and held in custody overnight at Chelsea police station. He is due to appear before Horseferry Road magistrates on April 10.

Blandford faces the press.

BRITAIN, TUESDAY 4

Scotland bans broadcast of BBC interview with Major

A television interview in which John Major promised two tax-cutting budgets before a general election in 1997 was banned in Scotland last night. A judge ruled that the *Panorama* interview should not be broadcast there because it could influence local elections being held in three days' time. The decision was upheld on appeal five minutes before the programme was due to be shown.

The Court of Session in Edinburgh ruled that the programme could not be broadcast after Labour and the Liberal Democrats protested that this would breach BBC guidelines on impartiality. Three judges then arrived at the same court from their homes to hear an appeal by BBC lawyers. After 60 seconds of discussion, they upheld the decision.

Mr. Alan Duncan, chairman of the Tory back bench constitutional affairs committee, described it as a "stinking judicial decision".

Major agreed to be interviewed at short notice last week. MPs saw it as the latest stage in a campaign to woo back middle-class voters in the run-up to local elections.

BBC director general, John Birt, said: "This judgement raises serious constitutional issues. The BBC has a deep commitment to impartiality."

A spokesman for Labour said: "Clearly Number 10, the Tory party, and the BBC forgot those elections were happening."

Georgia, US, Sunday 2. British-born killer Nicky Ingram (right) was executed at 9.15 p.m. today. "The order of the court has been carried out", prison doctors stated, declaring Ingram dead after nine minutes strapped to the electric chair, where 2,000 volts was sent through his body.

LONDON, SATURDAY 1

Girl who symbolized Sarajevo's suffering dies

Irma Hadzimuratovic, the severely injured Bosnian girl whose plight inspired a mission to airlift wounded children from the former Yugoslavia, has died in her sleep at Great Ormond Street children's hospital.

She arrived in London in August 1993, aged five. The mortar shell that exploded in a Sarajevo market killed her mother and left Irma badly injured in her stomach, spine, and brain.

In Sarajevo, surgeons operated by daylight and candlelight to rebuild her bowel, but she then developed signs of brain damage. An appeal to the United Nations to evacuate her failed and her surgeon, Eno Jaganjac, wept on television, saying that in Sarajevo she had one day to live, whereas in the West her injuries could easily be treated.

Early the next day, Irma was flown to Great Ormond Street, where she had a three-hour skin graft to cover a wound in her back which had infected her spinal fluid. Despite her frailty, Irma gradually grew a little stronger and learnt English, before suffering complications which prevented her from eating and finally led to her death. Her father and younger sister were with her when she died.

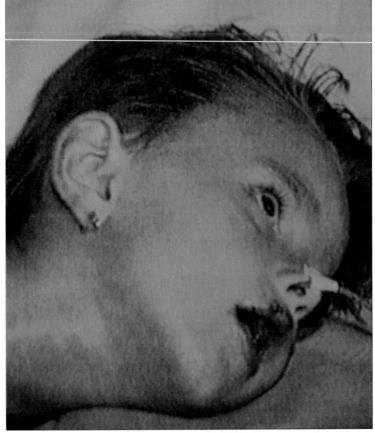

Bosnia airlift girl Irma Hadzimuratovic loses her fight for life.

LONDON, FRIDAY 7

Cancer victim spent nine hours on trolley

A woman with cancer has died the day after spending nine hours lying on a hospital trolley in a side room in casualty because no bed could be found for her. Maggie Curtin, a 47-year-old mother of three, died at Northwick Park Hospital in Harrow, north London.

Her husband, Mike Curtin, discovered she was dead by finding her body in the ward bed, after the hospital had asked him to come in without giving a reason. Mr. Curtin was telephoned by the hospital at 5.15 p.m. on the day after the nine-hour wait.

"They just asked me to come in. I realized later I had been called in because she had died. I went straight on to the ward and I saw her bed had curtains pulled round it. When I pulled back the curtains I found her lying there dead. Nobody was with her. I went to pieces."

Mr. Curtin has written to the hospital to complain and sent copies of his letter to Health Secretary Virginia Bottomley, his local Conservative MP Hugh Dykes, and the Labour MP Ken Livingstone. Michael Cole, chief executive of the hospital, has ordered an investigation into the death.

Mr Curtin said: "The only person I haven't heard from is Mrs. Bottomley." He went on to add, "My wife died because of the state that the health service is in."

April

S	M	T	W	T	F	S
						1
2	3	4	5	6	7	8
9	10	11	12	13	14	15
16	17	18	19	20	21	22
23	24	25	26	27	28	29
30						

New York, 9
Robert McNamara, the prime architect of US strategy in Vietnam, breaks down in tears on TV and admits that his policy on Vietnam had been wrong.

Tajikistan, 9
Tajikistan appeals for international help after its border guards are fired on from Afghanistan.

Augusta, Georgia, 9
Bob Crenshaw wins the US Masters for a second time.

Walsall, 9
A 35-year-old man, Paul Nixon, is killed as mass brawling breaks out between Manchester United and Crystal Palace fans outside a pub prior to the FA Cup semi-final between the clubs.

Tokyo, 9
Voters make some surprise choices in selecting TV personalities for the governorships of Tokyo and Osaka.

London, 10
The Marquess of Blandford is gaoled for 30 days for stealing £10 worth of drugs from a chemist's shop.

Sheffield, 10
Six officers from the South Yorkshire police force who say their careers were ruined by the Hillsborough tragedy have their claims dismissed by Mr. Justice Walker.

London, 11
Jonathan Aitken MP calls a press conference to announce that he is to sue the *Guardian* newspaper for libel over stories that he procured call girls for Saudi princes.

London, 12
Dr. David Hope, who has been targetted by groups aiming to "out" gays, is to be the new Archbishop of York, the second highest position in the Anglican church.

Cambridge, 13
A 51-year-old woman has a test-tube baby after lying about her age to doctors.

Death
Maraji Desai, former Indian prime minister, aged 99, April 10.

Hamburg, Saturday 15. Fifty years ago today, British soldiers of the Allied forces entered the concentration camp of Belsen. Most camps were located further east, and this was the first time that troops of the western allies had come across such scenes of horror.

BLACKPOOL, SATURDAY 15
Leftist teachers jostle David Blunkett at NUT conference

There were disturbing scenes at the conference of the National Union of Teachers. Labour Party spokesman on education, David Blunkett, was surrounded by members of the Socialist Workers' Party as he arrived to address the conference. Shouting "Sack the Tories, not the teachers", the demonstrators made it impossible for Mr. Blunkett, who is blind, to continue to the main chamber. He and officers of the union went into a side room while the demonstrators chanted outside.

The Labour Party has changed its attitude to education recently, and has accepted Conservative Party reforms such as tests for all pupils at certain ages and a national ranking of schools. When he was able to give his speech, Mr. Blunkett warned teachers not to strike over class sizes.

NEW YORK, MONDAY 10
Smoking ban in New York restaurants comes into force

An endangered species: the smoker.

The anti-smoking lobby is celebrating a significant victory. Regulations that seriously limit smoking in New York's restaurants come into effect today. The new rules essentially ban smoking in dining areas where there are seats for more than 35 people.

Smoking is permitted in a bar area or separate lounge only if dining tables are at least 2 m (6½ ft) away. Many restaurant owners believe that without the opportunity to relax and smoke before or after their meal, diners will spend less on drink, and profits will fall heavily.

TOKYO, FRIDAY 14
Easter alert in Tokyo after sect phone threats

Police are out in force in Tokyo and its suburbs. Shoko Asahara, leader of the Aum Supreme Truth sect, has prophesied that the Easter weekend will see a terrible disaster befall the city, a disaster worse than the Kobe earthquake of January. The earthquake, he said, would be "as minor as a fly landing on one's cheek" compared with this new disaster.

Asahara's sect is held to be responsible for the devastating nerve gas attacks on the Tokyo underground system. The fear is that Asahara's followers will use the stocks of nerve gas they have built up to make an attack on the Shinjuku entertainment district. A woman whose daughter joined the cult said that her daughter had recently phoned her and warned her not to go to Shinjuku.

Police have set up road blocks across the capital, and are stopping cars and searching motorists. Wearing chemical-warfare clothing, police have also raided centres known to be used by the cult. Up to 100,000 police, one third of Japan's police force, are believed to be involved in the security operation.

Hospitals have been advised to build up stocks of nerve gas antidotes. Many businesses, including shopping centres, have decided to close for the weekend, just in case. (→April 21)

New York, Friday 14. Burl Ives, much-loved singer of American folk ballads, has died aged 85. He was also a successful actor on stage and screen.

TEL AVIV, SUNDAY 9

Suicide bombers kill seven in Gaza Strip

One of the wounded Israeli soldiers hit by the suicide bomb blast near Kfar Darom. Over 45 people were injured in two attacks.

The prospects for a lasting peace in Israel were jolted when Palestinian suicide bombers struck at Israeli targets within the Gaza Strip today.

In the first attack, near Kfar Darom, a van pulled up next to a bus carrying Israeli soldiers back from their weekend leave. The driver then activated the explosive, killing himself and seven Israeli soldiers in the blast. There were also nine casualties.

The second attack took place on a convoy near the town of Netzarim. In this, a car pulled up near a security convoy, and exploded. Five Israeli policemen were injured in the blast. Israel's premier, Yitzhak Rabin, was clearly shocked by the attacks, but vowed that he would not abandon the peace negotiations with the Palestinians and neighbouring Arab states. He did, however, warn: "The Palestinian authority must prove that it can act against these groups." (→ April 16)

WASHINGTON DC, THURSDAY 13

US to threaten Japan with sanctions

Frustrated by lack of progress in lengthy free trade negotiations with Japan, the White House has decided to impose punitive tariffs on the Japanese unless they agree to open up their domestic market to US automobiles and auto parts. The tariffs will come into effect if no clear progress has been made within the next three weeks.

The situation is exacerbated by the recent drastic fall in the value of the dollar against the yen, and that has convinced US administration officials that they cannot afford to delay action any longer. (→ May 16)

Athens, Monday 10. In a three-month experiment to try to solve the city's enormous pollution problems, the government has banned traffic from the historically important Ermou area.

CORNWALL, TUESDAY 11

Cornwall in show of solidarity with Canada vs Spain

The maple leaf was strongly in evidence in the Cornish town of Newlyn for the visit of Mr. Royce Frith, the Canadian high commissioner. Mr. Frith was visiting the fishing port to give thanks for the support expressed by Cornish fishermen for Canada in its confrontation with the Spanish trawlers that were trying to take Greenland halibut from the Grand Banks.

The Cornish are as worried as the Canadians by the large Spanish fishing fleets that are moving into waters traditionally fished by other nations. The diplomatic niceties are interesting: as a member of the European Union, Britain officially supports the Spanish in the negotiations with the Canadians, but most Britons, and certainly all those connected with the fishing industry, feel strongly that the Spaniards should be prevented from extending their operations. There is also suspicion that the Spaniards are using illegal nets. (→ April 16)

LIMA, SUNDAY 9

Fujimori easily re-elected in Peru

Fujimori supporters celebrate victory.

Alberto Fujimori, the incumbent president of Peru, has been re-elected by a large majority in today's election. His majority will probably be close to 60 per cent, which means that there will be no need for a second round of voting.

President Fujimori's main rival was Javier Pérez de Cuéllar, former secretary general of the United Nations. He has polled 22 per cent of the votes. Pérez de Cuéllar has complained about election fraud, but the result is unlikely to be overturned.

S	M	T	W	T	F	S
						1
2	3	4	5	6	7	8
9	10	11	12	13	14	15
16	17	18	19	20	21	22
23	24	25	26	27	28	29
30						

Britain, 16
National "phone day" as new codes come into force around the country.

Singapore, 17
The trial of Briton John Scripps, accused of international serial killing, begins. (→ November 10)

Teheran, 17
Iran bans the use of TV satellite dishes, and announces that the American TV programme *Baywatch* is a corrupting influence.

London, 18
Eric Cantona, Manchester United's French star, is ordered to do 120 hours of community service for kicking an abusive spectator. (→ October 1)

Athens, 20
Two men die in a terrorist bomb blast − a naval officer and almost certainly the terrorist himself. Police said the explosives were similar to those used by terrorists in attacks over the past few months.

Lyons, 20
The mayor of Lyons, Michel Noir, is given a suspended jail sentence after being found guilty of embezzlement.

Sierra Leone, 20
Six Britons held hostage by a rebel group are released on Sierra Leone's border with Ghana.

Yokohama, 21
There is another gas attack on the underground. 300 people were taken to hospital. The Aum Supreme Truth cult is again suspected of having planned the attack. (→ May 3)

London, 21
It is announced that retail sales have slowed, signalling that the recovery in the economy is still fragile.

Washington DC, 21
US State Department formally complains to Saudi authorities about their failure earlier in the month to co-operate in catching Imad Mugniyeh, one of the world's most dangerous terrorists.

Death
Milovan Djilas, Yugoslav dissident, April 20 in Belgrade, aged 83.

HEBRON, SUNDAY 16
Israel shoots three Hamas fighters

Israeli security forces killed three members of the Palestinian separatist group Hamas today. Dressed as Palestinians, the Israelis ambushed the Hamas men in an olive grove. After the shooting, the Israelis imposed a curfew on the town of Hebron.

The Israelis maintained that the three men had been on their way to attempt a terrorist attack. The dead included two individuals who had also been wanted for previous attacks. During the past six months, over 60 Israelis have died in terrorist attacks, as Hamas militants have made a determined attempt to derail the peace process. (→ May 8)

WESTMINSTER, THURSDAY 20
"Cash for questions" Tories suspended

The two Tory MPs in the "cash for questions" row were tonight suspended from the Commons without a vote being taken. David Tredinnick was suspended for four weeks and Graham Riddick for two. The penalties are heavy, but the all-party Privileges Committee felt that, by agreeing to take £1,000 from a reporter for tabling questions, their behaviour was "below the standards of the House".

TORONTO, SUNDAY 16
Agreement reached in Canadian fishing dispute

Spanish trawlers seized by the Canadian authorities during the dispute.

After a long period in which it looked as though they would fail, the negotiations between the European Union and Canada over fishing rights on the Grand Banks came to a successful conclusion this weekend. Agreement was reached on Saturday night, and endorsed by the EU in Brussels today.

The key to the agreement is an undertaking to maintain a close inspection of fishing on the Grand Banks. Independent monitors will be present on all vessels fishing there, and they will inspect both the fishing equipment used and the catch records. Satellites will track fishing vessels in the area.

This dispute, over what the Canadians saw as over-fishing of the Greenland halibut by Spanish fishing vessels, threatened to set Canada against the EU, but the Canadians are happy that the new deal will conserve fish stocks.

TAHITI, SUNDAY 16
Brando's daughter commits suicide

Cheyenne Brando.

Cheyenne Brando, daughter of film star Marlon Brando, committed suicide in her brother's home in Tahiti. She hanged herself after her mother left the house to go to church.

Cheyenne, Marlon Brando's daughter by his third wife, Tarita Teriipia, had led a troubled life. In May 1990, her brother Christian shot and killed Cheyenne's Tahitian lover, Dag Drollet; she was charged with complicity, but the charges were dropped in 1993. Cheyenne had a son by Drollet, born after his father's death. A drug addict, who after a car accident had needed to have plates implanted in her head, she had twice tried to commit suicide before.

Florida, Friday 21. Tessie O'Shea, popular singer and variety performer, died at Leesburg, aged 81. Her ample frame earned her the nickname of "Two Ton Tessie".

Russians claim capture of last Chechen stronghold

Colonel-General Anatoly Kulikov, commanding Russian forces in the breakaway republic of Chechnya, today claimed a significant breakthrough in his troops' operations. He announced that the town of Bamut was now in his hands. If so, this will mean that the last rebel stronghold in the lowlands has fallen, and the whole of the built-up north and west of the republic is under Russian control.

This success does not mean that the rebel forces of Dzokhar Dudayev are finally defeated, but it does mean that they are no longer able to put up significant resistance in the most populous areas of Chechnya – a far cry from early 1995, when they held up the Russian army in savage street fighting in the centre of the capital, Grozny. Their best recourse is now to fight a small-scale guerrilla struggle in the mountains, attempting to wear the Russians out. (→ May 15)

Russian troops in relaxed mood as their offensive meets with success at last, after months of frustration and low morale.

Hutus killed as Rwandans close refugee camp

Refugee camps have mushroomed across central Africa because of the Tutsi-Hutu conflict.

There was more death and misery in this benighted nation today, when soldiers of the Rwandan Patriotic Army, mainly Tutsis, tried to close the Kibeho camp, containing thousands of displaced Hutus. The camp had been surrounded by government soldiers since Tuesday, and the refugees feared an attack. Government soldiers fired into the air and ordered the Hutus to return to their home. Lorries were available to take Hutus back to their homes from the camp, but the operation was proceeding slowly. According to a UN spokesman, soldiers began to fire into the crowd when one of the refugees tried to grab a rifle. At least 13 people died in subsequent shooting.

The government believes that the refugee camps harbour many of the militiamen responsible for the mass slaughter of Tutsis in 1994, and has ordered the closure of all camps in southwest Rwanda, which contain up to 250,000 people. (→ April 23)

300 rescued as ferry hits rocks

Near disaster was closely averted when a catamaran carrying 300 passengers from the channel island of Jersey to the island of Sark struck rocks soon after leaving the port of St. Helier. The Mayday call was sent out at 10.07 a.m., and rescue services were soon on the scene. The catamaran had been holed in her port hull as she tried to pass through a narrow passage near reefs.

The rescue vessels arrived swiftly and three ferry boats took off most of the passengers. There were 50 injured as people leapt from the stricken catamaran: many of the injured sustained broken legs jumping into life rafts.

Why the catamaran struck the rocks is still a mystery. According to the harbourmaster of St. Helier, Captain Roy Bullen, the passage should have been safe until 10.30 a.m., but it is agreed that it can be a risky route. There was a heavy sea, and this may account for the fact that the catamaran, travelling at the relatively high speed of 35 knots, could not steer the right course.

Rome, Sunday 16. In his Easter message, the Pope urged the Palestinians and the Kurds to renounce violence.

CSA reform cuts support payments

New Child Support Agency rules that come into force today will reduce the payments that many single parents receive to raise their children. Payments will now be capped so that no one has to pay more than 30 per cent of their income. The agency will also take account of so-called "clean break" settlements between partners, in which a couple has agreed to a division that includes monetary settlement, or a capital asset such as a house. More than 400,000 absent parents will have their charges re-assessed under the new rules in the latest phase of this contentious legislation.

Oklahoma terror bombing shocks a nation

At 9.02 a.m. on Wednesday April 19, a car bomb exploded immediately outside the Alfred P. Murrah building in Oklahoma City, which housed Federal government offices. It left a gaping, nine-storey hole on the north face, festooned with trails of cable, masonry, and office equipment. Hundreds of people were buried in the rubble.

As the papers went to press that evening, 26 deaths were confirmed, including 12 children who had just been dropped off by their parents at a first-floor day centre. Federal authorities began their investigations on the assumption that Muslim extremists had carried out the attack.

A day later, however, with the death toll at 53, two white males were named as suspects: they had rented a truck 390 km (245 miles) north of Oklahoma City using false papers. On Friday, two men described as army deserters, Timothy McVeigh and Terry Nichols, were arrested. The theory was that a white supremacist militia was seeking revenge for the FBI assault on the Branch Davidian sect in Waco, Texas, exactly two years earlier. Later, Nichols' brother James was also brought in for questioning, and McVeigh was charged with malicious damage and destruction of Federal property.

On Sunday 23, with the death toll nearing 80, and with 100 still missing, the nation found itself united in grief as a national day of mourning was proclaimed. At an emotional memorial service for the victims of the bombing, held at the State Fairgrounds Arena, President Clinton addressed 10,000 mourners who were paying their respects to friends and relatives, innocent victims of the horrifying terrorist attack. He pledged to seek powers for a domestic counter-terrorism agency.

The Reverend Billy Graham summed up the general bewilderment over the bombing when he asked: "Why would God allow this to happen?" (→April 25)

Rescue workers dig through the devastation the day after the bomb blast.

A blood-spattered victim is helped away from the Federal building for medical attention.

Oklahoma's feelings were plain to see.

The grim rescue

Twenty-month-old bomb victim P.J. Allen recovers from burns and other injuries as her grandmother, Doris Watson, waits in anguish.

Some of the 10,000-strong crowd who gathered at the Oklahoma State Fairgrounds Arena on April 23, to mourn the victims.

An aerial view of the devastated Federal building.

A rescue worker searches through the wreckage.

Sniffer dogs are employed to seek out the missing.

Rescue workers take a break from their grim task.

S	M	T	W	T	F	S
						1
2	3	4	5	6	7	8
9	10	11	12	13	14	15
16	17	18	19	20	21	22
23	24	25	26	27	28	29
30						

Rwanda, 23
It is revealed that an estimated 2,000 Hutus have been massacred in Kibeho in the past few days.

The Hague, 24
The International Tribunal for the former Yugoslavia names Radovan Karadzic and Ratko Mladic as war crimes suspects. (→ May 2)

London, 25
Letter bombs are sent to Conservative ministers William Waldegrave and Tom King. It is thought animal rights activists are responsible.

London, 25
A junior doctor who claimed he was made suicidal by overwork receives £5,600 in an out-of-court settlement from the Camden and Islington Health Authority.

Washington DC, 25
Finance ministers of the group of seven leading industrial nations announce that the decline in the dollar on international exchanges had gone far enough, but there is no promise of definite action.

Kurdistan, 25
Turkey pulls 20,000 troops out of northern Iraq, where they have been hunting members of the Kurdish Workers' Party.

Buenos Aires, 25
The Argentine army admits that it sanctioned the killing and torture of civilians during the "Dirty war" against leftist guerrillas in the 1970s.

London, 26
It is announced that the Churchill family will receive £12 million from the national lottery for the archives of Sir Winston Churchill. Critics believe that many of documents should already be the property of the state.

London, 26
Police raid a house in Bow and find £18 million in counterfeit money.

London, 27
The Office of Fair Trading finds that endowment mortgages that people were persuaded to take out are more risky and expensive than conventional repayment loans.

Blair wins vote to rewrite Clause 4 at special Labour conference

Tony Blair today won an important victory in the campaign to transform the Labour Party, securing an overwhelming majority in favour of ditching the party's 77-year-old commitment to nationalization.

Delegates at a special conference in Westminster's Methodist Central Hall voted in favour of rewriting Clause 4 of Labour's constitution. A total of 65 per cent of the votes were cast in favour of the move despite stiff opposition from the largest union affiliate, The Transport and General Workers' Union.

Blair thanked the delegates with an emotional speech, saying: "I'm proud to be the leader and it's the party I'll always live in and die in." In an attempt to appease union critics, he said Labour would fight to keep the railways under public control and would "re-nationalize" the health service. He stressed that Labour had to continue reforming if it was to win the next election. (→ May 4)

Blair secures a two-to-one majority in his battle to rewrite Clause 4.

Two brothers accused of conspiring with Oklahoma bomb suspect

As investigations continue into the the bombing in Oklahoma City last week, two brothers were charged today with engaging in a bomb-building conspiracy with Timothy J. McVeigh, the man accused of setting the blast. James D. Nichols, 41, and Terry L. Nichols, 40, are not yet linked directly with the Oklahoma bombing. They are accused of building bottle bombs and experimenting with explosives in 1992 and 1994 with former Army sergeant McVeigh. The conspiracy charges are intended to keep them in custody while investigators dig deeper. (→ May 6)

Terry L. Nichols, above, and James D. Nichols, right.

Gas explosion in South Korea kills 100

A gas explosion beneath a crowded road in the South Korean town of Teagu killed ten children on their way to a school picnic. Over 100 commuters are also feared dead.

A spark, possibly caused by tunnelling drills being used to construct an underground railway system, ignited a leak from a gas pipe at 7.30 a.m., blasting to pieces a 250-m (835-ft) stretch of road and hurling cars and buses into the air. A vast fireball erupted from below the ground, killing rush-hour commuters and pupils crossing the road on their way to school.

Ten children and one teacher were confirmed dead. This number is certain to rise, because dozens of people are believed to be buried in the tunnel beneath the debris and because many of the 150 or so injured are in a critical condition.

Almost 4,000 soldiers, police, and firefighters were rushed to the scene to begin the rescue operation.

PARIS, MONDAY 24

Jospin tops first round in French poll

Socialist candidate Jospin, dazed by his success in the first round of presidential voting.

The Socialist candidate in the French presidential election, Lionel Jospin, confounded all predictions to come top of the poll in yesterday's first round of voting. The totally unexpected result was a blow for the Gaullist candidate, Jacques Chirac, who had been anticipating a clear run.

Late night estimates gave Jospin 23.3 per cent of the vote, Chirac 20.1 per cent, and the other Gaullist, Edouard Balladur, 18.8 per cent, which knocks him out of the race.

A left-right struggle will now ensue, as Chirac and Jospin scramble for the votes of the defeated candi-dates in the second round on May 7. Initial estimates last night revealed that Chirac would still win; one poll gave him 60 per cent. Other commentators thought Jospin might well pick up centrist votes from Balladur.

However, Balladur urged his supporters to vote for Chirac, who will also be hoping to pick up votes cast for the far-right candidates, such as Jean-Marie Le Pen, who won 15 per cent in the first round.

Jospin will be chasing the votes cast for the far left: 8.7 per cent Communist, 5 per cent Trotskyist and 3 per cent Green. (→ May 7)

NEW YORK, THURSDAY 27

Anarchist bomber claims 16th victim

A serial bomber has now described his motives in greater detail after his sixteenth attack in 17 years killed an executive in California earlier this week. The FBI said that the man, known as Unabomber, sent three letters that were delivered on Monday, shortly before a package bomb explosion killed Gilbert Murray, president of the pro-logging California Forestry Association.

Two letters went to survivors of previous bombs. In the third, to the *New York Times*, Unabomber repeated claims to be a member of an anarchist group and defined his targets as leaders in technological fields considered destructive to the environment. Investigators who have spent years on the case believe he is a man in his forties operating alone. (→ September 19)

London, Monday 24. Chris Evans, star of TV shows *The Big Breakfast* and *Don't Forget Your Toothbrush*, makes his Radio 1 debut as DJ on the breakfast show. The station hopes he will win back audience share.

LONDON, MONDAY 24

Four Weddings scoops five BAFTAs

Hugh Grant won the Best Actor award for his portrayal of a reluctant bridegroom.

LONDON, TUESDAY 25

Party whip restored to Euro rebels

John Major moved to heal the Conservative Party's damaging rift over Europe last night by restoring the whip to eight Tory rebels. They were invited back after five months in the cold, in an attempt to close ranks in the run-up to next week's local elections in England and Wales.

The decision to restore the whip unilaterally without extracting assurances of future good behaviour represented a climbdown by Major, in the face of growing right-wing anger at the continued exclusion of the rebels. Senior Tories are believed to have warned the Prime Minister of the threat of a leadership challenge after next week's elections if he perpetuated the split within the party.

The British hope of the Oscars, *Four Weddings and a Funeral*, won homegrown revenge on the American favourite *Forrest Gump* yesterday, by scooping five prizes in the British Film and Television Academy Awards in London. The film failed to pick up any Oscars earlier this year.

Four Weddings was named Best Film, and Mike Newell won the David Lean Award for the Best Achievement in Direction. The film, which has taken more than £160 million at the box office worldwide, also won the Lloyds Bank People's vote for the Most Popular Film. Hugh Grant won Best Actor in a Leading Role and Kristin Scott Thomas won Best Supporting Actress.

Hugh Grant said: "I absolutely adore getting prizes and I want to thank BAFTA. I'd like to apologize to John Travolta, but he should realize that BAFTAS are a little bit flag-waving." *Pulp Fiction*, starring Travolta, was named Best Original Screenplay.

Los Angeles, Tuesday 25. Ginger Rogers, the world-famous dancer and actress who starred in 80 films, died at her home in California today, aged 83.

May

S	M	T	W	T	F	S
	1	2	3	4	5	6
7	8	9	10	11	12	13
14	15	16	17	18	19	20
21	22	23	24	25	26	27
28	29	30	31			

London, 1
Schools inspectors say children are suffering because many teachers have a poor grasp of the three Rs.

Los Angeles, 1
Judge Ito excuses another juror, the seventh so far, in the O.J. Simpson trial. (→ May 8)

Sierra Leone, 1
Rebel troops surround Sierra Leone's capital city, Freetown.

Washington DC, 1
US secretary of state, Warren Christopher, claims Iran has been trying for a decade to develop nuclear weapons.

New York, 2
Sixteen Bronx policemen are arrested after a two-year undercover investigation by the Bureau of Internal Affairs.

London, 2
Rupert Murdoch submits the lowest bid for Channel 5 – just £2 million.

Beijing, 3
Japanese premier, Tomiichi Murayama, pledges to make "peace last forever" on an historic visit to Beijing.

Swansea, 3
A baby is delivered by caesarean section to Karen Battenbough, who has spent ten weeks in a coma following a car crash.

Tokyo, 3
Police arrest the "justice minister" of the Aum Supreme Truth cult. He is suspected of the gas attack on the Tokyo underground which killed 12 people and injured more than 5,000. (→ May 11)

Ankara, 4
Turkish troops withdraw from northern Iraq after a six-week search-and-destroy mission against rebel Kurd bases.

Copenhagen, 6
A ten-year study claims that moderate consumption of wine can enhance longevity.

Oklahoma, 6
The search for further victims of the bombing is abandoned, with the death toll at 158. (→ May 23)

Fresh fighting between Serbs and Croats: Zagreb shelled

ZAGREB, TUESDAY 2

A blood-spattered victim of the rocket attack in Zagreb waits to be taken to hospital.

Five people died and 121 were injured when five rebel Serb rocket-propelled cluster bombs hit the centre of the Croatian capital city of Zagreb today. The attack arrived without warning in the mid-morning. The bombs smashed into houses and a school playground in the busy area, spreading panic and shock. Many passers-by were injured by flying shrapnel from the warheads. One rocket landed only 100 m (95 yd) away from the US Embassy. The attack was launched from rebel Serb positions about 25 km (40 miles) away. It appears to have been in retaliation for yesterday's successful end to the Croatian military operation to capture territory in Slavonia, which the Serbs also claim.

US, British and German citizens were warned to leave Zagreb in case of further attacks, in what is an escalation of the Balkan conflict. (→ May 7)

Death on the streets of Croatian capital Zagreb as conflict breaks out once more.

Street riots as Major visits Derry

LONDONDERRY, WEDNESDAY 3

Angry crowds hurled missiles at the police as street violence erupted during Prime Minister John Major's visit to the city, threatening next week's peace talks between the government and Sinn Fein.

The violence broke out as demonstrators gathered outside the town's museum to demand the release of republican prisoners. The violence grew worse as stones, bottles, and other missiles were thrown as the police attempted to disperse the crowd, forcing the prime minister to abandon temporarily his plans to visit the city centre.

Mr Major left Ulster in the evening indicating that he would seek a denunciation of the riots from Sinn Fein before agreeing to proceed with next week's peace talks. (→ June 17)

Road protestors in tree-top battle

BLACKBURN, MONDAY 1

A tree-top protester taunts the bailiffs.

Anti-motorway protesters today fought off attempts by bailiffs to reclaim the "tree-top village" they have been occupying to prevent construction of the M65 extension in Stanworth Valley near Blackburn. More than 300 security men and police took part in the operation, which resulted in ten arrests and the removal of only 15 of the protesters.

LONDON, THURSDAY 4

Conservatives trounced in local elections

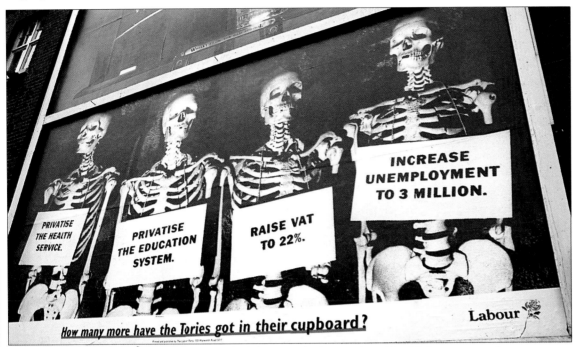

The Labour Party's message got through to voters in local elections as the Conservatives achieved their worst-ever result.

The Labour Party has had an overwhelming victory in the local elections, gaining 1,799 seats and winning control of 44 councils, many of them in the Conservative Party's traditional heartland of central and southern England.

The final results give the Labour Party control of 155 councils, while the Conservatives retain control of only eight. The Liberal Democrats control 45. The results leave the Conservatives without a single local council in Scotland or Wales.

Labour won 48 per cent of the vote, their highest share in any election since 1966, while the Conservative's share fell to 25 per cent, their worst-ever performance.

Commentators have explained the results as due in part to the electorate's belief that Tony Blair's leadership has created a "new" and more responsible Labour Party. But voters were also responding to the country's slow recovery from economic recession, to accusations of sleaze against Tory politicians, and to the Conservative Party's internal divisions, particularly over Europe.

While reinforcing Tony Blair's leadership of the Labour Party, the results have again called into question John Major's authority. Many expect a leadership challenge to him during the summer. (→ May 14)

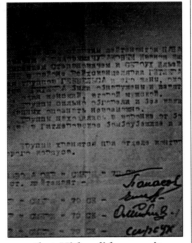

Berlin, Tuesday 2. New evidence proves that Hitler did commit suicide with his lover Eva Braun in April 1945. The evidence also reveals that Hitler's remains were not destroyed until 1970. (Shown above, left, Hitler's jacket and, right, a Soviet intelligence report.)

LONDON, SATURDAY 6

Will Carling in "old farts" row

Will Carling, 29, has been sacked as England rugby union captain after describing the sport's ruling body, the Rugby Football Union, as "57 old farts". The sacking comes only three weeks before the start of the Rugby Union World Cup in South Africa. RFU officials decided Carling was guilty of "conduct prejudicial to the interests of the Union". Carling said that he was "totally shocked" but that he would "give the new man all the help I can." It is thought that many of Carling's team-mates are unhappy with the decision and may push for his reinstatement. (→ May 8)

Will Carling with the Princess of Wales.

LONDON, MONDAY 1

Dangerous smog levels in heatwave

The May heatwave has brought trouble for Britain's asthma sufferers and may even have caused the death of 17-year-old sufferer Hayley Jones, who collapsed and died in Liverpool.

High temperatures in urban areas mean that sunlight has reacted with exhaust fumes to create ozone, which acts as a lung irritant for many asthma sufferers. Victims may experience watery eyes, runny noses and breathlessness.

Doctors said that there was no cause for alarm, but added that the government should regulate ozone levels more stringently.

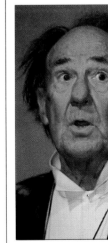

London, Tuesday 2. The classical and comedy actor Sir Michael Hordern has died, aged 83, after a long illness.

May

S	M	T	W	T	F	S
	1	2	3	4	5	6
7	8	9	10	11	12	13
14	15	16	17	18	19	20
21	22	23	24	25	26	27
28	29	30	31			

Newmarket, 7
Sunday horse racing is introduced to Britain with the 1,000 Guineas meeting.

Sarajevo, 7
A Serb mortar attack kills nine in a suburb of Sarajevo.

Los Angeles, 8
The O.J. Simpson murder trial reaches a crucial stage as the prosecution introduces results of DNA tests. (→ June 15)

London, 8
Will Carling apologizes for offensive remarks about the game's administrators and is reinstated as England rugby captain 72 hours after being demoted.

Rio de Janeiro, 8
Police shoot dead 14 drug pushers in a gun battle in Nova Brasília.

Rome, 8
Former prime minister Silvio Berlusconi sees his Freedom Front Party suffer heavy losses in Italian local elections.

Moscow, 9
Prime Minister John Major and President Bill Clinton attend Russian VE Day anniversary celebrations.

Edinburgh, 9
A ruling by Scotland's Court of Session saves the West Highland railway sleeper service from closure.

New York, 9
An anonymous bidder pays £18 million at Sotheby's for a portrait from Pablo Picasso's Blue Period.

London, 9
Every Metropolitan police officer is to be issued with body armour and CS gas.

London, 11
Rupert Murdoch, owner of News International, apologizes for a story in the *News of the World* about the Earl and Countess Spencer.

Johannesburg, 11
A runaway locomotive crushes over 100 workers to death in a Transvaal mine.

Tokyo, 11
Masami Tsuchiya of the Aum Supreme Truth cult confesses to making the nerve gas Sarin for the cult's terror campaign. (→ May 16)

Chirac elected French president on second ballot

The new French president, Jacques Chirac, waves to supporters.

Jacques Chirac has become French president after achieving a narrow victory over the Socialist candidate Lionel Jospin. A nerve-racking campaign ended with his garnering 52.7 per cent to Jospin's unexpectedly high 47.3 per cent before the votes in France's overseas territories had been counted. Chirac had previously contested the 1981 and 1988 presidential elections but despite his defeats in those contests and his unpopularity in presidential election polls taken earlier this year, the conservative mayor of Paris had remained single-minded in pursuit of France's highest political office.

Ministers in first Sinn Fein meeting for 23 years

Michael Ancram, British Northern Ireland minister, yesterday met representatives of Sinn Fein. It was the first official encounter between the two sides for 23 years but it ended in deadlock after they found little room for agreement on vital aspects of the Irish peace process. The talks are a turning point, however: after eight months of the IRA ceasefire, Britain has finally recognized Sinn Fein, the IRA's political wing. (→ June 17)

Ebola outbreak in Zaire

A new outbreak of the deadly Ebola virus has struck Kikwit, south of the Zairean capital Kinshasa. The town has now been quarantined. A total of 49 people have died in one month after this latest manifestation of the virus, which is regarded by scientists as a Level 4 pathogen, making it more dangerous than AIDS, which has a Level 3 classification. The Ebola virus liquefies human organs, causing its victims to die in agony. A satellite link will connect a hospital for victims with international experts. (→ May 24)

Israeli PM announces release of 250 Palestinian prisoners

Israel made a further conciliatory gesture towards the Palestinians yesterday when it released 250 prisoners. The freed Palestinians signed documents promising not to take part in further attacks on Israel.

The gesture was timed to coincide with the Islamic festival of Eid al-Alha and drew criticism from some quarters. Israel's justice minister, David Libai, expressed doubts over whether the gesture could be justified on legal grounds. Also, the right-wing Israeli party, B'Tdezek, went to court in a failed effort to stop the action. A further 200 prisoners, held following violence that was directed at Israelis, are also expected to be released by the Palestinian Authority in Gaza and Jericho. (→ May 22)

**Kashmir, Thursday 11.
A two-month siege of Muslim separatist guerrillas was ended when Indian troops stormed them and killed 42 at the site of an Islamic shrine.**

Nolan committee recommends stringent controls

The Nolan report on ethics has been published with seven recommendations for Members of Parliament. It advises that they should exercise selflessness, accountability, openness, integrity, objectivity, honesty, and leadership. The guidelines, the tightest ever faced by members, also recommend that MPs should not be employed by political lobbying bodies and that earnings from consultancies should be revealed. The report by Lord Nolan, a high-ranking appeal judge, is designed to restore public faith in MPs after a host of allegations of corruption. (→ May 14)

LONDON, MONDAY 8

Millions celebrate as Britain marks the fiftieth anniversary of VE Day

The Queen, the Queen Mother, and Princess Margaret, all of whom took part in the original VE Day celebrations, greet the crowds.

The spirit of Britain's past came to life yesterday as millions of people throughout the land celebrated the fiftieth anniversary of the allies' Victory in Europe. The Queen joined a 150,000 all-ticket crowd in Hyde Park, for the final phase of the proceedings which included a two-minute silence for the victims of the World War II. The Queen then lit a beacon and set off a spectacular fire-work display. Other public celebrations also took place at venues throughout the United Kingdom.

During the day, a crowd gathered outside Buckingham Palace and was treated to a lunchtime concert and flypasts by wartime aircraft and aerobatics from the Red Arrows. The most touching scenes were to be found in Hyde Park, where veterans of the conflict were reunited. Some had not seen each other since the original VE Day.

The Red Arrows (above) perform their aerobatics above Buckingham Palace. Sir Harry Secombe, Dame Vera Lynn, and Cliff Richard (right) perform at a lunchtime concert outside the palace.

S	M	T	W	T	F	S
	1	2	3	4	5	6
7	8	9	10	11	12	13
14	15	16	17	18	19	20
21	22	23	24	25	26	27
28	29	30	31			

Liverpool, 14
Blackburn Rovers lose 2-1 to Liverpool at Anfield, but win the Premier League Championship because the other contender, Manchester United, needing a win, only drew at West Ham.

Dharamsala, 14
The Dalai Lama names a six-year-old as the reincarnation of the Panchen Lama, the second most important figure in Tibetan Buddhism. The last Panchen Lama died in 1989.

Buenos Aires, 14
President Carlos Menem is re-elected as president of Argentina, with just under half of the votes cast. He has more than a 10% lead over both his rivals.

Southern California, 14
New Zealand's yacht *Black Magic* wins its fifth consecutive race against *Young America* to take the America's Cup to New Zealand for the first time. It is only the second time that the Cup has left the US.

Cairo, 15
Egypt's Antiquities Council announces that US archaeologists have found the largest ancient Egyptian tomb yet discovered. It was built for the 50 sons of Ramses II and has 67 chambers.

Chechnya, 15
Russian troops resume their offensive, attacking villages near the border with Dagestan. (→ June 14)

Beijing, 15
In defiance of international opposition, China conducts an underground nuclear test, four days after signing an extension of the nuclear non-proliferation treaty.

London, 16
Nurses vote overwhelmingly to end their no-strike rule, because of their anger at government policy.

London, 17
Lord Mackay outlines proposals to cap the budget on legal aid.

London, 19
Anthony Williams is jailed for seven and a half years. The Scotland Yard clerical officer used money allocated to fight international crime to fund his life style as a Scottish laird.

WESTMINSTER, SUNDAY 14

More trouble for Tories: Major bars Nolan from examining party donations

There was fresh trouble for the Tory Party as an official spokeswoman for Prime Minister John Major revealed that the Nolan committee enquiring into standards in public life had been barred from looking into how political parties were funded. The phrase the spokeswoman used was: "His remit is his remit and it doesn't include party funding."

It is known that some members of the Nolan committee wish to look at how political parties are funded, and feel that a proper examination of standards of public life would necessarily include such an area. Lord Nolan himself has said that he is unhappy about these calls from other committee members. He agrees that his committee has a narrow remit, and that it should investigate along a narrow path: as "a watchdog, not a bloodhound", as he put in a radio interview today.

However, the Nolan committee is widely seen as having a remit to look into accusations of sleaze within the Tory Pary, whose funding is the subject of many rumours. It is known that there have been anonymous donations to the Conservative Party from abroad, while businessman Asil Nadir, wanted on fraud charges, also gave money. Critics say Major can only wish to keep Nolan away from this area if he has something to hide.

LONDON, THURSDAY 18

Feminist Greer in public row

Germaine Greer.

Germaine Greer, Australian-born author, academic and journalist, has launched a vitriolic personal attack on Suzanne Moore, a writer for the *Guardian* newspaper, accusing her of "disloyalty" and of being a "lipstick feminist". Ms Greer was herself a columnist for the *Guardian* until the paper refused to print an article attacking Ms Moore.

Ms Greer's anger relates to the claim – repeated in an article by Ms. Moore – that she had a hysterectomy as a young woman. Ms Moore says she has been misquoted. Ms Greer nevertheless attacks Ms Moore and in an article for the *Spectator* describes Ms. Moore as having "hair bird's-nested all over the place and three fat inches of cleavage."

PARIS, TUESDAY 16

Pakistan cricketer Imran Khan marries Goldsmith heiress

Former Pakistan cricket captain Imran Khan and Jemima Goldsmith, 21-year-old daughter of millionaire financier Sir James Goldsmith, were married here today. The brief ceremony was conducted by an Imam from a Parisian mosque in Sir James's house. The chief witness was Pakistan's ambassador to Paris.

Imran's marriage has caused consternation among the orthodox Muslim community in Pakistan, where he has political ambitions. He had previously stated that he would marry a Pakistani, but it is thought that his bride's conversion to Islam may dampen the controversy.

The newly wed couple.

Tokyo, Tuesday 16. Sect leader Shoko Asahara is arrested on suspicion of organizing the Tokyo subway gas attack. (→ June 22)

LONDON, SATURDAY 20

Thatcher's autobiography lambasts Major

Former prime minister Lady Thatcher.

Margaret Thatcher was insisting tonight that the second volume of her autobiography, *The Path to Power*, which is published next month, is not intended as a direct attack on her successor as Conservative leader, John Major. But revelations about the contents of the book have sent shock waves through the Tory Party.

Lady Thatcher argues that the present deep trough in Tory popularity is due to Major not taking a sufficiently strong stand in defending Britain's interests during the negotiations for the Maastricht treaty and for being

less tough than she would have been in subsequent talks with the other members of the European Union. She also makes trenchant comments about the problems with the exchange rate mechanism, which was a source of great dispute during her premiership.

In the next few days, the cabinet will formulate its policy for the Inter-Governmental Conference between the EU member states. Lady Thatcher's intervention has given great suport to the Euro-sceptics in the coming arguments and debates.

Los Angeles, Thursday 18. The star of TV series *Bewitched*, Elizabeth Montgomery, has died, aged 57.

ROME, SATURDAY 20

Prosecutors apply to bring Silvio Berlusconi to trial

Magistrates today decided to press for the trial of former prime minister, Silvio Berlusconi, on corruption charges. They claim that £120,000 in bribes was paid to government officials to secure favourable tax breaks.

Signor Berlusconi has admitted that directors of his companies may have made such payments, but his defence is that in the prevailing atmosphere of the time and under pressure from tax inspectors who were themselves corrupt, the men who ran his companies had little choice but to comply.

The future of Berlusconi's holding company, Fininvest, which currently owns three TV stations, hangs in the balance, in any case. The Italian parliament is at present debating whether to hold a referendum on limiting the ownership of television stations to one per owner.

Former prime minister Silvio Berlusconi.

LONDON, SUNDAY 14

National Grid chairman gets share windfall

There was fresh acrimony at Westminster today over revelations that David Jefferies, chairman of the National Grid, made a large profit from trading in some of his share options before public trading in the shares had even begun. The amount that he made has been estimated at over £360,000. which effectively doubled his present salary. Shadow Chancellor Gordon Brown described the news as "the biggest outrage of all". Mr. Brown also warned that other directors of the National Grid could receive sums of up to £1.1 million before the sale of the National Grid in the summer.

The National Grid distributes the electricity from the generating companies. It recently set up a share-options scheme for employees. Mr. Jefferies bought his shares at around £3 per share, but sold them, through a stockbroker, at more than £9 per share.

The news comes at a time when there is widespread public disquiet about the amounts of money that the directors of utilities are making. Public opinion sees the utilities as more or less monopolies, and believes that those who run them should not be unduly rewarded. It has been estimated that directors of the privatized utilities hold more than £40 million in share options.

HAMPSHIRE, FRIDAY 19

Couple sent to jail for lying about minor traffic accident

Patricia and David Whitehead.

There was shock in court when Mr. Justice Kennedy jailed a husband and wife with three children under the age of ten for lying to police about a traffic accident. David Whitehead and his wife, Patricia, were convicted of perverting the course of justice. They had told the police that Mrs. Whitehead was driving their car when it was involved in an accident with a motorcycle. A week later, they admitted that the driver had in fact been Mr. Whitehead. The Howard League for Prison Reform voiced a general sentiment when it said: "Our view is that prison should be reserved for serious and violent offenders."

Wembley, Saturday 20. Everton beat Manchester United 1-0 in a dour game to win the FA Cup. Paul Rideout was the goal scorer.

May

S	M	T	W	T	F	S
	1	2	3	4	5	6
7	8	9	10	11	12	13
14	15	16	17	18	19	20
21	22	23	24	25	26	27
28	29	30	31			

Kashmir, 21
Twenty-two people die in violent protests against the policies of the Indian government.

Barcelona, 21
Two paintings and a sketch bought in a Barcelona flea market are authenticated as genuine Picassos.

Westminster, 22
Tory MP Jerry Wiggins apologizes to fellow Conservative Sebastian Coe for having used his name as a front when putting down a motion.

London, 23
An official investigation censures Islington council for being too concerned about political and racial sensitivities to investigate child abuse claims properly.

Oklahoma, 23
The ruins of the bombed Federal building are finally demolished.

Germany, 23
Germany's highest court rules that former East German spymasters cannot now be prosecuted, but those already serving sentences are not to be freed.

Zaire, 24
Deaths from the latest outbreak of the deadly Ebola virus reach 108.

South Africa, 25
The opening match of the rugby World Cup is a triumph for South Africa as they defeat Australia 27-18.

Perth, 26
The Scottish Nationalist Party wins the Perth and Kinross by-election.

London, 27
The debate over pay for the chiefs of the privatized utilities is inflamed by the news that an Electricity Board chief received a bonus of £500,000.

London, 31
The trial for fraud of the sons of newspaper magnate, Robert Maxwell, opens today. Maxwell died in mysterious circumstances aboard his yacht in 1991.

Death
Jean Muir, fashion designer, aged 66, May 28.

2,500 feared dead in Russian earthquake

The inhabitants of Neftegorsk search for their belongings in the devastated town.

Thousands of people are still unaccounted for after an earthquake measuring 7.5 on the Richter scale flattened the town of Neftegorsk in the north of Sakhalin Island during the small hours of the morning.

The disaster was made worse by two factors. Firstly, a series of after shocks made rescue work difficult, and, secondly, the geographical position of Neftegorsk, tucked away on the north of Sakhalin Island and thousands of miles away from Moscow in Russia's far east, meant that rescue workers and equipment had to fly in from long distances.

Three hundred deaths were registered soon after the first shock, but it is feared that the final casualty toll may well approach 2,500. In addition, massive ecological damage is feared as the earthquake also damaged an oil pipeline.

Surgeon saves passenger's life

Professor Angus Wallace saved the life of a fellow on a Hong Kong to London flight today. The drama began when the passenger, Pauline Dixon, began complaining of pains in her arm. She soon had difficulty breathing, and Wallace diagnosed a collapsed lung. Operating with a coat hanger, a pair of scissors, an oxygen mask, and a plastic bottle, all sterilised in five-star brandy, he saved the passenger's life – and then drank the rest of the brandy.

Wallace with his life-saving tools.

Tributes as Wilson dies

One of the leading lights of post-war British politics died today, when Lord Wilson, 13 years Labour Party leader and victor in four of the five General Elections he contested, passed away in his sleep.

There were tributes from all sides of the political divide. Conservative Prime Minister John Major said Wilson was "one of the most brilliant men of his generation".

Wilson held his first cabinet post at the age of 31 (the youngest cabinet member since 1806), became leader of the Labour Party in 1963 and

Harold Wilson at a party conference.

prime minister in 1964. He resigned as prime minister in 1976, and later entered the upper house as Lord Wilson of Rievaulx.

Learner drivers to take written test

There will soon be a new test for learner drivers – one that will be given before the learner is allowed to take the practical driving test itself. The new test is a written exam, containing 35 questions. It will come into force from July 1996.

Announcing the new hurdle that learners will have to face, Minister for Road Safety Steven Norris claimed that "in having to prepare for a theory test people will become better drivers". He also said that he hoped the pass rate for the practical test would rise from the present 50 per cent when the written test eventually came into operation.

The exam will consist of multiple-choice questions chosen at random from a possible 600, which will be published beforehand (together with the answers). The questions will cover a broad range of topics, linked to the requirements of the practical test. It will cost a learner upwards of £10 to take the new written test.

BOSNIA, FRIDAY 26

Serbs take UN troops hostage in retaliation for NATO air strikes

Some of the 200 UN troops taken hostage by Bosnian Serb forces are paraded for the TV cameras.

The atmosphere is tense in Bosnia, as the Bosnian Serb forces under Ratko Mladic seem, once again, to have outsmarted the international community. NATO air strikes were ordered in against the Bosnian Serb capital of Pale on Thursday, to try to force the Serbs to pull their heavy guns back from around Sarajevo and other designated safe havens. International outrage was fuelled by a Serb shell that killed 71 Bosnians in Tuzla on Thursday. At first, the bombing was seen as a welcome show of resolution from the Western powers, which have watched with fuming impotence as the Bosnian Serbs have ignored all ultimatums to make them draw back.

In a sudden move, however, the Bosnian Serbs dramatically turned the tables by taking members of the UN peacekeeping forces hostage, and showing them on television. Nearly 200 soldiers have been taken by the Serbs, who now have the upper hand. In the game of bluff and double bluff, it is now up to the UN and NATO to formulate an effective response in a situation where they have once again lost the initiative. Further air strikes have been called off for the moment. (→ June 7)

JERUSALEM, MONDAY 22

Israel retreats on Jerusalem land annexation

The Israeli government of Yitzhak Rabin today effectively abandoned controversial proposals to annex Palestinian land in East Jerusalem. In total, an area of about 130 acres had been earmarked to be expropriated. It has been a feature of Israeli policy towards Jerusalem that it has never agreed that Palestinians have land rights in the historical capital of the Jewish state.

The proposal to expropriate the land was defeated by what was, in any reckoning, an unlikely alliance. The small Israeli Arab parties within the Knesset (which usually support the Labour government) tabled a motion of no confidence over the issue. Right-wing parties, including the Likud, threatened to support the motion because the combined votes would have brought down Rabin's government. Paradoxically, Likud supports land annexation in East Jerusalem. (→ June 25)

Virginia, Monday 29. Actor Christopher Reeve, star of the Superman series of films, was today seriously injured in a fall from a horse while competing in an equestrian competition at Charlottesville. Reeve was thrown when his horse refused a jump. He has badly injured his neck and back and may be paralyzed. (→ October 17)

North Sea, Tuesday 23. The remaining Greenpeace activists occupying the Brent Spar rig in protest against plans to sink the rig in the mid-Atlantic were brought ashore. (→ June 16)

WASHINGTON, DC, TUESDAY 23

Gunman shot and wounded in White House grounds

There was drama at the White House today when secret servicemen shot and wounded an intruder who had climbed the security fence.

Leland William Modjeski, 37, sometime psychology student but more recently sacked as a pizza delivery man, got over the fence armed with a .38 revolver, later found to be unloaded. He refused to stop when ordered, and headed towards the Jacqueline Kennedy Garden, getting to within 32 m (30 yd) of the White House. One guard moved to stop him, but when other officers noticed that Modjeski was carrying a weapon, they opened fire, hitting him in the arm, but also wounding one secret serviceman. This is the fourth time in recent months that an intruder has attempted to get into the presidential residence.

June

S	M	T	W	T	F	S
				1	2	3
4	5	6	7	8	9	10
11	12	13	14	15	16	17
18	19	20	21	22	23	24
25	26	27	28	29	30	

Newlyn, 1
A Cornish fisherman claims that his nets were deliberately cut by a Spanish trawler 160 km (100 miles) off Land's End.

Vienna, 1
The Austrian parliament votes a £32 million fund for victims of the Nazis.

London, 2
A memorial service is held for playwright John Osborne. At the door is a notice, believed to be from his wife on behalf of her late husband, barring by name certain people, including Sir Peter Hall.

London, 2
Kevin Maxwell tells the court at his fraud trial that he does not think his father Robert committed suicide.

Beijing, 4
On the sixth anniversary of the Tiananmen Square massacre, democracy movement leader Chen Ziming, currently on parole, calls for the release of all China's political prisoners.

London, 5
A Scrabble player sues three tournament officials for allowing him insufficient time to go to the toilet.

London, 5
A leaked excerpt of the Scott enquiry accuses former Foreign Office minister William Waldegrave, of lying to Parliament. (→ June 19)

London, 6
A Church of England report issued today says that unmarried couples who are living together should be welcomed into the Church, thereby dropping the idea of "living in sin".

Tokyo, 6
Shoko Asahara, leader of the Aum Supreme Truth religious cult, and six followers are charged with the Tokyo gas attack. (→ June 22)

London, 7
A High Court judge upholds the ban on homosexuals serving in the armed forces, but says it is "with hesitation and regret".

Death
Dilys Powell, film critic and radio personality, aged 93, June 3.

BELGRADE, WEDNESDAY 7
Serbs release most UN hostages

UN troops in Pale, following their release by the Bosnian Serbs.

The application of international pressure on the Serbs, following the seizure of over 320 UN hostages late last month, continues to bear fruit. A Serbian official announced here today that a further 108 soldiers had been released, following the 121 set free last Friday. There remain 149 in Serb hands, but according to a spokesman for the Serbian president, Slobodan Milosevic, who has joined the calls for their freedom, they should be released soon. The Bosnian Serbs captured the men following NATO airstrikes on their positions, and they are insisting that there should be no more NATO attacks. (→ June 8)

Holland, Monday 5. Ethiopian runner Haile Gebresilasie knocks nine seconds off the world 10,000 metres record.

TOKYO, TUESDAY 6
Japanese express remorse over war

After weeks of arguing, the Japanese government agreed tonight on a motion making an apology of sorts for its conduct during World War II. The depth of the apology depends on how one translates the word *hansei*, which can mean either "remorse" or "reflection". Giving the word its stronger meaning, the motion says, "Recalling many acts of aggression and colonial rule in modern world history, we recognize and express deep remorse for these kinds of actions carried out by our country in the past."

CAPE CANAVERAL, THURSDAY 1
Woodpeckers delay launch of space shuttle

The latest problem to hit the troubled space shuttle programme has emerged from the air. Woodpeckers have been found pecking away at the craft, causing sufficient damage to call into question next week's planned launch.

The birds have been chipping away into the insulating foam around the launcher's fuel tank. A total of 71 separate holes have been found in the insulating material.

NASA scientists have been experimenting with low-tech ways of detering this natural hazard. They have resorted to blowing air horns in the hope that the noise will drive the birds off. They have also placed decoy owls around the launch pad to see if these will frighten the woodpeckers away.

HONG KONG, THURSDAY 8
Boat people riot in Hong Kong

Vietnamese boat people protest in Hong Kong against repatriation.

Over 800 rounds of tear gas were fired by police this morning at 50 Vietnamese protesting against their imminent deportation from a detention centre in Hong Kong back to Vietnam. The rioters attacked the police with spears and home-made weapons and set fire to the administration block in the camp, apparently in the hope of destroying the records necessary for their deportation. However, the papers were elsewhere.

The violence follows a riot last month in Hong Kong and another four days ago at a camp in Malaysia when 1,000 people broke out and had to be turned back by water cannon. Officials are worried that the resistance will make the planned repatriations impossible.

Downed American pilot rescued in Bosnia

Happy to be going home: Captain Scott O'Grady wih a fellow officer after his rescue.

US Air Force pilot, Captain Scott O'Grady, has returned to safety after being shot down by a Serb missile. In a daring, text-book mission he was plucked by American marines right from the heart of the Serb-held territory in the north of Bosnia following six days on the run from the Serb forces seeking him.

Captain O'Grady had been moving around in wooded terrain since he bailed out. An F-16 pilot heard a radio message sent out by O'Grady calling for help. Within five hours a rescue helicopter, supported by three others and two jet fighters, released a team of marines who pulled him on board. There were no casualties during the operation, although the mission was shot at by the Serbs. The success of the rescue, and O'Grady's hero status, has gone some way to temporarily head off public criticism in the US of its involvement in the Bosnian conflict. (→ June 25)

Washington DC, Sunday 4. Bob Dole's wife pledges to sell her shares in Disney after discovering one of its subsidiaries distributes *Priest*, a film branded as immoral by her husband.

MISSOURI, SATURDAY 10

"Smoker's gene"

Scientists at the Washington University School of Medicine in Missouri have published the findings of research that suggest that the propensity to smoke could be genetic. They have been examining over 2,000 pairs of twins, half of whom are identical and half fraternal. The identical twins, who have the same genes, were found to have far more similar smoking habits than the fraternal twins, whose genes are different. Personality characteristics were found to be much less important. One of the team, Dr. Pamela Madden, said, "Our evidence indicates that strong genetic effects are responsible for both starting smoking and for long-term smoking."

Mexico commits to new round of privatization

The Mexican government is planning a huge sell-off of state-owned enterprises. This will be the country's third round of major privatizations in ten years. Previous offloading of state assets has attracted criticism for the apparent lack of organization shown by the government. This time the stars of the sale are the airports, communication satellites, as well as the railway system.

Mexico has been under a lot of pressure from creditor nations, especially the United States, to cut public spending and to raise cash. The previous sales have concentrated more on the amount of revenue raised, rather than the nature of the services that the nation requires. For example, the telephone system was sold as a single concern to a monopoly that has maintained the service in the same poor state as before.

A government official admitted that the same mistakes could be made again: "The pressure for that kind of thing to continue is pretty strong."

Asians riot in Bradford for two nights

An Asian youth shows his anger during the street violence.

Riots have broken out on the streets of Bradford for the second night running as Asian youths clashed with police. About 1,000 youths went on the rampage, throwing petrol bombs and stones, and setting fire to cars and furniture. The riot took place in the Manningham district, where community leaders and young people have in recent weeks been working with the police to tackle the area's notorious prostitution problem.

The rioting started on Friday night when a 15-year-old who had been playing football in an alleyway had an altercation with policemen in a patrol car. When another youth protested he too was arrested.

Local people claim that the police responded insensitively to the incident. A spokesman for the community called for calm: "We want the situation defused as much as anyone. The economic prosperity of this community is being damaged and we don't want it to go on." West Yorkshire police have promised an investigation into the riots.

New York, Sunday 4. *Sunset Boulevard*, by Andrew Lloyd Webber, wins seven Tony Awards, including Best Musical and Best Actress in a Musical for Glenn Close.

June

S	M	T	W	T	F	S
				1	2	3
4	5	6	7	8	9	10
11	12	13	14	15	16	17
18	19	20	21	22	23	24
25	26	27	28	29	30	

Colombia, 11
A bomb kills 28 people, many of them children, at a music festival in Medellin.

Bosnia, 13
Bosnian Serbs free all but 26 of the remaining hostages, including the last British ones. (→ June 18)

London, 13
Henry Kissinger is to be given an honorary knighthood for his contribution to Anglo-American relations.

London, 13
Michael Heseltine orders an official enquiry into possible Iranian arms deals by a company of which Treasury Chief Secretary Jonathan Aitken was a director.

Rugby, 14
Rugby School boys are in revolt over the appointment of the school's first head girl.

London, 14
Two police officers are acquitted of the manslaughter of Joy Gardner, who died in July 1993 while being taken for deportation.

West Midlands, 14
A baby boy dies of breathing difficulties after being taken to four hospitals in eight hours.

Northampton, 16
Working with the FBI, police find forged US gold and silver deposit certificates worth $700 million (£440 million).

Hamburg, 16
A Shell petrol station is firebombed and thousands of others boycotted in protests against the company's planned dumping of the Brent Spar oil platform in the North Sea. (→ June 20).

Madrid, 17
Felipe González, Spanish prime minister, finds himself in the centre of a row over the tapping of the phones of many top people in Spain, including King Juan Carlos.

Death
Arturo Benedetti Michelangeli, brilliant but temperamental concert pianist, in Switzerland aged 75, June 12.

France announces resumption of nuclear tests in Pacific

The New Zealand government has reacted angrily to an announcement by newly elected French president Jacques Chirac, that France will resume nuclear testing in the South Pacific. President Chirac said that the first of eight tests will take place in September, and that they will continue until May 1996. After the tests, he maintained, France would sign a comprehensive test ban treaty.

President Chirac had attacked the decision by former president, François Mitterand, to agree to a moratorium in 1992, and in the election campaign he was critical of his rival, Edouard Balladur, for agreeing to the moratorium. He said tonight, "I have consulted all the military and civil experts. They were unanimous in telling me that if we wanted to guarantee the sureness, safety, and reliability of our nuclear force, we were obliged to complete this series of tests." (→ September 10)

London, Saturday 17. Cliff Richard is awarded a knighthood by the Queen. He will be known as Sir Cliff, rather than by his real name, Harry Webb.

Adams pulls Sinn Fein from preliminary talks

Sinn Fein leader Gerry Adams.

Gerry Adams today warned that violence could re-erupt at any time, as he pulled Sinn Fein – the political wing of the IRA – out of preliminary talks with the British government.

Speaking on BBC Radio from South Africa, where he is scheduled to meet President Mandela, he said that as far as he was concerned exploratory talks had finished. They have been going on for six months, but Sinn Fein now wishes to conduct a formal meeting with Sir Patrick Mayhew, the secretary of state for Northern Ireland.

However, Sir Patrick has turned down the request, as the IRA has not responded to the government on decommissioning its weapons. "There is always a danger, unless we deal with the root causes of conflict, that the danger of slipping back into conflict remains," Mr. Adams warned. (→ July 3)

O.J. struggles to fit the incriminating gloves

The attention in the O.J. Simpson trial today turned to his hands, as the prosecution insisted that he try on a pair of gloves tendered in evidence. One of the blood-stained gloves was found at the scene of the murder, the other, according to the prosecution, on a path at O.J.'s home.

O.J. struggled with the leather gloves, having manifest difficulty in getting them on, and muttering, "too tight, too tight", as he tried. Defence counsel claimed that they were obviously too small. However, he did eventually get them on, and some spectators considered them a snug fit. The gloves are crucial to the prosecution's case.

The former football star has exceptionally large hands, and the gloves are extra large in size. A buyer at Bloomingdale's department store testified that Nicole Simpson bought such a pair of gloves from the shop in December 1990. (→ July 27)

Does the evidence fit O.J. like a glove? The jury must decide whether they are "too tight".

Chechen rebels take 2,000 hostage in hospital

Chechen gunmen earlier today swept through a town in southern Russia, and occupied a hospital, taking around 2,000 patients and staff hostage. Earlier in the day, 37 policemen and soldiers plus an unknown number of civilians were killed as the men fought their way through the town of Budyonnovsk, some 110 km (71 miles) north of the Chechen border. According to various reports the gang numbers between 50 and 250; they are led by Shamil Basayev, third in the rebel Chechen hierarchy.

The raid answers Russian fears that the fighting would spread from Chechnya into Russia itself, now that the rebels have been driven into hiding. The gunmen have threatened the lives of the hostages, saying that ten hostages will be killed for every gunman, and five killed for every Chechen injury. The rebels are demanding that Russia withdraws from Chechnya, that President Yeltsin enters into negotiations with the Chechen leader, and that they are allowed to talk to reporters. Moscow is now gripped by fears of terrorist attack. (→ June 20)

Rebels and hostages in the hospital of the southern Russian town of Budyonnovsk.

BA directors receive rises as high as 47 per cent

Those critical of the earnings of executives in the privatized industries were given further ammunition today by the announcement from British Airways of huge increases in the salary packages of its top board members. When bonus payments and share appreciation rights are included, Finance Director Derek Stevens has been given the largest increase: 47 per cent.

The chairman, Sir Colin Marshall, received a salary increase of 15 per cent, and when company contributions to his pension are taken into account, his total package comes to just short of £906,000 per annum. The non-executive deputy chairman, Sir Michael Angus, was paid £67,000 for the year, working on average half a day each week.

Cape Town, Sunday 11. England beat Australia 25–22 in the Rugby Union World Cup semi-final. The tense, evenly balanced match hung on the last kick of the game, as Rob Andrew scored a dropped goal that gave England the points for victory.

Mother and ex-wives spoil record jackpot party

Two men were today handed a cheque for over £22 million as the winners of the biggest lottery jackpot to date. But while the two were enjoying the champagne, relatives, ex-wives, and former friends of one of them, Mark Gardiner, were delivering a more poisonous cocktail.

Mr. Gardiner's mother said that her decision to adopt him was the worst she had ever made. She said that his drinking made the family's life a misery. Such was the rift between them that he changed his surname. His two former wives have been selling their stories to the press, while his third, estranged, wife is planning legal action to claim some of the winnings. A former colleague said that Mr. Gardiner was hated at work, and that he rued the day he once saved Gardiner's life.

June

S	M	T	W	T	F	S
				1	2	3
4	5	6	7	8	9	10
11	12	13	14	15	16	17
18	19	20	21	22	23	24
25	26	27	28	29	30	

Sarajevo, 18
Serbs free last 26 UN peace-keepers held hostage. (→ June 25)

New Delhi, 18
The latest deaths in northern India's hottest weather this century brings the death toll to 525 as temperatures hit 45° C (113° F).

Luxembourg, 19
European finance ministers agree to drop their target date of 1997 for the introduction of a single European currency. Under the Maastricht treaty it will have to be introduced by the beginning of 1999.

France, 19
Municipal elections give the National Front control of three towns in southern France, including Toulon.

London, 19
The first sponsored London Underground train, decked with the livery of United Airlines, goes into service.

Moscow, 20
Chechen rebels release their remaining hostages, used as human shields to see them back to safe territory in Chechnya. (→ July 24)

Scotland, 20
Tony Blair suspends the ruling Labour group in the Monklands district council in Scotland following accusations of abuses of power.

Washington DC, 21
The CIA asserts that China has sold vital components for missile systems to Iran and Pakistan.

Los Angeles, 22
Michael Jackson apologizes for anti-semitic lyrics on his new album, and pledges to amend future pressings.

London, 23
Douglas Hurd announces that he is standing down as foreign secretary.

Johannesburg, 23
Rupert Murdoch signs a £340 million deal with the southern hemisphere rugby-playing nations.

Deaths
Princess Margaret's unsuccessful 1950s suitor, Group Captain Peter Townsend, aged 80, June 19.

Jonas Salk, pioneer discoverer of the first polio vaccine, aged 80, June 23.

Major resigns as Conservative leader

John Major stunned the political world tonight by announcing his resignation as leader of the Conservative Party in order to submit himself for re-election. The move is designed to silence his right-wing critics and to end the damaging speculation about his leadership. Challenging his opponents to stand against him, he told them that it is now time "to put up or to shut up". Mr. Major continues as prime minister in the meantime.

Talk of a leadership challenge this autumn has been rife for some time. Speaking on a hot summer's afternoon from the garden at number 10 Downing Street, Mr. Major said that he had made his decision because "I am not prepared to see the party I care for laid out on the rack like this any longer."

By announcing the election before any stalking horse candidate can be put forward, Mr. Major has seized the initiative. In a concerted show of loyalty, his Cabinet colleagues greeted his decision as a courageous and imaginative move. However, at least two Cabinet members, Michael Heseltine and Michael Portillo, have been mentioned as possible challengers for Mr. Major's job. Heseltine is favoured by many Tory MPs who feel he has the best chance of leading the party to victory in the next general election. Many Euro-sceptics on the right of the party, openly hostile to Mr.

John Major announces his resignation in the rose garden of 10 Downing Street.

Major's policy on the European Union, favour Portillo.

If Mr. Major won the re-election contest, he would, he said, lead the party to the next general election and beyond. To win on the first round of this ballot among Tory MPs, a contender needs both an overall majority and at least 15 per cent more votes than any other candidate. If no-one clears both these hurdles there is a second ballot at which further candidates can, if they wish, choose to enter the fray. (→ July 4)

Michael Portillo: a leadership contender?

Iraq arms sales accusations

Leaks from the draft report of the Scott enquiry, broadcast on ITN's *News at Ten*, accuse the government of deliberately misleading Parliament about a change of policy on the sale of arms to Iraq during the Iraq–Iran war. The leaks specifically blame three junior ministers of the time, Alan Clark and Lord Trefgarne, who have since left government, and William Waldegrave, currently in the Cabinet. Mr. Waldegrave tonight said he would prove that he had not lied to Parliament.

New York, Friday 23. Disney's *Pocahontas* opens in American cinemas, after the world's biggest ever premiere in Central Park.

LONDON, TUESDAY 20
Shell abandons plan to sink Brent Spar

In the face of massive objections from the environmentalist movement, Shell UK announced that it will not, after all, dump the ageing Brent Spar oil platform in the North Sea. Instead, it will seek to dismantle the platform on dry land.

The decision is being hailed as a victory by Greenpeace, which had taken occupation of the platform while it was being towed from its original mooring towards the proposed dumping ground off the Outer Hebrides.

The environmentalists' campaign has been reinforced by a boycott of Shell petrol stations, particularly in Germany and the Netherlands.

Shell's U-turn is extremely embarrassing for the British government, which had publicly backed the company's original decision, having been persuaded by Shell that disposal at sea

The Brent Spar oil platform.

was less expensive and considerably safer than disposal on land. John Major had given the company his personal support at a G7 summit meeting over the weekend.

TOKYO, THURSDAY 22
Japanese police storm hijacked jet

At dawn this morning police successfully stormed a hijacked airliner at the city of Hakodate, on the northern island of Hokkaido. The 365 passengers and crew on board the All Nippon Airways Boeing 747 were released. The only serious injury of the incident was a neck wound inflicted on one of the passengers by an object resembling a large ice pick that was carried by the hijacker.

The plane was hijacked shortly after it left Tokyo yesterday, but was allowed to fly to its scheduled destination. The lone hijacker threatened the pilot with a time bomb. He is reported as belonging to the Aum Supreme Truth sect accused of the Tokyo underground gas attack, and is said to have demanded the release of the sect's leader. (→ July 4)

Long Island, Sunday 18. The US Open is won by Corey Pavin, his first major championship.

MOSCOW, TUESDAY 20
Zhirinovsky in TV orange-juice brawl

Russia's extreme nationalist politician Vladimir Zhirinovsky increased his reputation for aggressive behaviour tonight by assaulting a fellow guest live on television. He was taking part in a chat show with an old adversary, Boris Nemtsov, an economic reformer praised by western bankers. The debate degenerated into personal abuse, and when Mr. Nemtsov accused Mr. Zhirinovsky of having syphilis, Mr. Zhirinovsky stood up, swore at him, and threw a glass of orange juice in his face. He followed it up with the glass as the show was blacked out.

JOHANNESBURG, SATURDAY 24
South Africa wins World Cup

South Africa is celebrating after beating New Zealand 15–12 in the final of the Rugby Union World Cup. The South Africans effectively shut the Kiwi phenomenon Jonah Lomu out of the game. The team's success has united people of all races, as blacks have joined in the cheering of what under apartheid was an almost exclusively white sport.

WASHINGTON DC, THURSDAY 22
Senate blocks Clinton's nomination for surgeon general

Republicans in the US Senate have rebuffed President Clinton's choice of Henry W. Foster Jr. as surgeon general. A procedural motion to have the nomination considered failed by just three votes. It was the second time the motion had failed by that margin, and it was agreed that after two failures it would be withdrawn. Dr. Foster had been criticized for performing a number of abortions on mentally retarded women and for not having been open in admitting them. He claimed that he was victim of power play among Republican presidential hopefuls. President Clinton has not been lucky in his choices for surgeon general. The previous incumbent was sacked after advocating teaching masturbation.

EASTBOURNE, TUESDAY 20
Suicide boy rescued

A 15-year-old boy was rescued today after spending three days on a ledge on Beachy Head with a broken leg and broken ribs.

Martin Hinchcliffe threw himself from the highest cliff on the south coast of England in a suicide bid after a row with his girlfriend. His fall was deflected by rocks and he came to rest in a crevice about a quarter of the way down the cliff face. He was rescued by four men who abseiled down the cliff after a passer-by heard his calls for help.

South Africa's victory celebrations.

Berlin, Thursday 22. A 24-year-old dream is realized as the artist Christo and his wife Jeanne-Claude supervise the completion of the wrapping of the Reichstag. It will be under cover for two weeks.

June

S	M	T	W	T	F	S
					1	2	3
4	5	6	7	8	9	10
11	12	13	14	15	16	17
18	19	20	21	22	23	24
25	26	27	28	29	30	

Sarajevo, 25
Bosnian Serb sniper-fire and shelling kills at least nine civilians in Sarajevo, including four children.

West Bank, 25
Israeli soldiers kill two Arabs and injure more than 30 others during a protest in Nablus calling for the release of 5,000 Palestinian prisoners. (→ July 30)

Bonn, 26
The German government resolves to send armed forces to the Balkans for the first time to support UN peace-keepers.

Qatar, 27
The crown prince of Qatar, Hamad Bin Khalifa al-Thani, forces his father to leave the country.

Haiti, 27
President Jean-Bertrand Aristide describes the Haitian elections as "a major step forward for democracy", despite widespread claims of vote rigging and counting irregularities.

Oregon, 27
British women Sally-Anne Croft and Susan Hagan, former followers of cult leader Bhagwan Rajneesh, go on trial charged with conspiracy to murder the US attorney for the region.

India, 28
Madhya Pradesh in central India is designated a "tiger state" to protect the threatened animal from poachers and settlers.

Geneva, 28
America and Japan reach a broad accord on the automotive trade, ending their two-year dispute.

Sri Lanka, 28
Tamil rebels kill 161 people in five separate attacks.

Johannesburg, 28
Mandela sets up a Truth Commission to expose human rights abuses committed during the apartheid era.

Germany, 28
IRA member Donna Maguire is convicted of attempting to bomb a British army barracks in Germany, but is freed because she has spent nearly six years in jail on remand.

Houston, 29
The US space shuttle *Atlantis* docks smoothly with the Russian *Mir* space station 392 km (245 miles) above central Asia.

At least 63 killed as South Korean store collapses

The tangle of concrete and steel left by the collapse of a crowded department store in Seoul.

A five-storey department store in Seoul packed with shoppers, collapsed today, killing at least 63 people and injuring more than 850.

Injured people – some unconscious, others crying for help – were carried out of Seoul's Sampoong Department Store in a steady stream. Helicopters ferried many to hospitals because evening rush-hour traffic slowed ambulances.

The disaster has left South Koreans anguished over yet another tragedy attributed to slipshod construction and poor government foresight. Two fatal gas explosions in the last six months killed 113 and a bridge collapse killed 32. The government has promised to punish those responsible for the latest disaster.

England finally beat West Indies

Cork has Richie Richardson LBW.

England today claimed their first victory against the West Indies at Lord's since 1957, bringing the score to 1-1, with four Tests still to play.

Dominic Cork, 23, the Derbyshire all-rounder, has been credited with swinging the balance in England's favour, after producing the best bowling performance by an England debutant this century. His second innings analysis showed 7 for 43, to which he reacted modestly, saying: "We have got great team spirit and are confident we can go on from here."

John Redwood challenges Major

The Tory leadership contest erupted into a battle today between John Major and his former cabinet colleague John Redwood.

After resigning as Welsh secretary, Redwood declared his intention to stand against Major, blowing apart any assumption of Cabinet unity. Cabinet heavyweights immediately closed ranks behind the Prime Minister, claiming that a lurch to the right under Redwood would make the Tory party unelectable and that only Major could reunite the party.

Redwood, a prominent Thatcherite, said that he was "devastated" by Major's decision to call a leadership contest. "Your decision to resign leaves our party in limbo when it needs firm but understanding leadership," he said.

Major said that he expected to win the election comfortably. (→ July 4)

John Redwood resigns as Welsh secretary and challenges Major for the premiership.

LOS ANGELES, TUESDAY 27

Hugh Grant arrested on prostitute charge

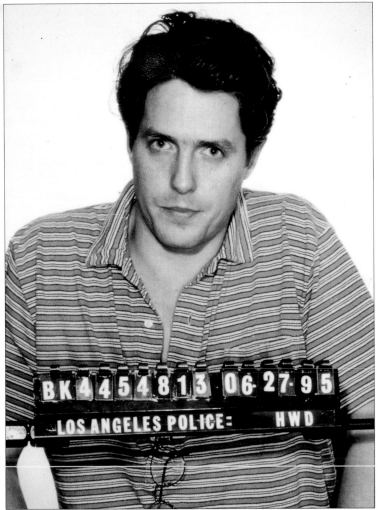

Hugh Grant "embarrassed" when arrested for indecent conduct near Sunset Boulevard.

Hugh Grant, star of *Four Weddings and a Funeral*, was arrested in Hollywood today, charged with lewd conduct with a prostitute in a public place.

Los Angeles police officer Lorie Taylor said: "Grant was observed to drive a vehicle up to a prostitute and allow her to get into it. They drove a short distance to a residential street and engaged in lewd conduct. Vice officers walked up on the car and observed the act. Both the prostitute, 23-year-old Divine Brown, and Grant were taken into custody."

Grant, 34, whose girlfriend is the actress and model Elizabeth Hurley, said: "I did something completely insane. I have hurt people I love and embarrassed people I work with. For both things I am more sorry than I can say." (→ July 11)

Divine Brown, accused of soliciting.

CAIRO, MONDAY 26

Attempt on Mubarak's life

Egypt's president Hosni Mubarak survived an assassination attempt without injury this morning when several gunmen carrying automatic weapons opened fire on the motorcade carrying him to the opening of an African summit meeting in the Ethiopian capital, Addis Ababa.

Mubarak was rushed back to Cairo, where he vowed that the attackers, believed to be Islamic fundamentalists, would "pay dearly for their actions". Two gunmen and two Ethiopian policemen were killed in the assault, but no bullets penetrated the armoured car in which Mubarak was travelling.

Islamic extremists have long conducted an armed campaign against the Egyptian government and in recent years have killed more than 700 people. Mr. Mubarak, who has already been the target of two assassination attempts, came to power in 1981 when militant Muslims killed his predecessor as president, Anwar Sadat, at a rally in Cairo.

At the New York trial of Sheikh Omar Abderahman, the cleric accused of planning a bombing campaign in the US, there were suggestions of a murder plot against the President in 1993, while last year two soldiers and a civilian were executed for their roles in a further plot to kill Mr. Mubarak.

Scotland, Wednesday 28. Roads began to melt and railway tracks overheated as temperatures in Scotland reached 30° C (86° F). Scores of people were admitted to hospital with dehydration and sunburn, and even the elephants at Edinburgh zoo were affected.

DEVON, THURSDAY 29

Lisa Clayton sails round world alone

Lisa Clayton, aged 36, arrived in Dartmouth today after 286 days and 49,600 km (31,000 miles) at sea. She is the first woman to circumnavigate the globe from the northern hemisphere non-stop and unassisted.

Her 12 m (39 ft) yacht, *Spirit of Birmingham,* has taken her from Britain to the Cape of Good Hope, across the Southern Ocean past New Zealand, across the Pacific to Cape Horn, and back north across the Atlantic. During the trip, aided neither by supply drops nor by putting into port, her only contact with the world was via fax. (→ August 2)

California, Thursday 29. Lana Turner dies, aged 75. Her films included *The Postman always rings Twice* (1946).

July

S	M	T	W	T	F	S
						1
2	3	4	5	6	7	8
9	10	11	12	13	14	15
16	17	18	19	20	21	22
23	24	25	26	27	28	29
30	31					

London, 1
Californian tennis player, Jeff Tarango, yet to win a match at Wimbledon after seven tournaments, is disqualified after accusing an official of corruption. He is later fined a record £10,000.

London, 3
The first radio station aimed at women, Viva!, is launched.

Cheshire, 4
The Master of Foxhounds for the Cheshire Hunt, David Woolley, and his son Josh, are injured by a letter bomb.

Lancashire, 4
Relatives of Frederick Brown exhume his body from a Freckleton graveyard and rebury him in Lytham St Anne's, after a two-year battle to use the words "dad" and "grandad" on his headstone.

Gwent, 5
Eight die when a coach crashes on an A40 roundabout at Raglan.

County Durham, 6
Graeme Alderton of Peterlee receives a ten year prison sentence for manslaughter, having killed his three children in a house fire, which he started in an attempt to be rehoused.

Nottingham, 7
The murder conviction passed on Emma Humphreys, 27, who stabbed her violent drug-addict boyfriend to death in 1985, is quashed and reduced to manslaughter. Miss Humphreys is freed.

Ipswich, 7
Jason Mitchell, 24, a paranoid schizophrenic "released into the community", receives life sentences for three murders, including that of his father.

London, 7
Michael Foot, former leader of the Labour Party, wins "substantial" damages against the *Sunday Times* for suggesting that he was a KGB agent.

Death
Bert Hardy, the pioneer photojournalist famous as the chief photographer on *Picture Post* magazine, in Surrey, aged 82, July 3.

LONDON, THURSDAY 6
Condon says most muggers are black

Metropolitan police commissioner Sir Paul Condon.

Metropolitan police commissioner Sir Paul Condon today urged Britain's ethnic community leaders to recognise that most muggers are black. He referred to a recent survey in which 80 per cent of mugging victims had described their attackers as young black males. Criminologists were more circumspect. Professor Bob Reiner of the London School of Economics said, "contact crimes are the only kind where the victim gets a view of the perpetrator." "Victims don't always get it right," he added.

Angry Labour MP Bernie Grant has described Sir Paul's comments as a licence for racists. "People will just think that every young black person is a mugger because the police commissioner says so."

TOKYO, TUESDAY 4
Gas attacks cause panic in Japan

Security was tightened across Japan after a renewed spate of gas attacks on the country's rail system. The new wave of attacks began on Monday when hundreds of travellers in Yokohama complained of sore eyes and throats; 50 were taken to hospital but none was seriously injured.

Today two gas bombs containing sulphuric acid, sodium cyanide crystals, and timing devices were found in station lavatories in Tokyo.

Police have no firm idea of who planted these devices. Nevertheless, despite repeated denials, suspicion continues to fall on the Aum Supreme Truth cult. (→ October 4)

SARAJEVO, SATURDAY 8
Serbs bombard Srebrenica

As Bosnian Serb artillery continues to bombard the Muslim enclave of Srebrenica, UN peace-keeping forces appear powerless to prevent the fall of this safe haven.

Several outposts held by Dutch UN troops were captured during fighting on the outskirts of the town and one Dutch soldier was killed. Bosnian president, Alija Izetbegovic has appealed to world leaders to protect the enclave. (→ July 11)

Las Vegas, Monday 3. Pancho Gonzalez, tennis player, dies aged 67. In 1969 he played the longest match in Wimbledon history – five hours 12 minutes.

NEW DELHI, TUESDAY 4
Hostages taken by Kashmiri rebels

Two Britons and two Americans have been kidnapped by armed Kashmiri rebels while trekking through thick forest to the east of Srinagar.

The kidnappers belong to one of several Muslim groups fighting for Kashmiri independence from India. Kashmir has been under direct federal rule since its elected state government was deposed in 1990, shortly after separatists began their armed struggle. The kidnappings are believed to be part of a campaign to draw western attention – particularly that of the USA – to the problems in Kashmir. (→ July 9)

London, Saturday 8. Steffi Graf wins the Wimbledon ladies' singles. Meanwhile, her father, Peter (above), has mounting tax problems. (→ July 17)

LONDON, TUESDAY 4

Major wins leadership election

John Major emerges from 10 Downing Street after the leadership election result.

The gamble taken by Prime Minister John Major last month, when he resigned as Conservative leader and called an election, paid off handsomely today when he was re-elected by a substantial majority. He defeated John Redwood by 218 votes to 89. There were also eight abstentions and 12 spoiled papers. Two Tory MPs did not vote. Mr Major needed only 165 votes – half of those entitled to vote – to win, so this result now gives him a clear mandate to continue unchallenged as prime minister until the general election.

Mr. Major started the leadership contest in order to clear the air after months of whispered discontent from the "Euro-sceptic" right wing of the Conservative Party. After his victory the Prime Minister was keen to stress that there would be "no recriminations". However, this will not extend to the reappointment of John Redwood in the expected Cabinet reshuffle later this week. (→ July 5)

LONDON, WEDNESDAY 5

Heseltine becomes deputy PM

After his victory in the Conservative leadership election, John Major announces a Cabinet reshuffle that rewards MPs who remained loyal to him. Mr. Major has created a new position – deputy prime minister – which he has awarded to Michael Heseltine, formally president of the Board of Trade. Other moves involve Brian Mawhinney, who replaces Jeremy Hanley as party chairman; and Malcolm Rifkind, formerly minister of Defence, who becomes foreign secretary in place of Douglas Hurd, who is retiring. As expected, the "Euro-sceptics" have done badly in this reshuffle, although they will be somewhat placated by right-winger Michael Portillo's move to defence.

Michael Heseltine assumes a new role.

BELFAST, MONDAY 3

Riots in Ulster after paratrooper Lee Clegg is released

Dozens of cars and vans were set ablaze on the streets of Belfast and Londonderry today in the worst disturbances since the start of the IRA cease-fire last year. Army bomb-disposal experts were called in to deal with suspect vehicles and a cache of petrol bombs was seized by police in the Ardoyne. Tonight, Crumlin Road in Belfast was blocked by about 100 demonstrators demanding the release of Republican prisoners. The violence was sparked off by the release from Wakefield Prison of Private Lee Clegg, the British paratrooper who had been serving a life sentence after being convicted in 1993 of murdering an 18-year-old Belfast joyrider.

Karen Reilly had been a passenger in a stolen car that drove through an army checkpoint in September 1990. She was killed by a bullet fired by Private Clegg after the car had passed. He was released after the Life Sentence Review Board decided he had been punished sufficiently. (→ July 10)

Aftermath of the riots in Belfast after Private Clegg's release.

July

S	M	T	W	T	F	S
						1
2	3	4	5	6	7	8
9	10	11	12	13	14	15
16	17	18	19	20	21	22
23	24	25	26	27	28	29
30	31					

Sri Lanka, 9
The Sri Lankan government sends 10,000 troops to combat in a major offensive against Tamil Tiger guerrillas. (→ August 7)

New York, 9
The murder rate in New York has dropped to its lowest level since 1970.

New York, 9
Seventh Avenue is flooded when a water main is severed.

Rome, 11
The Pope apologizes to women for the Catholic Church's discrimination against them in the past.

Union, SC, 10
Susan Smith, accused of drowning her two sons, is passed competent to stand trial after controversy over her mental stability. (→ July 22)

Washington DC, 11
President Clinton announces that full diplomatic relations with Vietnam are to be restored after a 22-year break.

Washington DC, Tuesday 11
Federal prosecutors are seeking the death penalty in the trial of Timothy J. McVeigh, accused of blowing up the Federal building in Oklahoma City. (→ August 10)

Washington DC, 12
President Clinton backs the right of parents to expect religion to have a place in American schools.

London, 14
John Major announces that £300 million will be spent to revive sport in state schools.

Chicago, 13
Twelve die in Chicago in the US heat wave as temperatures hit 41° C (106° F).

London, 14
A national strike by train drivers closes down virtually the entire rail network.

London, 15
Lancashire defeats Kent at Lords to take the Benson & Hedges Cup, despite a brilliant century from Kent's Aravinda de Silva.

LONDON, THURSDAY 13
UK house sales hit new low

There is more gloomy news for the property market as figures released today show house sales for June down 14.3 per cent on the same month last year. The figures, from the Corporate Estate Agents Property Index, also show that sales for June were 6.1 per cent down on May, and that the first half of 1995 is 15.5 per cent behind the corresponding period in 1994.

The CEA monitors activity in around 4,000 estate agents nationwide. Peter Constable, the CEA spokesman, said that the housing market desperately needed a confidence-boosting package from the government.

KASHMIR, SUNDAY 9
American hostage escapes rebels

An American hostage, John Childs, made a daring escape from his Kashmiri captors at the weekend. The lives of another American, Donald Hutchings, and two Britons, Keith Mangan and Paul Wells, were still hanging in the balance last night as the Kashmiri rebels who are holding them hostage set a deadline for their demands. They want 22 imprisoned Muslim rebels to be released by the Indian government by Saturday.

London, Sunday 9. Pete Sampras celebrates his third consecutive Wimbledon title, after defeating the former champion Boris Becker in four sets.

SARAJEVO, TUESDAY 11
Serbs overrun Srebrenica

The struggle for Srebrenica is over. Bosnian Serbs took over the town yesterday. One of six Muslim "safe havens" established under the protection of NATO, Srebrenica is the first of the designated safe areas to fall to the Bosnian Serbs. Its capitulation is a massive blow to the UN.

As the Bosnian Serbs increased the severity of their attacks on the town, NATO planes responded by destroying two of the tanks involved in the assault. However, when the Bosnian Serbs threatened to execute 32 Dutch peace-keepers they are holding as hostages, plans to continue the defence of the enclave were abandoned. Along with 20,000 refugees, 400 Dutch peace-keeping troops fled the area. Another "safe haven", Zepa, is thought to be the next to fall to Bosnian Serbs. (→ July 16)

Bosnian Muslim refugees flee Srebrenica, which fell to Bosnian Serb forces.

PORTADOWN, MONDAY 10
Loyalist confrontation with RUC ends in violence

A two-day stand off between 1,000 Orangemen and the RUC erupted into violence tonight as police fired rubber bullets into the crowd. The demonstrators responded with sticks, stones, and bottles.

The demonstrators had set out for their traditional pre-July 12 Orange march on Sunday. Their route through the predominantly Roman Catholic Gavarghy estate was blocked by the police after nationalists there had staged a sit-down protest. The loyalists insisted that they should be allowed to continue on their traditional route to celebrate the Protestant victory at the Battle of the Boyne. Harold Gracey, the Orange Order's district master, called for support, and the crowd swelled to over 1,000. The trouble began when some of the demonstrators ran across fields in an attempt to outflank the police and reach the Gavarghy road. Serious fighting broke out and at least three police officers were injured.

The violence highlights rising tensions in Northern Ireland; following the release last Monday of Private Lee Clegg, and the loyalist marching season now in full swing, the peace process is under strain. (→ August 12)

LOS ANGELES, TUESDAY 11
Hugh Grant makes TV confession

Hugh Grant (left) looks thoughtful during his televised interview with Jay Leno.

Actor Hugh Grant was fined $500 plus costs, put on probation, and instructed to participate in an AIDS education programme as a Los Angeles court found him guilty of "lewd conduct" with a prostitute, Divine Brown.

Later, while discussing the matter on TV, Grant paid tribute to the support of both his girlfriend Elizabeth Hurley and his father, and put on a performance that won over the studio audience on *The Tonight Show with Jay Leno*. "I've done an abominable thing and she's been amazing about it," the Englishman said of Hurley. "And, contrary to what I read in the paper today, she's been very supportive and we're going to try to work it out."

The star of the hugely successful 1994 movie *Four Weddings and a Funeral* had been booked to appear on Leno's show before being arrested on Sunset Boulevard with Brown. His appearance was scheduled to publicize his new film *Nine Months*.

Grant looked nervous as Leno asked him tough questions, but by the end of the show his apparently genuine remorse had convinced members of the studio audience that he deserved to be shown understanding for his actions. (→ July 18)

MOSCOW, TUESDAY 11
President Yeltsin taken to hospital with heart condition

The Russian president, Boris Yeltsin, 64, was taken to the Moscow Central Clinic today with a recurrence of his serious heart trouble.

President Yeltsin has been plagued by health problems in recent months, and suspicions are growing both in Russia and abroad that he may no longer have the strength to continue as leader. Worries over his health are exacerbated by indications that the president also has a serious, long-standing drinking problem.

It has been widely suspected inside Russia that Yeltsin has not been running the government for a while. He is regarded in some quarters as a figurehead, with day-to-day decisions being taken by Prime Minister Viktor Chernomyrdin.

Even when Yeltsin has been well, he has found himself at times upstaged by Chernomyrdin. While Yeltsin was meeting with world leaders at the Group of Seven summit in Canada in June, the Prime Minister was carrying out official duties that emphasized his increasingly important role as a statesman.

Chernomyrdin has also been the focus of commanding performances in the Russian parliament. Western observers and investors would have few fears if he were to replace Yeltsin, who has become unpopular with the Russian people. (→ July 24)

President Boris Yeltsin: back in hospital with heart trouble.

AUCKLAND, SUNDAY 9
French seize *Rainbow Warrior II*

France defied world public opinion when its navy commandos seized the Greenpeace ship *Rainbow Warrior II*. The environmentalists had sailed into French waters off Mururoa Atoll in protest against continued French nuclear testing in the area. Tear gas was used and two dozen Greenpeace activists arrested as President Chirac showed the world that France will not flinch despite widespread condemnation of its nuclear policy. The New Zealand prime minister, Jim Bolger, commented that the French actions had been "over the top". (→ September 1)

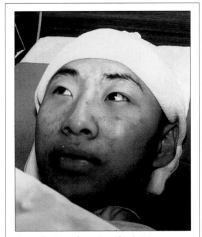

Seoul, Sunday 9. Choi Myong-Suk is pulled from beneath a collapsed South Korean department store. He survived nine days in a 1 m (3¼ ft) space.

BOULDER, COLORADO, THURSDAY 13
Creation of super atom predicted by Einstein is announced

After 70 years, a theory that was first proposed by Albert Einstein and the Indian physicist Satyendra Bose has finally been tested, and a new "super atom" has been created.

This new type of matter is produced when thousands of atoms are cooled to a temperature just above absolute zero. Electrons, which orbit around the nucleus of every atom, then spread out, dissociate from the nucleus, and finally act like a single entity. The successful experiment, which used atoms of the metallic element rubidium, took place on June 5, and the results have just been published. Dr. Carl Wieman of the National Institute of Standards and Technology said of the "super atom" in the publication *Science*, "It really is a new state of matter. It has completely different properties from any other kind of [solid, gas, or liquid]."

Dr. Eric Cornell, his colleague, added, "The sample in our lab is the only chunk of this stuff in the universe, unless it is in a lab in some other solar system." The Colorado success ends a race in which more than a dozen laboratories in America and Europe sought to be first to create the "super atom".

S	M	T	W	T	F	S
						1
2	3	4	5	6	7	8
9	10	11	12	13	14	15
16	17	18	19	20	21	22
23	24	25	26	27	28	29
30	31					

London, 16
A new book, *The Lodger* by British author Stewart Evans, claims that Jack the Ripper was an American.

Bradford, 16
Scientists have, for the first time, isolated the cells that regulate hair growth and are moving closer to discovering a cure for baldness.

Rio de Janeiro, 16
Up to 40 people are feared dead after several explosions at the Brazilian navy's main weapons base.

Bonn, 17
Wimbledon tennis champion Steffi Graf is considering quitting Germany after raids by tax inspectors on her home. (→ August 2)

Brussels, 17
The European Union signs a far-reaching trade pact with Russia.

Los Angeles, 18
Divine Brown, the prostitute arrested along with actor Hugh Grant, pleads not guilty to a charge of lewd conduct and seeks a trial.

Kiev, 18
The Ukraine is fighting a crop-destroying plague of locusts.

Madrid, 18
Vicki Moore, the British animal rights campaigner gored by a bull at a village fiesta, is to fly home.

Tallahassee, Florida 18
Dr. Rolando Sanchez is suspended amid allegations that he cut off a patient's toe without her consent. In February he amputated the wrong leg from another patient.

London, 19
Tory MPs vote against measures designed to make them reveal earnings from outside sources.

London, 20
The Queen Mother is recovering well after a cataract operation.

London, 20
The Royal Opera House, Covent Garden, is to receive a £55 million grant from the lottery fund.

South Carolina, 22
Susan Smith is found guilty of murdering her two sons, Michael and Alex. (→ July 29)

WASHINGTON DC, SUNDAY 16
US prepared to send helicopters to Gorazde

US helicopters currently under mothballs but which could quickly be whisked into action in Bosnia.

The US appears to be on the verge of taking drastic action to halt the advance of the Bosnian Serbs on the Muslim "safe areas". President Clinton is said to be considering using a fleet of US helicopters to transport 1,000 French troops to help defend the designated Muslim "safe area" of Gorazde. Such an action would almost certainly lead to the loss of American lives.

General John Shalikashvili, the chairman of the Joint Chiefs of Staff, is discussing operational matters in London with Field Marshal Inge, chief of the British Defence Staff, and Admiral Lanxade, chief of the French Defence Staff.

Secretary of State Warren Christopher, said, "No decisions have been made…we operate in the context of the fact that President Clinton has decided, and I think the American people want to keep it that way, that we will not inject American troops into Bosnia, except to use them to withdraw allied forces."(→ July 17)

LINCOLN, WEDNESDAY 19
Dean of Lincoln cleared of adultery

The Dean of Lincoln has been cleared by a Church court of "conduct unbecoming the office and work of a clerk in holy orders" and of indulging in "intimate sexual acts with a person" other than his wife.

The dean claimed to be the victim of a conspiracy: the allegations against him emerged only after he had spearheaded an investigation of cathedral affairs that potentially threatened the position of several individuals. The investigation followed the exhibition in Australia in 1988 of the cathedral's valuable copy of the Magna Carta, which led to a loss of £60,000.

London, Monday 17. Sir Stephen Spender, the poet, novelist, and critic who came to prominence in the 1930s, has died, aged 86.

CHICAGO, SUNDAY 16
Heatwaves claim hundreds of lives

Temperatures of 41° C (106° F) have lead to scores of heat fatalities, filling Cook County morgue in Chicago to capacity, leaving some 300 bodies awaiting autopsies in funeral homes. Bodies brought to the full morgue are now having to be stored in refrigerated trucks. Cook County medical examiner, Dr. Edmund Donoghue, expects that the final fatality count could be over 400 in Chicago alone.

In New York, declining temparatures were greeted with relief after the heat had climbed above 37.7° C (100° F) and had claimed 11 lives.

LONDON, THURSDAY 20
Suffolk is hotter than Miami

The fountains of Trafalgar Square are perfect for a cooling dip as temperatures soar.

Tropical style weather baked eastern and southern England today, and thousands of workers took the day off. Temperatures reached their peak in Honington, Suffolk, where the thermometer reached 32° C (90° F). This was higher than in Miami, or in Mediterranean cities such as Istanbul. The spell of hot weather is set to continue, although the weather forecast is for scattered thunderstorms in the next few days.

The hot weather has allowed many exotic species of insect and fish to survive on and around the shores of the British Isles. Off the Isle of Wight, for example, bathers were stung by poisonous weaver fish. (→ August 3)

BAGHDAD, SUNDAY 16
Two Americans released by Saddam

Two American citizens, sentenced to eight years prison for entering Iraq illegally, have been freed. David Daliberti and William Barloon had been working close to the Iraqi border in Kuwait and inadvertently strayed over the Iraqi border.

The man behind their release was Democratic congressman Bill Richardson, who has a history of intervening successfully in matters involving American citizens abroad. Mr. Richardson flew into Baghdad for a meeting with Saddam Hussein on Saturday, and persuaded the Iraqi leader to release the two men.

St Andrews, Scotland, Friday 21. Golfing great Arnold Palmer played his last-ever round in the British Open amid emotional scenes.

SARAJEVO, MONDAY 17
Thousands of Muslim refugees flee from Serbs

Thousands of Bosnian Muslims who had been feared missing after the fall of Srebrenica have emerged in Bosnian territory after managing to outwit Serbian troops.

"We don't know for sure, but we estimate that about 3,000 people crossed last night," said one relief official. The refugees were in a state of exhaustion after making a tough 30-mile (19-km) trek through forested areas. To escape they had negotiated a dangerous escape route past Serbian troops. Approximately 40,000 people were hounded out of Srebrenica last week when Serbian troops overran the town. There are grave fears for 5,000 Muslim men taken away by the Serbs for "questioning".

The Serbs' next target appears to be another of the UN's so-called "safe havens", Zepa, southeast of Srebrenica. They have, however, said that they will shoot 79 UN peacekeepers in the town if NATO jets threaten them. (→ July 23)

QUEENSLAND, SUNDAY 16
Blair makes pro-competition speech

Labour leader Tony Blair has made conciliatory noises improving the party's relationship with Rupert Murdoch, the Australian owner of News International and the most powerful media figure in Britain today.

Mr. Murdoch's newspapers, which include the *Sun* and the *Times,* were seen as staunch Conservative allies during the Margaret Thatcher era. Now Murdoch appears willing to embrace "new" Labour: he paid for Blair's trip to Australia. In return, Blair gave a speech that stressed Labour's commitment to open competition while denouncing the restrictive practices of the British establishment, a subject that is also close to Murdoch's heart. A weakening of the previously close relations between News International and the Conservative Party would mark a significant change in British domestic politics.

Traditionalist members of the Labour Party were guarded in their comments about Mr. Blair's speech. Although the need for the party to change in order to achieve power may be recognized, a *rapprochement* with Mr. Murdoch, the epitome of international capitalist acquisitiveness, is unlikely to be welcomed; too friendly a relationship could be seen to undermine Labour's socialist principles and long tradition of supporting the workers rather than the bosses.

Buenos Aires, Monday 17. One of the greatest drivers in the history of motor racing, Juan Manuel Fangio, has died at the age of 84. Fangio, who won five Formula One World Championships between 1951 and 1957, later became an international ambassador for the sport and president of Mercedes-Benz in Argentina.

July

S	M	T	W	T	F	S
						1
2	3	4	5	6	7	8
9	10	11	12	13	14	15
16	17	18	19	20	21	22
23	24	25	26	27	28	29
30	31					

Southampton, 24
Premiership footballers John Fashanu, Hans Segers and Bruce Grobbelaar are charged with fixing matches.

Moscow, 24
President Boris Yeltsin leaves hospital almost two weeks after being admitted with heart problems. (→ August 7)

London, 25
Channel 4 awards its chief executive, Michael Grade, a 20% salary increase, taking his annual earnings to £450,000.

The Hague, 25
Radavan Karadjic and Ratko Mladic, leaders of the Bosnian Serbs, are formally charged with war crimes.

Johannesburg, 27
Footprints preserved in volcanic ash show that there were humans in Africa who were walking upright 3.7 million years ago.

London, 29
Conservative MP Dudley Fishburn is to resign at the next election because he finds that being an MP is an undemanding job.

Tomislavgrad, 30
An escalation of the war in the former Yugoslavia looks certain with the increasing mobilization of Croatian and Bosnian Serb troops. (→ August 5)

Jerusalem, 30
The Israeli government is to seek the extradition of Mousa Mohamed Abu Marzook, a leading member of the terrorist group Hamas, who has been detained in the US. (→ August 2)

Union, SC, 29
Susan Smith, who killed her two young children, is sentenced to life imprisonment.

Death
Charlie Rich, US country singer and composer of "Behind Closed Doors" and "The Most Beautiful Girl", aged 62, in Hammond, Louisiana, July 25.

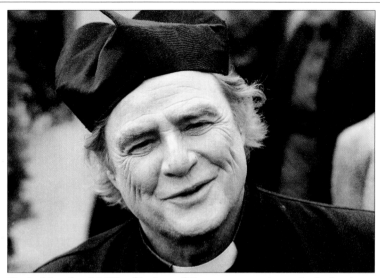

Cork, Monday 24. The filming of *Rapture*, a movie set in Ireland and starring Marlon Brando (above, on set), has been suspended after its backers encountered financial problems.

LITTLEBOROUGH, THURSDAY 27
Lib Dems win Littleborough

A fiercely contested by-election has ended in victory for the Liberal Democrats. Chris Davies, 41, a communications consultant, beat off a close challenge from Labour to win the Littleborough and Saddleworth seat with a 1,993 majority.

The election is another severe blow for John Major's beleaguered Conservative government. The by-election came after the death of Tory MP Geoffrey Dickens who won the seat with a majority of 4,494 at the 1992 general election. The Conservatives have now failed to win any of the 33 by-elections since 1989.

LONDON, WEDNESDAY 26
Diane Modahl wins drugs appeal

Diane Modahl, the British athlete who was sent home from last year's Commonwealth Games when she failed a drugs test, has had a four-year ban overturned. Modahl, one-time Commonwealth Games 800-metres champion, had the ruling rescinded because of the British Athletics Federation's doubts over the methods employed when the suspect urine sample was taken at an athletics meeting in Lisbon last year.

BRISTOL, SUNDAY 23
Parents to sue over wire left in baby

A 16-month-old baby had a 30-cm (12-in) piece of wire left in his body after a heart operation at Bristol Royal Infirmary. The wire was left in his body for ten days and was only discovered after an X-ray was taken of the boy, Jonathan Clapton, shortly before he was due to be discharged from the hospital.

Jonathan's parents are now planning to sue the hospital. Mrs. Sharon Clapton, the baby's mother, said, "We could not believe it… He could have died. I just don't want anyone else to go through the same suffering. We have spoken to a solicitor and we want to sue the hospital."

PARIS, TUESDAY 25
Paris Metro bomb kills 4

Emergency aid for the wounded after the bombing on the Paris Metro.

Four people were killed and 60 injured, ten severely, when a terrorist bomb ripped through a Metro train in central Paris. The explosion took place during the evening rush-hour at St Michel station, close to Notre Dame Cathedral, one of the French capital's most popular tourist sites.

Police investigators discovered evidence the bomb had been hidden under a seat on the train. Paramedics set up emergency hospital facilities in a cafe close to the scene of the explosion while the most badly injured victims were transported to hospital by helicopter.

"There was a blast and the train door blew out," said one survivor. "There was a deafening explosion. Everyone got down on the ground. There was not much panic," said another. Algerian extremists are suspected of having been behind the bombing. (→ August 17)

Paul Barker.

Robert Gee.

GREAT BRITAIN, SUNDAY 30
Three children murdered

Two young boys were murdered near Ellsemere Port today. Robert Gee and Paul Barker, aged 12 and 13 respectively, had gone fishing. When they had not returned by late afternoon, their parents searched for them before alerting the police. The bodies of the children were found in the evening; both had been attacked with a knife. Police have warned parents of other children in the area to be particularly careful.

In another tragic incident, in Llandudno, seven-year-old Sophie Hook was murdered after being abducted from a tent in the garden of her uncle's house. (→August 1)

LOS ANGELES, THURSDAY 27
O.J.'s lawyers argue that sock and glove were part of frame up

Defence lawyers for O.J. Simpson have started putting their case: that the former American footballer is the victim of a police conspiracy.

They claim that certain police officers tampered with forensic evidence in a bid to strengthen the case against Simpson. The three key pieces of evidence that the defence alleges were interfered with are a bloodied sock, a bloodied glove and laboratory tests that were subsequently leaked to members of the press. The defence also alleges that one officer in particular, Detective Mark Fuhrman, is a racist and that his bias led him to alter evidence in the Simpson case.

Mr Herbert MacDonell, who is a member of the International Association of Blood Stain Pattern Analysts, gave evidence that threw doubt on the incriminatory nature of the bloody sock that was offered as evidence by the police. (→ August 15)

A glove found at the scene of Nicole Simpson's murder is shown to the jury.

LONDON, SUNDAY 23
1,200 UK troops bound for Sarajevo

British troops, who will be deployed in strengthening defences around UN "safe areas".

A 1,200-strong force of British troops is heading for Sarajevo after a joint warning from British, French and US government military officers that further Bosnian Serb aggression in the UN-designated "safe areas" would not be tolerated. The joint communique was delivered to the Bosnian Serb commander Ratko Mladic, in Belgrade.

The troops' first task will be to make safe the only passage into Sarajevo. Fifty British Warrior tanks are moving into position around the dirt track over Mount Ignam that provides that access. They are to respond with fire if the Serbs resume their bombardment of the track. The British will be joined by 500 French Foreign Legionnaires, who will be backed up by 12 light tanks and other armoured vehicles. This is the first real deployment of the UN's Rapid Reaction Force. (→ July 25)

WESTMINSTER, TUESDAY 25
Clarke share options climbdown

The Chancellor of the Exchequer is preparing to change his plan to introduce tax on share options, after it became clear that all employees in share options schemes—not just directors—would be penalized. Taxing directors' shares was a step which had been recommended by the Greenbury Committee, set up to investigate executive pay and conditions. However, the committee distanced themselves from the measure when it became clear large numbers of employees would be affected. Kenneth Clarke said, "I am prepared to look at any sensible suggestions".

Seattle, Wednesday 26. Al Hendrix, father of rock star Jimi, who died in 1970, has won the rights to his son's music after years of legal battles.

August

S	M	T	W	T	F	S
		1	2	3	4	5
6	7	8	9	10	11	12
13	14	15	16	17	18	19
20	21	22	23	24	25	26
27	28	29	30	31		

Merseyside, 1
Steven Heaney, of the Wirral, is charged with the murders of Paul Barker, 13, and Robert Gee, 12, stabbed to death while fishing near their homes in Eastham.

Coventry, 1
Six Co-op executives are gaoled at Coventry Crown Court for their part in a £5.6 million fraud, in which they were offered lavish bribes by wholesaler Gordon Faulkner to order stock from his company.

Germany, 1
Motor-racing champion Michael Schumacher marries Corinna Betsch in a registry office at Manheim.

London, 2
British yachtswoman Lisa Clayton has been asked by the World Sailing Speed Record Council to substantiate her claim to be the first woman to sail single-handed and non-stop around the world from the northern hemisphere. (→ August 29)

Yorkshire, 2
Michael Tierney is accused of threatening behaviour after ramming a woman with his trolley in a supermarket, in a fit of "trolley rage".

Bristol, 2
Janet Martin, 37, and her daughter Jasmina, 3, are killed as they stand on the pavement when a driver has a heart attack at the wheel.

London, 3
Metropolitan Police commissioner Paul Condon launches Operation Eagle Eye, which is aimed at cutting London street crime.

Teheran, 5
Leading members of the Islamic regime in Iran are put on trial accused of wholesale embezzlement from two of the country's banks.

Death
Ida Lupino, the British-born actress who described herself as "the poor man's Bette Davis", and who turned to writing, directing, and producing in the 1950s, in California, aged 77, August 3.

JERUSALEM, WEDNESDAY 2
Israeli settlers clash with police on the West Bank

Israeli soldiers and settlers in violent confrontation on the West Bank.

There was tension in Israeli settlements on the West Bank tonight after a day of clashes and protests. The settlers bitterly oppose Premier Yitzhak Rabin's plan to hand over the West Bank to the Palestine Liberation Organization. Settlers occupied hills near the settlements of Beit El and Kidumin, as police kept a watchful eye, but at the hill of Al-Khader, to the south of Jerusalem, there was violence as soldiers forced settlers to disperse. There were also violent scenes in Jerusalem, when settlers gathered outside the police headquarters where Rabbi Shlomo Riskin, whom they regard as their spiritual leader, was being held. Riskin was released late today. (→ August 21)

NOTTINGHAM, FRIDAY 4
Lottery millionaire to go to jail

Lee Taylor-Ryan won £6.5 million on the lottery. But his luck ran out today when the jury at Nottingham Crown Court found him guilty of dealing in stolen cars. Ryan was clearly astonished at the verdict and the judge warned him that he could expect a custodial sentence, not probation. Ryan arrived at court in a Bentley, and is at present having a mansion constructed, at a cost of £1 million. He has already served several borstal and prison sentences.

Lee Ryan, lottery winner, who will shortly begin a prison sentence.

ISLE OF WIGHT, WEDNESDAY 2
Royal Yacht to go on sale

The government has decided to put the Royal Yacht, *Britannia*, up for sale. It was decided last summer that the vessel would be retired, but there was no decision about what should become of her. Now, she will be sold to whoever offers the most money and the best proposal. Isle of Wight council, for one, has expressed great interest. Councillors would like to use *Britannia* as a museum and conference centre, moored off the island's south coast. They have already discussed this idea with Heritage Secretary Virginia Bottomley.

M4 Motorway, Thursday 3. In a journey along the motorway, food guru Egon Ronay slammed service-station food, saying some was inedible.

BONN, WEDNESDAY 2
Steffi Graf's father on tax charges

Peter Graf, the father of reigning Wimbledon champion Steffi Graf and her financial manager since the start of her tennis career, was arrested at his home in Brühl, near Bonn, and charged with tax evasion.

It has been confirmed that Miss Graf herself is also being investigated. Most high-earning German sports stars have emigrated for tax purposes but Graf has chosen to remain in Germany. Recently, it was revealed in the German magazine *Der Spiegel* that the Grafs have not made any tax declarations for four years.

Refugees flee Croatian advance on Knin.

BOSNIA, SATURDAY 5

Croats take Knin

In a bold offensive that could mark a turning point in the war in former Yugoslavia, the Croatians and their Bosnian Muslim allies have inflicted a major defeat on the Serb militias.

After 30 hours of intense fighting Croatian forces took Knin, the capital of Serbian-held Krajina, while the Bosnian Muslims attacked the Krajina Serbs from the rear. To the east of Knin, further Serb-held towns of strategic significance were under Bosnian government attack.

As the Croatians advanced on Knin, some 35,000 Krajina Serbs took to the roads leading out of the area in what UN officials termed the biggest single refugee movement of the war. Croatian sources claimed that corridors out of Serb territory had been left open to allow the escape of civilians, a growing tide predicted to reach 100,000.

On Friday, the Krajina Serb leader Milan Babic was in Belgrade, appealing for support from the Serbian army. But he secured only a promise of humanitarian aid.

Among the casualties of the Croatian advance on Knin were two Czech UN peace-keepers, killed in Gospic. Following the Croatian bombardment of the Serb capital, one UN official said that "almost the only people remaining in Knin were the dead and the dying". (→ August 9)

London, Friday 4. The Queen Mother celebrates her 95th birthday by greeting the large crowd of well-wishers outside Clarence House, her London residence.

ARGENTINA, TUESDAY 1

Jet and UFO in near-miss

During the early hours of Tuesday morning the pilot of an Aerolineas Argentinas jet, Jorge Polanco, reported a UFO that flew into the path of the plane before proceeding to cruise alongside it.

His observations were confirmed by Air Force major Jorge Oviedo and a number of other witnesses.

Simultaneously there was a total power failure in the city of San Carlos de Bariloche, forcing pilot Polanco to abort his landing approach.

GREAT BRITAIN, THURSDAY 3

Countryside on forest fire alert

Weeks of drought and high temperatures have left areas throughout England, Scotland, and Wales at high risk of forest and moorland fires.

In Devon, racing driver Nigel Mansell's Woodbury Park Country Club, a golf and leisure complex, was for a while menaced by a gorse fire, and Staffordshire beauty spot Cannock Chase has been closed to the public. The threat extended from the North Yorkshire Moors to Dartmoor. Only the Lake District was not considered to be at immediate risk.

ANTARCTICA, THURSDAY 3

Ozone hole over Antarctica widens

The sea ice of the Antarctic begins to melt as the hole in the ozone layer above the continent deepens.

A study by the British Antarctic Survey, published ten years after its original revelation of a "hole" in the ozone layer above the ice, suggests that the danger continues to increase.

Ozone measurements at the Halley Research Station show values of less than 40 per cent of those recorded in the 1960s. Writing in the science magazine *Nature*, team members Jonathan Shanklin and Dr. Anna Jones suggest that the fall in ozone levels, previously limited to the Antarctic spring, can now be detected in summer as well.

Loss of ozone, which is essential for protection against the harmful effects of ultra-violet rays, is caused by increases in levels of chlorine and bromine in the atmosphere, brought about in turn by emissions of man-made chemicals, notably the CFCs that are used, for example, as aerosol propellants.

The recent Montreal agreement on control of ozone-destroying chemicals suggests that the problem will eventually diminish, but Dr. Jones predicts that the hole in the ozone layer will nonetheless last for decades.

S	M	T	W	T	F	S
		1	2	3	4	5
6	7	8	9	10	11	12
13	14	15	16	17	18	19
20	21	22	23	24	25	26
27	28	29	30	31		

Colombia, 6
Miguel Rodriguez Orejuela, one of the leaders of the Cali drug cartel, is arrested. Six of the top seven Cali drug barons are now in custody.

Moscow, 7
President Boris Yeltsin, 64, returns to work at the Kremlin four weeks after being admitted to hospital with acute heart trouble.

Sri Lanka, 7
A suspected Tamil suicide bomber causes an explosion at a government building in the Sri Lankan capital, Colombo, killing 22 people. (→ October 20)

Iraq, 8
Two of Saddam Hussein's daughters and their husbands, both generals in the Iraqi regime, flee to Jordan.

Oban, 8
On a walkabout in Oban, Argyll, Prince Philip asks a local driving instructor, "How do you keep the locals off the booze long enough to get them past the test?"

Washington DC, 9
In a magazine interview Marianne Gingrich, wife of the Speaker of the House, says, "I don't want him to be president and I don't think he should be." In the same article British woman Anne Manning claims an adulterous affair with Gingrich during his previous marriage.

Belfast, 12
As the anniversary of the IRA cease-fire approaches, police clash with Republican demonstrators in the Catholic-inhabited Lower Ormeau Road. There was also trouble in Londonderry, where the Protestant Apprentice Boys paraded on the city walls. (→ August 25)

Deaths
Brigid Brophy, novelist, critic, and political campaigner, whose works included *The Finishing Touch* and *Baroque 'n' Roll*, aged 66, August 7.

John Schofield, aged 29, BBC correspondent shot by snipers in Bosnia while reporting for Radio 4, August 9.

Phil Harris, band leader, comic, and voice of Baloo in Disney's *The Jungle Book*, aged 91, August 11.

Hiroshima remembers the A-bomb

In the Peace Park at Hiroshima, 50 years to the minute since the atomic bomb fell on the city, a bell was struck and a crowd of over 60,000 observed a minute's silence.

As the Peace Bell tolled one could notice the survivors present at the commemoration ceremony, many with the scars of half a century ago still visible. The centrepiece of the park is a memorial arch, beneath which a register of those who died is preserved within a stone chest.

Hiroshima stands on the delta of the River Ota, which 50 years ago was spanned by a T-shaped bridge that provided a target for *Enola Gay*, the B-29 plane that carried the four-ton atomic bomb which decimated the city.

Floating candles commemorate those who died 50 years ago.

With few exceptions, the buildings of Hiroshima were razed to the ground.

The bomb was released at 10,500 m (31,000 ft) and fell for 43 seconds before exploding. The temperature reached 3,000° C (5,400° F), and severe burning was suffered by people 4 km (2½ miles) away.

Hiroshima today is an industrial city of more than one million people. Its mayor, Takashi Hiraoka, in an historic speech, apologized for Japanese conduct during World War II, and warned that the horrors of Hiroshima could be repeated as long as there are nuclear weapons in the world's arsenals.

Wreaths were laid at the memorial and 1,500 doves were released. After the ceremony, the crowd dispersed to more private commemorations.

Gothenburg, Sunday 6. Linford Christie collapses with a hamstring injury at the end of the 100 metres final in the World Athletics Championships. He finished sixth, losing his title.

780,000-year-old European found

Reports in the journal *Science* suggest that human ancestors reached Europe from Africa at least 780,000 years ago, far earlier than was previously thought. The report is based on analysis of fossils and tools found in caves near Burgos, Spain.

The material does not match any species already described – neither *Homo erectus* nor Heidelberg Man, at 500,000 years old, thought until now to be among the earliest Europeans. The newly discovered humanoids could instead be primitive Neanderthals, who were eventually replaced by modern humans.

California, Wednesday 9. A generation mourned the death of Jerry Garcia, leader of the band the Grateful Dead, who died at a drug treatment centre.

Gothenburg, Monday 7. British athlete Jonathan Edwards smashes the world record for the triple jump in winning the gold medal at the World Athletics Championships. His leap of 18.29 metres exceeded his previous best, set in July, by 0.31 metres.

Yorkshire water leaks away

Yorkshire Water became the first of the privatized water companies to seek government powers to tackle problems exposed by the drought, provoking widespread protests from customers and environmentalist groups regarding its inefficiency.

The company made a pre-tax profit of £142 million last year, and yet it loses more than 100 million gallons of water every day through leaking pipes. It was seeking permission to take an extra three million gallons a day from the River Wharfe, and to ban non-essential use such as car-washing. (→ August 21)

Los Angeles, Thursday 10. Heidi Fleiss is found guilty of eight charges of tax evasion and money laundering through an account set up by her father.

OKLAHOMA CITY, THURSDAY 10

McVeigh and Nichols indicted by Grand Jury

Timothy J. McVeigh and Terry Nichols were indicted by a Federal Grand Jury on charges of blowing up the Federal building here on April 19.

It is alleged that the two conspirators financed the crime by robbing an Arkansas gun dealer. Then, they raided a Kansas quarry for dynamite and fuses and concocted a deadly explosive mixture of fertiliser and diesel fuel. McVeigh is further charged with parking a truck containing the explosives in front of the Federal building and setting off the bomb. At least 167 people died in the horrific blast.

The two accused are former army buddies, and a third ex-soldier, Michael Fortier, pleaded guilty to a separate indictment concerning his knowledge of the intention to carry out the bombing. (→ August 15)

WASHINGTON DC, WEDNESDAY 9

Spy plane photos indicate mass graves at Srebrenica

The chilling evidence of photographs taken from satellites and U-2 reconaissance planes over the Bosnian town of Srebrenica suggests that Bosnian Serbs have committed atrocities on a vast scale.

One photograph shows hundreds, possibly thousands, of Muslim men and boys being held in a field five miles north of the town, where thousands were rounded up by Bosnian Serbs last month. Another shows an extensive area of freshly-dug earth, consistent with the appearance of mass graves.

David T. Johnson of the US State Department said, "We've got some evidence from sensitive sources that tend to corroborate accounts of atrocities against the Bosnian men and boys who were prevented from leaving Srebrenica." This evidence will be presented to the United Nations Security Council.

The International Red Cross reports that more than 6,000 people are still missing following the fall of the town to the Bosnian Serbs.

The latest massacre is considered to be on a similar scale to that in 1991 when the Serbs overran the town of Vukovar, on the Danube. Thousands of people are still unaccounted for following that incident. (→ August 30)

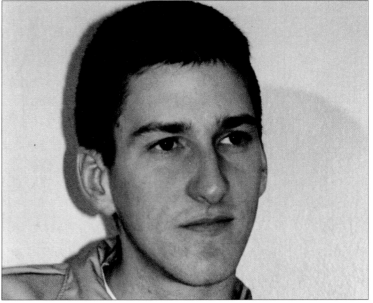

Timothy J. McVeigh, who is accused of causing the Oklahoma City bomb blast.

S	M	T	W	T	F	S
		1	2	3	4	5
6	7	8	9	10	11	12
13	14	15	16	17	18	19
20	21	22	23	24	25	26
27	28	29	30	31		

Srinagar, 13
Kashmiri separatists kill a kidnapped Norwegian tourist and threaten to kill other hostages unless India frees 15 militants.

Bogotá, 13
Bands of armed men kill at least 38 people in a series of raids in northwestern Colombia.

New York, 14
A mayoral advisory panel recommends that New York City abolish its municipal hospital system.

Bermuda, 14
In a referendum disrupted by Hurricane Felix, 74 per cent of the people of Bermuda vote against independence from Britain.

Los Angeles, 15
O.J. Simpson trial judge Lance Ito faces demands to withdraw from the case so that his wife, Margaret York, the highest-ranking woman in the LAPD, can give evidence about racist tapes. (→ August 31)

Washington, 15
The dollar soars to its highest level in six months after concerted buying by the US, Germany and Japan.

Oklahoma City, 15
Timothy J. McVeigh and Terry L. Nichols plead not guilty to charges of planting the bomb that killed 167 people in the Oklahoma City Federal building.

Boston, 16
A long-term study shows that the drug AZT does not help fight off the development of full-blown AIDS.

Moscow, 16
Rich Russians demonstrate outside former KGB headquarters against the large number of murders in the business community.

Washington, 17
The Pentagon orders equipment into the Persian Gulf after warnings that Iraq may be planning attacks on Kuwait or Saudi Arabia.

Death
Howard Koch, Hollywood screenwriter and one of the authors of *Casablanca*, dies in Kingston, New York, aged 93, August 17.

LOS ANGELES, MONDAY 14

Michael Ovitz becomes president of Disney corporation

Michael Ovitz with his wife, Jody.

In a surprise move, the Walt Disney Company today announced that its new president will be top Hollywood talent agent Michael Ovitz.

The appointment shocked an industry still reeling from the news announced only two weeks ago that Disney was to acquire ABC for $19.2 billion, thus becoming the world's largest entertainment company.

Ovitz will now work closely with Disney chairman Michael D. Eisner. Eisner had previously been criticized for failing to appoint a strong deputy after the death 16 months ago of his trusted lieutenant Frank Wells. Some commentators had expected the high-profile Disney studio chief Jeffrey Katzenberg to take over, but acrimonious disputes with Eisner led to his departure from the company.

PORT-AU-PRINCE, SUNDAY 13

Voting finally takes place in Haiti

A low turnout was reported at today's elections in Haiti, the first to be held in the country since President Jean-Bertrand Aristide was restored to power last autumn.

More significantly, however, there were no reports of disorder, in marked contrast to the earlier election in June. This had to be abandoned when the smaller parties rejected the results on the grounds that procedural irregularities had been unfairly advantageous to the President's Lavalas Party.

They refused to participate further in the political process until Pierre-Michel Sajous, the newly appointed elections officer, had promised greater accountability and that fair play would be seen to be done.

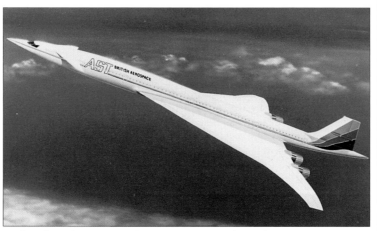

Paris, Thursday 17. An Air France Concorde with 80 passengers on board took 1 hour 22 minutes off its own round-the-world speed record early today. It flew from New York's Kennedy Airport to Acapulco, Mexico, via Toulouse, the United Arab Emirates, Bangkok, and Guam in 31 hours 27 minutes.

Mexico City, Thursday 17. New research shows that smog is not caused by car exhaust, but by leaks from tanks containing gas for cooking and heating.

BOGOTA, TUESDAY 15

Kidnapped British student found dead

Trevor Catton, the British student who was kidnapped seven weeks ago by guerrillas from his parents' weekend cottage 25 miles outside Bogotá, has been found murdered.

Mr Catton, who was 22, is the latest victim of the recent kidnapping spree by Colombian guerrillas. The British Embassy here would not comment on reports that the kidnappers had demanded a ransom of $500,000 for Mr Catton which had not been forthcoming.

LONDON, THURSDAY 17

Newspaper prints wrong anti-Blair story

The London *Evening Standard* has apologized for publishing an article attacking Labour leader Tony Blair. The newspaper believed that the piece had been written by Bryan Gould, Blair's former shadow cabinet colleague, but it turned out to have been the work of Nick Howard, the student son of Tory Home Secretary Michael Howard.

The *Standard* said that, by "extraordinary mischance", an article by Gould had been mixed up with an unsolicited fax from Howard.

LAS VEGAS, SATURDAY 19
Storm over Tyson's comeback victory

On his return to the ring after two years in prison, former undisputed World Heavyweight boxing champion Mike Tyson won his comeback fight easily, beating Peter McNeeley after only 1 minute 29 seconds of the first round of the contest.

The bout ended in controversial circumstances. Tyson landed two lefts and a right in quick succession. McNeeley fell backward, and while referee Mills Lane was ushering Tyson to a neutral corner, Vinny Vecchione, McNeeley's manager, climbed into the ring and effectively disqualified his fighter.

The outcome provoked storms of protest from fight fans at the ringside who had paid up to $1,500 a ticket to attend. Disappointment and anger were also expressed by members of the pay-to-view television audience of over a million who had paid an average of $40 a home.

The fight cost a total of $70 million to stage, and $25 million of that went to Tyson himself.

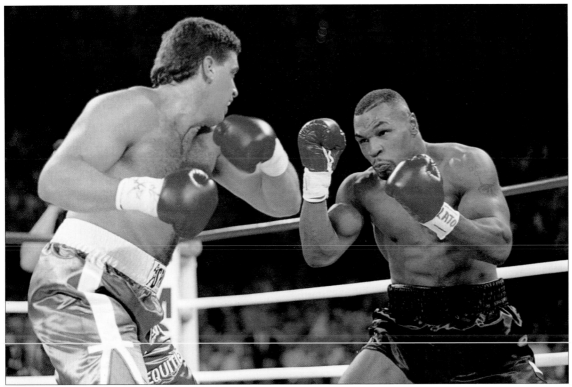

Peter McNeeley (left) and Mike Tyson during their 89-second confrontation.

PARIS, THURSDAY 17
Paris nail bomb injures 16

A bomb exploded in a dustbin near the Arc de Triomphe just after 5 p.m. today, injuring 16 people, three of them seriously.

The device, a canister of camping gas stuffed with nails and bolts, was placed at the Avenue de Friedland entrance to the Charles de Gaulle-Etoile metro station.

The bombing is the latest in a series of terrorist attacks in Paris that have occurred throughout the year. Although no group has claimed responsibility, the attacks are believed to be the work of the Algerian Armed Islamic Group. (→ August 31)

LONDON, TUESDAY 15
Celebrations mark VJ Day

Ceremonies in Britain marked the fiftieth anniversary of VJ Day, when the Japanese surrendered and brought an end to World War II. Today's events mark the start of a week of celebration and acts of remembrance.

The Japanese marked the anniversary by reiterating their deep remorse for the atrocities they perpetrated during the War. However this failed to satisfy many veterans. One of these, Viscount Slim, said, "The one word that is always missing is 'sorry'."

ISLAMABAD, THURSDAY 17
British woman climber dies on K2

Mountaineer Alison Hargreaves.

Alison Hargreaves, the 33-year-old mother of two who in May had become the first woman to climb Mount Everest without oxygen, is now known to have been killed in a huge avalanche on K2, the world's second highest mountain.

Reports suggest that she may have died on Sunday after having reached the summit and begun the descent along the Abruzzi Ridge of the 8,700 m (28,250 ft) mountain.

K2 forms part of the Karakoram range in Pakistan. It is a notoriously treacherous mountain and has claimed the lives of many experienced climbers over the years.

Charleston, Monday 14. After a two-and-a-half-year battle to become the first female cadet in the 152-year history of the military academy, The Citadel, Shannon Faulkner, aged 20, was unable to take the oath on her first day of training when she was overcome by the 38° C (100° F) heat and taken to the infirmary.

S	M	T	W	T	F	S
		1	2	3	4	5
6	7	8	9	10	11	12
13	14	15	16	17	18	19
20	21	22	23	24	25	26
27	28	29	30	31		

Yorkshire, 21
The first drought order of the long, hot summer is sanctioned by Environment Secretary John Gummer to Yorkshire Water, to protect supplies in the Bradford area. At the same time, water regulator Ofwat begins an inquiry into the water companies' competence to maintain supplies. (→ September 1)

Munich, 22
Germany's highest court has ruled that the Bavarian law requiring a crucifix to be hung in every classroom is unconstitutional, following a ten-year challenge by a parent, Ernst Seler.

London, 23
Lord Wakeham, chairman of the Press Complaints Commission, tries to pre-empt problems during the forthcoming school term by reminding the media that Prince William's privacy at Eton should be respected.

Belfast, 25
Northern Ireland Secretary Patrick Mayhew aims to keep the peace process alive by promising troop withdrawals, in a speech six days before the first anniversary of the IRA ceasefire. (→ August 31)

London, 25
The driver of a 15-ton Sherman tank, who hit a Jaguar while driving through a narrow street in Soho, is found guilty of careless driving. "I knew that it was going to be a bit of a tight fit", he says.

Bonn, 25
Eight former East German generals go on trial accused of manslaughter by operating a "shoot to kill" policy on the Berlin Wall. This is the biggest such trial of senior German officers since World War II.

London, 26
One of the most celebrated features of the August Bank Holiday weekend, the Notting Hill Carnival in west London, gets underway. It claims to be Europe's biggest street festival.

Death
Len Martin, the voice of the football results on BBC TV for 37 years, in Middlesex after a short illness, aged 76, August 21.

SHEFFIELD, FRIDAY 25

Rave priest suspended

Chris Brain used loud music and flashing lights during his Nine O' Clock Service.

The Reverend Chris Brain was admitted to a psychiatric hospital within hours of being banned from practising as an ordained minister of the Church of England by the Archbishop of York, the Most Rev. John Hapgood.

The New Age priest, founder of the controversial Nine O'Clock Service in Sheffield, has been in hiding for ten days since the Bishop of Sheffield, the Rt. Rev. David Lunn, forbade him to preach within his own diocese.

The developments take place in an atmosphere of allegations concerning financial irregularities and sexual contact with female worshippers in his congregation.

The church is increasingly having to confront potential problems caused by attempts to make its teaching relevant to a generation used to rave parties, drugs, and casual sex.

ZAIRE, TUESDAY 22

Zaire troops expel Rwandan refugees

About 750,000 Rwandans, almost all Hutus fleeing the Tutsi-led rebel government, have been squatting in camps at Goma, on the border between Zaire and Rwanda. Now Zairean soldiers have begun to forcibly expel the refugees, setting fire to huts and looting the camps.

This action began on Saturday but has increased daily, to the point where an estimated 10,000 were expelled in one day. A further 60,000 Rwandans, fearful of being murdered if they are forced to return home, have fled to the hills in an attempt to escape the soldiers.

MOSCOW, SUNDAY 20

3,000-year-old Siberian in ice

A 3,000-year-old tattooed man has been found, preserved in permafrost, in a Scythian burial mound in Siberia, near the borders with China and Mongolia.

The tattoo, covering his back and chest, is of an elk. The man had long, red, braided hair, and was dressed in embroidered trousers, fur coat, and boots. His horse was buried nearby.

The corpse has been moved to the Mausoleum Institute in Moscow, which looks after Lenin's body.

JERUSALEM, MONDAY 21

Bus bombing in Jerusalem

Another suicide bomber struck at the heart of the Israeli state when he killed himself and four passengers, including an American woman, in detonating a device aboard a Jerusalem bus. The toll of injured was put at 100.

The incident provoked protests against the government's negotiations with the Palestine Liberation Organization, whose leader Yasser Arafat said on television, "I condemn the attack completely".

The Islamic resistance movement Hamas has claimed responsibility for the bombing. (→ August 29)

Washington, Thursday 24. Workers at Bothell, preparing for the midnight launch of Microsoft Windows 95. It was the computer industry's most expensive launch ever, costing an estimated £200 million. Microsoft have paid the Rolling Stones $10 million (about £7 million) to use one of their songs, *Start Me Up*, for the launch.

FIROZABAD, NORTHEAST INDIA, MONDAY 21

Death toll could reach 500 in Indian train crash

Rescue workers anticipate finding more bodies as they cut their way into the wreckage.

The death toll of 350, following the collision of two passenger trains, both bound for New Delhi, was expected to rise as teams equipped with cranes and oxy-acetylene cutters worked on the crumpled coaches. The list of injured totals 500.

One of the express trains, between them carrying around 2,200 passengers, was stalled on the line after hitting a cow. Police are now seeking the signalman who gave a green light to the following train to continue on the same track. It hit the stationary train at about 60 mph, throwing coaches into the air.

A makeshift morgue is being established at nearby Firozabad, but in the meantime hundreds of corpses lie in fields alongside the track, awaiting identification.

Victims of the disaster included labourers, a team of athletes and their coaches, and about 60 soldiers.

TORONTO, SUNDAY 20

Monica Seles begins her comeback with a commanding victory

Monica Seles, now recovered from stab wounds inflicted to her back and shoulder by a fanatic in April 1993, marked her return to competitive tennis with a commanding victory at the du Maurier Ltd Open.

In winning her thirty-third title, 21-year-old Seles brushed aside the unseeded South African Amanda Coetzer, ranked number 27 in the world, 6-0, 6-1. "I wasn't sure I'd ever be back to play tennis again," said Seles who won all five rounds of the tournament in straight and one-sided sets. She said it was the mental scars caused by the horrific assault, rather than the actual physical injury itself, that took longest to heal.

Monica Seles proves unstoppable on her comeback, winning every set in Toronto.

California, Saturday 26. The former *Dallas* actor Larry Hagman was recovering in hospital today after having undergone a liver transplant.

WASHINGTON DC, SATURDAY 26

Russia prepared to supply Iran with nuclear reactors

A new diplomatic row has blown up between Washington and Moscow following the news that Russia was apparently prepared to supply Iran with two further atomic reactors. This flies in the face of the international initiative designed to prevent Teheran from being able to develop atomic weapons.

Russia has already supplied Iran with reactors, and in May President Clinton was in Moscow attempting to persuade the Russians to stop the trade. It is now said that a new deal was agreed this month, during a visit to Moscow by an Iranian delegation that included Reza Amrollahi, Iran's atomic energy chief.

The two 400 megawatt reactors are intended for the Neka nuclear research complex, part of Iran's concerted drive to develop nuclear technology. Pakistan and China have also shown themselves to be willing to deal with the Iranian regime.

One diplomatic source was quoted as saying, "If the Russians are prepared to sell Iran this kind of equipment it is only a matter of time before Teheran develops its own nuclear warhead." Meanwhile, Moscow still remained defiant.

Manchester, Saturday 26. Bruce Bursford has set a new unofficial world record speed of 207 km per hour (128 mph) on a specially designed stationary bike.

August

S	M	T	W	T	F	S
		1	2	3	4	5
6	7	8	9	10	11	12
13	14	15	16	17	18	19
20	21	22	23	24	25	26
27	28	29	30	31		

Paris, 27
The International Rugby Football Board bows to the inevitable and confirms that Rugby Union can become professional.

Belfast, 28
James Molyneaux, leader of the fiercely loyalist Ulster Unionist Party, announces his retirement. (→ September 8)

Fairford, Gloucestershire, 29
A U-2 pilot is killed when his reconaissance plane, thought to be headed for Bosnia, turns back to RAF Fairford after developing problems, and crashes.

London, 29
After a month scrutinizing documents provided by yachtswoman Lisa Clayton, the World Sailing Speed Record Council confirms her as the first woman to sail non-stop and single-handed around the world starting from the northern hemisphere.

Gaza, 29
Palestinian police arrest dozens of suspected Muslim militants in the Gaza Strip, as part of a crackdown on opponents of the peace talks between Israel and the Palestine Liberation Organization.(→ September 28)

London, 30
Variable speed limits are introduced on Britain's busiest stretch of motorway, ten miles of the M25 south of the M4. At the most congested times limits will be reduced to improve traffic flow.

Isle of Wight, 30
A stamp collector who paid £1 for an album at a car boot sale reveals that he has sold two of the stamps, Trinidadian and dating from 1847, to a private collector for £95,000.

Monrovia, Liberia, 31
People throng the streets of the West African country to celebrate peace after six years of civil war.

Death
Daily Express cartoonist Carl Giles, best known for the fictional family that included umbrella-wielding Grandma and many rowdy children, in Ipswich, aged 78, August 27.

Judge rules on Fuhrman tapes in O.J. trial

Detective Mark Fuhrman (left), whose racist comments on tape are vital to the defence.

In a dramatic development in the trial of O.J. Simpson, Judge Lance Ito ruled that the jury should only hear two of 41 instances on tape where Detective Mark Fuhrman refers to blacks as "niggers". Just 15 seconds of tape will be played to them, culled from more than 14 hours displaying Fuhrman's racial bigotry and boastful disregard of the law.

The tapes, made over a period of years by screenwriter Laura Hart McKinny, who was seeking background material on police procedures, were considered a trump card in the defence hand, allegedly proving that Fuhrman is so racist that he could, for example, have "planted" the blood-stained glove on Mr. Simpson's property. The lead defence lawyer Johnnie L. Cochran Jr. said, "To say we are outraged and livid by this ruling would be a master understatement". (→ September 6)

London, Tuesday 29. Comedian Michael Barrymore, whose private life has been under much tabloid scrutiny, wins three National TV Awards.

20 Muslims arrested in France

In early-morning raids in Paris and Lyons, 20 Muslim fundamentalists were arrested and weapons, forged travel documents, and a gas canister were seized.

The canister resembled those used recently in three bombs, two of which exploded, killing three and injuring dozens. Investigators have been tracing the attacks back to a fundamentalist cell in Algeria. The police revealed that those arrested included French citizens. (→ October 17)

Head of college suspended

The headmaster of one of the country's most exclusive private schools, Dulwich College, has been suspended following an allegation that he sexually harassed a female member of staff. Anthony Verity, 56, was replaced by his deputy "pending further investigation of certain matters", in the words of a note sent to parents. The move comes in reaction to an allegation made last term. Mr. Verity strenuously denies the charge.

Draw at Oval ends great Test series

England skipper Mike Atherton, with a match-saving 95, saw his side to a second successive draw against the West Indies. The magnificent six-match series ended with two wins each.

The visitors began the summer series with a commanding win at Headingley, and on past evidence the odds were hugely against England being able to get back into the series.

However, England won at Lord's, only to be crushed in the Third Test at Edgbaston. They fought back at Old Trafford to square the series, even though the West Indian Brian Lara made centuries in the last three Tests.

For England Dominic Cork was a match-winner and, on his recall, wicket-keeper Jack Russell proved that he could bat at this level.

Graham Hick dodges a bouncer.

Panic as Japan's largest credit union collapses

As rumours of impending collapse spread, desperate depositors beseiged the Kizu Credit Co-operative in Osaka, Japan's largest such financial organization. When the doors were closed many had still not managed to withdraw their money, although government sources assured them that deposits would be honoured.

This was a dramatic manifestation of a deep crisis in Japan's banking system, caused chiefly by hundreds of billions of dollars in bad mortgage debts. A few hours after the panic, the Ministry of Finance and a consortium of major banks announced a rescue package for the equally troubled Hyogo Bank in Kobe.

A Finance Ministry spokesman strove to damp down further panic by saying that the worst of the financial crisis was over, but this view was contradicted by industry analysts, who estimate that billions more in bad debts remain, a legacy of the collapsed property boom of the 1980s.

First anniversary of cease-fire in Northern Ireland

Belfast citizens celebrate a year of peace after a quarter of a century of violence.

A year ago the Irish Republican Army announced a cessation of their violent campaign against British occupation of Northern Ireland, a gesture that was followed in October by a cease-fire by Protestant "loyalist" paramilitaries as well.

After 25 years during which violent, politically motivated death was almost a daily occurrence there has been just one such murder in a year, when an IRA gang shot a post office worker while carrying out a robbery, although self-appointed vigilante groups on both sides have continued to mete out punishments.

But progress towards all-party peace talks has proved painfully slow. The British demand for decommissioning of weapons before negotiations has been one sticking point, while hardline loyalists cannot envisage talking to those whose goal is a united Ireland. Meanwhile, ordinary people enjoy the peace, however uneasy it may be. (→ September 8)

NATO bombs Serbs

NATO's rapid reaction force scores a direct hit on an armaments dump.

As a direct response to the shelling of Sarajevo market from Bosnian Serb positions around the city on Monday, when dozens of civilians died, NATO warplanes carried out a retaliatory action in the early morning.

The attacks were concentrated on positions to the south and east of the city, in the direction of the Bosnian Serb headquarters at Pale.

An estimated 100 NATO aircraft were involved in the action, drawn from the forces of the US, Britain, France, Spain, and the Netherlands. No NATO casualties were reported.

In Washington DC, a Defense Department official said that 24 military targets had been hit. These were identified as surface-to-air missile sites, artillery batteries, ammunition depots, and control centres. The spokesman confirmed that, should the Serbs respond violently, NATO action will intensify. (→ September 1)

Shevardnadze survives car-bomb assassination attempt

The Georgian leader Eduard A. Shevardnadze sustained superficial injuries when a car bomb exploded near his vehicle as he was on his way to sign a new constitution for Georgia. He had just departed from the parliament building in Tbilisi.

Several other people were injured but there were no fatalities. Mr. Shevardnadze appeared on television, dazed and cut on the face.

His press secretary, Ramaz Sakvarelidze said, "It's clear that Shevardnadze's enemies tried to assassinate the head of our state to stop the signing ceremony".

Mr. Shevardnadze has confirmed that he will run for the post of president, which is to be restored under the new constitution. (→ November 5)

Eduard Shevardnadze, target for bombers.

September

Sarajevo, 1
NATO air strikes against the Bosnian Serbs are suspended for 24 hours to accelerate peace talks in Belgrade. (→ September 14)

Johannesburg, 1
One man is killed and more than 20 injured during a clash between blacks and whites in Kuruman in South Africa's northern Cape.

Tahiti, 1
On the eve of a scheduled nuclear test, French commandos board two Greenpeace ships and tow them towards their base at Mururoa. (→ September 5)

Paris, 1
Riot police break up Greenpeace protest against France's resumption of nuclear tests in the Pacific. (→ September 5)

London, 1
Environment Secretary John Gummer calls in Yorkshire Water boss Sir Gordon Jones to try to avert threatened water cuts after the long summer drought. (→ September 19)

Beijing, 1
Chinese authorities attempt to curb free discussion by delegates at the World Conference on Women. (→ September 15)

London, 2
British boxer Frank Bruno beats American Oliver McCall to take the WBC World Heavyweight title.

London, 2
Warwickshire win cricket's NatWest Trophy, beating Northamptonshire by four wickets in a one-day match.

London, 4
Lloyds Bank is to pay £77,529 damages for lending a couple money to renovate a house just before the collapse of the property market.

London, 4
Greenpeace apologizes to Shell for overestimating the pollution risk from the Brent Spar oil installation.

London, 6
A £2.5 million sponsorship agreement is signed for the RAF aerobatic team, the Red Arrows.

LOS ANGELES, WEDNESDAY 6

Detective in O.J. case pleads the Fifth Amendment

Courting controversy in the O.J. trial: Detective Mark Fuhrman (left) and Judge Ito.

The detective at the heart of the O.J. Simpson case, Mark Fuhrman, invoked the Fifth Amendment when he took the witness stand today, refusing to answer possibly incriminating questions. Simpson's chief lawyer, Johnnie Cochran, whose case rests on the allegation that Fuhrman falsified evidence, said, "What more does anyone need out there?"

Detective Fuhrman, who is alleged to have boasted of his racism, was asked questions such as, "Have you ever falsified a police report?" and "Did you plant or manufacture any evidence in this case?" After each question was put to him, the detective looked to his lawyer before stating to Judge Ito, "I wish to assert my Fifth Amendment privilege." (→ September 22)

WASHINGTON DC, MONDAY 4

Colin Powell remains undecided over whether to run in presidential election

Colin Powell meets the public in San Bernardino, California.

Colin Powell, chairman of the US Joint Chiefs of Staff during the Gulf War, will wait until November to decide whether he is going to stand as a candidate in the next presidential election. Speculation has been growing for much of the year that the 58-year-old retired general will run as a centrist Republican candidate. But he has carefully avoided answering direct questions from reporters on that subject or on his political views.

He is about to embark on a tour of the US that will see him visit 23 cities to promote his autobiography, *My American Journey*. The publicity generated will be enormous. Television and magazine interviews as well as book signing sessions will guarantee he stays firmly in the public eye during the forthcoming weeks. The interest has been generated by his potential candidature and his book's revelations on the Gulf War. (→ September 19)

PARIS, MONDAY 4

Runaway spends 70,000 francs at Disneyland

Tiring of life in his parents' Paris hotel, a 12-year-old boy stole 70,000 francs (about £9,300) from their till and ran away to spend it all on the competing attractions of the top hotel at EuroDisney to the east of the French capital.

As police and family frantically searched for him, Lamine Ghalmi checked into the luxury £150-a-night Disney hotel and repeatedly went on all the rides and visited all the attractions at one of Europe's leading theme parks.

On checking in, Ghalmi allayed any suspicions the concierge might have had by telling him, "I'm here with my mother but she is busy and told me to take the room."

After a few days Lamine became bored with the charms of the Magic Kingdom, so he hired a chauffeur-driven stretch limousine at £375-a-day to ferry him to and from Parc Asterix, another theme park on the outskirts of Paris.

Lamine was eventually tracked down and reunited with his family after ten days in the hotel. Despite her anguish, his mother was quite forgiving. She told reporters, "He always seems sure of himself and people believe him. The main thing is he came to no harm. He knows it was a very naughty thing to do."

St. Maarten, Thursday 7. The 140-mph hurricane Luis devastates the Dutch/French Caribbean island of St. Maarten.

France carries out underground nuclear test at Mururoa Atoll

One of the French commandos who stormed the Greenpeace vessel Rainbow Warrior.

A demonstrator shows her feelings.

There have been riots in Tahiti in protest at the French programme of nuclear testing.

France exploded a nuclear bomb at 2:30 p.m. local time today in defiance of international protests. The device was buried deep below the coral-ringed Mururoa Atoll, about ,200 km (750 miles) southeast of the Pacific island of Tahiti.

Until now the French themselves have released few details about the exact weaponry being tested, but today the country's defence ministry announced that the explosion was the equivalent of less than 20,000 tonnes of TNT. (For the purposes of comparison, the nuclear bomb exploded at Hiroshima in 1945 had a force of 15,000 tonnes of TNT.) This

is the first in a series of tests which the French plan to carry out between now and May 1996. After that, they have promised to renounce nuclear testing for ever and sign a comprehensive global test ban treaty.

The tests were originally ordered by the French president, Jacques Chirac, shortly after he took office in the spring. He insists that the tests are essential to confirm the accuracy of the latest generation of nuclear warheads and to perfect computer simulation techniques that would obviate the need for any further explosions. The French also maintain that the testing is safe because the basalt rock

around the exposion prevents any radioactivity leaking into the sea.

Worldwide protests against French policy continued throughout the build-up to today's explosion. Tens of thousands of people have taken part in demonstrations in Australia, New Zealand, and Japan. French goods are widely boycotted throughout the South Pacific region.

Greenpeace called the explosion "an outrage". New Zealand and Australia have withdrawn their ambassadors to France. The US expressed regret and hoped France would join the moratorium on further tests. (→ September 10)

Privatized industry merger talks spark "ransom" row

A political storm blew up today when the northwestern regional electricity company Norweb confirmed that it was in merger talks with North West Water. Between them, the two businesses have nearly 5 million customers and a combined turnover of £4 billion.

The proposals were widely condemned and described as holding the consumer to ransom. Labour spokesman Nigel Griffiths said, "The government privatized water, electricity, and gas, saying that it would create competition. Now we have the prospect of huge privatized monopolies." It is feared that if the merger goes ahead there will be further substantial job losses: both companies have already shed thousands of jobs since privatization.

Ulster Unionist leader poses new threat to Major

David Trimble was elected leader of the Ulster Unionists today in succession to James Molyneaux, who stood down earlier this year.

Trimble, the 50-year-old MP for Upper Bann, is seen as a hard-liner who may well be less biddable than his predecessor in the Northern Ireland peace process which is now at a delicate stage of negotiation.

The new leader has been particularly uncompromising on the decommissioning of IRA weapons and he will not take the Unionists into all-party talks until he is convinced of the IRA's commitment to exclusively peaceful means. He is particularly sceptical about "symbolic gestures" such as the surrender of token quantities of weaponry and Semtex explosives.

Prime Minister John Major is dependent on the continued support of the Ulster Unionists both to advance the peace talks and to maintain his slim overall majority in the House of Commons. (→ September 21)

September

S	M	T	W	T	F	S
					1	2
3	4	5	6	7	8	9
10	11	12	13	14	15	16
17	18	19	20	21	22	23
24	25	26	27	28	29	30

London, 10
The charity album *Help*, recorded to raise funds for Bosnian war victims, goes straight to Number 1 in the album charts after one day's sales.

Moscow, 10
Vladimir Zhirinovsky, the far-right nationalist, assaults a female MP by pulling her hair during a disturbance in the Russian Parliament.

London, 11
Janet Street-Porter quits *Live TV*, the Mirror Group's cable service that she herself founded.

Brighton, 12
Labour leader Tony Blair stresses his commitment to modernization at the TUC conference. (→ September 27)

Paris, 12
The French army is guarding the Channel Tunnel entrance as part of the French government's anti-terrorist measures.

London, 13
Scotland Yard is accused of allowing a Yardie gangster who was also their informer to enter the country.

Great Yarmouth, Norfolk, 14
A woman is charged with the murder of 18-year-old student Rachel Lean, who was found stabbed to death near an RAF base at the weekend.

London, 14
A leaked draft Cabinet paper which refers to a shortage of funds for state schools causes further damage to John Major's government.

London, 14
Eurotunnel's banks freeze interest payments on the beleaguered company's loans for 18 months. (→ October 6)

Mold, Wales, 14
Nuclear Electric is fined £250,000 for ignoring safety procedures at its power station in Wylfa.

London, 14
German government investigators reveal that roughly 32,000 British workers employed in Germany are also dole claimants in Britain.

Death
Jeremy Brett, the actor famous for his portrayal of Sherlock Holmes, London, aged 59, September 12.

PARIS, SUNDAY 10

French nuclear tests will continue

President Chirac refuses to allow world opinion to stop French nuclear tests in the Pacific.

France will continue nuclear testing in its territory in the Pacific – that is the new defiant message from French president Jacques Chirac. He suggested that political motives rather than worries about environmental effects of the testing were behind antipodean antipathy towards French nuclear testing in the Pacific.

In an interview on French TV he said that objections to the tests from Australia and New Zealand are "not really anti-nuclear". Instead, he added, critics in those countries are "motivated by their wish to see us out of the Pacific".

The President insisted that he would not allow French defence policy to be swayed to any degree by agitators, opinion polls, or international condemnation.

At Mururoa Atoll, where the tests are being held, eight protesting MPs, from Sweden, Luxembourg, Japan, Italy, and Australia were arrested by French commandos. (→ October 1)

New York, Sunday 10. Pete Sampras took four sets to beat Andre Agassi and win the US Open Championship for the third time in five years.

NEWCASTLE, WEDNESDAY 13

Bannister says black athletes are best

Sir Roger Bannister, the first man to run a mile in under four minutes, has told the British Association for the Advancement of Science that he believes black athletes have natural advantages over whites.

Sir Roger, a neurologist, claimed that genetic factors provide black competitors with an advantage. Black athletes in general have a lower body-fat content than white runners, for example. According to Sir Roger, climatic factors in an athlete's upbringing can benefit their performance. He also believes that the three-and-a-half-minute mile will eventually be run.

Southeast Asia, Wednesday 13. The Worldwide Fund for Nature says one tiger in southeast Asia is killed every week and they now face extinction.

PARIS, TUESDAY 12

Alfred Dreyfus officially absolved

The French army has finally given Captain Alfred Dreyfus an official pardon for crimes on which he was convicted more than a century ago.

General Jean-Louis Mourrut, chief historian of the French army, said the charge of high treason on which Dreyfus was convicted was "a judicial error and a military conspiracy". Dreyfus was Jewish and the case exacerbated anti-semitic feeling prior to the First World War. A civil court reversed the ruling in Dreyfus's lifetime and he was reinstated in the army. Until now, however, the army had not commented on the case.

Alfred Dreyfus, the wronged soldier.

BELGRADE, THURSDAY 14

NATO halts Serb bombing in new peace hopes

The Bosnian town of Sbrinje (formerly Foca) after one of the NATO bombing raids that have devastated Serb-held areas.

NATO's bombing of the Bosnian Serbs was halted yesterday. The tactic appeared to have had its desired effect with the imminent withdrawal of the Serbs from around Sarajevo. On Wednesday, US peace envoy Richard Holbrooke had a meeting with Serbian leaders Radovan Karadzic, General Ratko Mladic, and President Milosevic in Belgrade. It was agreed that the Bosnian Serbs would withdraw their weapons from around the besieged city. The order to cease bombing the Bosnian Serbs was then given by NATO secretary general, Willy Claes.

With the Bosnian Serbs in retreat and suffering from NATO's bombing, worries have arisen that the conflict could be exacerbated by Bosnian Muslims launching attacks on a weakened enemy. "It is no secret that I made interventions to parties urging them not to exploit the situation," said Claes. (→ September 18)

Pasadena, California, Sunday 10. Actress Candice Bergen has won a fifth Emmy for her role in the comedy *Murphy Brown*.

BEIJING, FRIDAY 15

UN women demand change

Sexual freedom and an end to violence against women were the two main resolutions adopted by the United Nations' Fourth World Conference on Women, which ended today. In particular, the 5,000 delegates condemned trafficking in women and genital mutilation of girls. However, some of the views that were upheld by the conference, such as its implicit recognition of homosexual relationships, were rejected by representatives of Islamic countries and by the Vatican.

LONDON, TUESDAY 12

Internet usage is 50 per cent porn

The Internet is being extensively used by paedophiles and pornographers, according to Professor Harold Thimbleby of Middlesex University. He told the British Association for the Advancement of Science that research had shown that close to 50 per cent of those who used the worldwide computer service for leisure purposes did so to send or receive pornographic material.

"If you want to know about any perversion at all," said Professor Thimbleby, "there are full details that are easily accessible by my nine-year-old son." He added that because of the nature of the Internet and the lack of extensive controls on the type of material that it contains, governments had not yet become fully aware of the extent of harmful material that was being transmitted freely across their national boundaries, and which they can barely control.

Among the perversions on the Internet that the professor brought to the association's attention were child pornography and bestiality.

CAMBRIDGE, TUESDAY 12

Pigs' hearts to be used in transplants

Scientists hope to use pigs' hearts for transplants within a year.

Hearts, lungs, and kidneys from specially bred pigs could be transplanted to humans in a major breakthrough announced by British research scientists. The first operation is planned for spring 1996 on the basis of research progressing at its current rate. The organs could be in widespread use by the end of the century.

Dr. David White, the founder of Imutran, the company that conducted the research, said, "This will give hope to hundreds of thousands of patients around the world who would otherwise die waiting for a heart, lung, or kidney." Every year in the UK, 6,000 people are on the waiting list for transplants but only half that number receive them.

Specialist pig breeders have cooperated with the research scientists to develop a unique herd of 300 transgenic pigs – each of which is given a human gene by the scientists at birth.

S	M	T	W	T	F	S
					1	2
3	4	5	6	7	8	9
10	11	12	13	14	15	16
17	18	19	20	21	22	23
24	25	26	27	28	29	30

Sarajevo, 18
The UN Secretary General, Boutros Boutros Ghali, says UN troops should withdraw from Bosnia.
(→ October 5)

Washington DC, 19
The House speaker, Newt Gingrich, is to be investigated after he received a $4.5 million book advance from Rupert Murdoch.

Los Angeles, 19
Police Chief Willie Williams files a law suit against the city to end a "smear campaign" aimed at him.

Washington DC, 19
Rainbow coalition leader Jesse Jackson leads African-American attacks on General Colin Powell, calling him the "black of choice" for whites. Quincy Jones says if Powell ran for president he would face "attack like you can't believe".
(→ November 8)

Ankara, 20
Turkey's first woman prime minister, Tansu Ciller, resigns. Elections should follow unless she can forge a temporary coalition with the conservative Motherland Party.

Britain, 21
The Halifax Building Society is accused of depressing the housing market by offering bonuses to sales staff who persuade vendors to drop their price.

London, 21
The government offers financial recompense to GPs for night work.

Atlanta, 22
CNN boss Ted Turner sells his Turner Broadcasting System to Time Warner in a $7.5 million deal.

Los Angeles, 22
O.J. Simpson tells the jury he will not testify in his own defence.
(→ September 27)

Austin, 23
Astronomers at the University of Texas predict that a chaotic "butterfly effect" caused by the gravitational fields of Mars and Jupiter could send asteroids crashing into Earth.

Beijing, 23
China says it will send vital uranium to Iran, which could help the Iranians produce a nuclear bomb.

HONG KONG, MONDAY 18

Pro-democracy candidates win clear victory in Hong Kong elections

A smooth transition to Chinese rule in Hong Kong now appears to be in jeopardy following an overwhelming vote for pro-democracy candidates in the British colony's first fully democratic election.

The Democratic Party and its allies won 29 of the 60 seats. The middle-of-the-road liberals took nine more, while the leading pro-Beijing party won only six. Governor Chris Patten described the election, the last under British rule, as "a couple of days that can never be erased from the history books".

China's Deng Xiaoping opposed the elections on the grounds that they would not encourage people who loved "the motherland and Hong Kong". China plans to scrap the Legislative Council in 1997.
(→ September 24)

Jubilant pro-democracy supporters after their poll victory in Hong Kong.

NEW DELHI, THURSDAY 21

Hindu idols around the world in milk-drinking "miracles"

Worshippers queue with milk for the Hindu god Ganesh.

Rumours that statues of the Hindu god Ganesh were drinking milk spread around the world today. They began in New Delhi where thousands queued with offerings. Milk prices soared. The story quickly spread to other temples in India. Soon people were lining up to feed milk to statues of Ganesh in places as far away as the Vishwa Temple in Lady Margaret Road, west London, where hundreds of worshippers turned up clutching bottles.

"When we tried feeding spoonfuls of milk to the gods, the milk disappeared," said one. Sceptics say that the stone is absorbent and the milk runs down it in a thin, invisible film.

BELFAST, THURSDAY 21

Adams says peace process is doomed

Sinn Fein president, Gerry Adams, has warned that the Anglo-Irish peace plan is near to collapse if Britain continues to insist on the IRA laying down its arms before all-party talks begin. This comes on the eve of a meeting between Prime Minister John Major and the Irish Taoiseach John Bruton at the European summit.

The problem remains that the IRA sees any handing over of arms as symbolic surrender. Burton believes that the IRA will not agree to this. But Major insists he is sympathetic to Adams' position, having to satisfy the "men of violence".

"I am not looking for people coming out, throwing their weapons at the feet of the British. That is not remotely what I have in mind," Major assured Sinn Fein. "I do sit here and try to put myself into Mr. Adams' head to see the difficulties he faces in order to determine what he is going to do." Adams accused the government of destroying peace by its rigid attitude. (→ September 29)

"Schoolboy" was 32-year-old man seeking a new start

Brian MacKinnon, 32, (centre) enjoys a meal with fellow pupils.

Brian MacKinnon, 32, changed his name to Brandon Lee, claimed he was 17, and went back to school at Bearsden Academy, Glasgow, thinking he might do better the second time around. He hoped to fulfil his ambition to become a doctor.

However, he made the mistake of going on holiday with two female classmates to Tenerife, where Spanish immigration officials found he had two passports. It now appears almost certain that he will lose his place at Dundee University's medical school.

Channel ferry runs aground

Some 245 passengers were trapped on board Stena Sealink's *Challenger* channel ferry after it ran aground on the beach at Calais. A second attempt by tugs to tow the ship off at high tide succeeded at 8.05 p.m. Trapped passengers were just yards from the shore. Free food and drink provided by ferry staff helped ease their plight. A vet was lowered on to the ship by

helicopter to inspect livestock. All passengers will receive a full refund, plus hotel accommodation in Calais. The operation to re-float the £31 million ferry cost £2.5 million. Human error is thought to be the cause of the accident, but Stena Sealink and both the British and the French maritime authorities are to undertake investigations.

The Stena Sealink Challenger, *beached only yards from shore.*

Unabomber manifesto published

The *Washington Post* published a special supplement carrying the manifesto of the Unabomber, a lone terrorist who has eluded the FBI since the late 1970s. So far he has killed three people and injured 23 others in 16 bombings. The *New York Times* backed the publication.

The Unabomber's manifesto was sent to the *Washington Post*, The *New York Times*, and *Penthouse* magazine after his last attack on April 24, when timber industry lobbyist Gilbert Murray was killed by a mail bomb. Murray had campaigned for logging in a habitat of the threatened spotted owl. The *Times* and the *Post* said that they were troubled by the decision to print the manifesto, but had made it on the advice of the Attorney General

The Unabomber's manifesto.

and FBI chief who urged publication for "public safety reasons". The Unabomber promised to stop his mailbomb campaign if his manifesto was published by next Sunday. But he reserves the right to attack property, and demands more space in the papers over the next three years.

Manchester, Tuesday 19. Queen of *Coronation Street*, Bet Gilroy – alias actress Julie Goodyear – is to leave *The Rover's Return* after 25 years with Britain's favourite soap. Her first appearance in the Street was in 1966, but she became a regular fixture in 1970.

Water boss hasn't had a bath

The managing director of Yorkshire Water, Trevor Newton, who is trying to encourage his 400,000 customers to accept water rationing, claims he has not had a bath or a shower for three months. He has also banned his wife from using their washing machine and urges consumers to place a litre bottle of water in their lavatory cisterns: "every time you flush, a litre is saved". Meanwhile, Yorkshire Water is applying for

an emergency drought order which could cut households off for 24 hours at a time. The dry summer has left reservoirs "desperately" low. Yorkshire Water plans to introduce cuts in Halifax in two weeks time. Bradford should follow suit a few days later. Newton believes that rotas will cut consumption by 25 per cent – if voluntary cuts do not get there first. But few of his customers are eager to follow his example. (→ October 1)

September

S	M	T	W	T	F	S
					1	2
3	4	5	6	7	8	9
10	11	12	13	14	15	16
17	18	19	20	21	22	23
24	25	26	27	28	29	30

London, 24
Railtrack has to print 300 pages of corrections to its timetable. Two supplements are needed in order to make the schedule accurate.

Hong Kong, 24
Governor Chris Patten's demand that the colony's 3.5 million passport holders be allowed into Britain after China takes over in 1997, is rejected by Home Secretary Michael Howard.

Washington DC, 24
Former US secretary of state, James Baker, reveals that Iraq planned to invade Saudi Arabia after taking over Kuwait at the start of the Gulf War.

Athens, 24
Greek newspapers print pictures of Prime Minister Andreas Papandreou's wife in the nude.

Freetown, 25
Aid agencies warn that the threat of starvation looms in Sierra Leone.

London, 26
Humphrey, the Number 10 cat that had been given up for dead, returns to Downing Street after going missing for three months.

London, 27
Former Olympic swimming coach Paul Hickson, 48, has been jailed for 17 years for indecently assaulting the teenage girls he trained.

Leeds, 27
Liz Davies, prospective parliamentary candidate for Leeds North East, is rejected by Labour's national executive for being too left wing.

Los Angeles, 27
The voice of O.J. Simpson's murdered wife is heard in court. Assistant Prosecutor Christopher Darden plays a tape recording made when she called the police pleading for help. (→ September 29)

Belfast, 29
The IRA refuse to hand over their weapons. They call British demands for decommissioning "ludicrous". (→ November 10)

Paris, 29
France places its forces in the Indian Ocean on alert following a call from the government of the Comoros Islands asking for help to put down a coup d'état. (→ October 4)

Sting accuses accountant of theft

Sting accuses his accountant of fraud.

Rock star Sting claims that his accountant stole £6 million. Keith Moore, 51, who was paid more than £800,000 a year by the lead singer of rock band the Police, denies 15 theft charges. The prosecution maintains that Moore diverted Sting's money into his own property. Southwark Crown Court was told that Sting hired a private dective to trick Moore into a taped confession.

Final summing up in O.J. case

The longest-sequestered jury in American legal history soon face the prospect of freedom as the summing up in the O.J. Simpson trial begins. But first they have to make one momentous decision – should O.J. regain his freedom too?

There were originally 12 alternates plus 12 jurors but that has now dwindled to 12 jurors with just two alternates. At one time, a mistrial seemed inevitable. The jury has heard testimony from 126 witnesses – 72 for the prosecution and 54 for the defence. They saw 857 exhibits and sat through testimony that filled more than 200 volumes.

The trial has been televised and has been compulsive viewing for a huge section of the American people. The lawyers for the prosecution and defence – Marcia Clark, Johnnie Cochran, F. Lee Bailey, and Robert Shapiro – as well as the judge Lance Ito, are household names.

The defence successfully shifted the central issue of the trial on to race, painting key police witness Mark Fuhrman as a racist. (→ October 3)

National Grid chairman spurns government call to waive £200,000

The directors of the National Grid are being attacked for executive greed for refusing to forego special dividend entitlements when the company is floated. The Grid's chairman, David Jefferies, will get £200,000. His current salary is £328,000 a year. The government has already announced that domestic electricity consumers will receive a £50 rebate in the new year and that bills will be cut by another £40 in a series of reductions already in the pipeline. But this pales in comparison to what the directors will receive. Even Sir Keith Stuart, chairman of the newly privatized electricity company Seeboard dubbed the Grid's directors "fat cats". The Department of Trade value the National Grid at £3 billion, though City analysts say it is worth £3.5 billion.

Will Carling and wife to separate: his friendship with Princess Di blamed

England rugby captain Will Carling, 29, and his wife, 30-year-old PR consultant Julia, are to separate after 14 months of marriage. Carling left the couple's home in Putney today carrying several suitcases.

Since August their marriage had been dogged by talk of "secret trysts" that had allegedly taken place between Carling and the Princess of Wales. Carling admitted having had a "close friendship" with the princess but had said that he would not be seeing her again.

Will and Julia Carling in happier times.

Provence, Sunday 24. A teenage boy slays his parents and brother, then opens fire at random in the next village. Eight more people are killed before Eric Borel, 16, turns the gun on himself. "It was like he was hunting birds," said a witness in Cuers.

NEW YORK, SUNDAY 24
Europeans win Ryder Cup

The European team snatched Ryder Cup victory in the penultimate match when 33-year-old Irishman Philip Walton halved the 18th to clinch the game by one hole. Europe won 14½ to 13½ against what was thought to be a stronger US team. This is Europe's first win since 1989, and their first on US soil since 1987.

Golf victory for Europe.

WASHINGTON DC, THURSDAY 28
Israel agrees to give Palestinians autonomy in the West Bank

An historic agreement giving the Palestinians self determination on the West Bank of the Jordan was signed today at the White House. The so-called "occupied West Bank" will no longer be patrolled. Israeli troops will begin to withdraw within ten days and the pull out should be complete in six months.

The agreement was signed by Israeli prime minister, Yitzhak Rabin, and the PLO's Yasser Arafat, whose name, until two years ago, was synonymous with terrorism. But although peace has been agreed on paper, militant Palestinian groups and Jewish settlers denounce the accord. Both see their leaders as traitors. But Americans see their president basking in another unexpected foreign policy triumph. (→ October 25)

Israel's Yitzhak Rabin and the PLO's Yasser Arafat sign the historic accord.

HOLLYWOOD, TUESDAY 26
Macaulay Culkin sacks father

Macaulay Culkin.

Home Alone star Macaulay Culkin and his brother, wannabe child star Kieran, have split from their manager father. Kit Culkin, who has proved to be one of Hollywood's toughest negotiators, can now see his children only with a judge's permission. When Kit pulled Kieran off a movie set without warning Macaulay and his brother fled to find sanctuary with their mother. Patricia Culkin fears "if Kit deliberately botches this deal, no-one in Hollywood will want to work with our children again."

STRASBOURG, WEDNESDAY 27
European Court rules against Britain over "Death on the Rock" shootings of IRA members

The European Court of Human Rights condemned the killing of three IRA members in Gibraltar in 1988. Sean Savage, Daniel McCann, and Mairead Farrell were shot dead by undercover SAS men who thought they were about to detonate a car bomb. They were unarmed and their car did not contain a bomb. But another car hired by Farrell left in Spain did contain a Semtex bomb.

The Court ruled that the British government had breached the European Human Rights Convention which guarantees the right to life. Prime Minister John Major was "appalled" by the Court's ruling. Deputy Prime Minister Michael Heseltine said it would not change the government's policy on terrorism. The Court ordered the British government to pay costs, but did not order compensation as the victims were engaged in terrorism.

LONDON, WEDNESDAY 27
Leading publishers pull out of price-fixing agreement

The Net Book Agreement which has fixed book prices for nearly 100 years is breaking down as three major publishers pull out. HarperCollins, Random Century, and Penguin – who publish more than half the titles in the UK – will cease to set a minimum price from October 1. The booksellers Waterstones and WH Smith, who together control a quarter of the retail market, say they will now start discounting.

The publishing trade expects there to be a price war over best sellers. Small book shops will inevitably be put under financial pressure.

WASHINGTON DC, MONDAY 25
Nancy talks of Ronald Reagan's Alzheimer's

Nancy Reagan.

Former first lady Nancy Reagan has talked to *Newsweek* magazine about her husband, ex-president Ronald Reagan, and his suffering from Alzheimer's disease. She characterized his deterioration as the "long goodbye". Ronald Reagan first revealed that he was suffering from Alzheimer's in November 1994. One positive aspect to her husband's disease, said Mrs. Reagan, was that it had brought her family closer together.

S	M	T	W	T	F	S
1	2	3	4	5	6	7
8	9	10	11	12	13	14
15	16	17	18	19	20	21
22	23	24	25	26	27	28
29	30	31				

London, 1
The Water Service Association warns that water restrictions could last until the end of the year.

Ankara, 1
An earthquake in the southwestern town of Dinar kills at least 64 people and injures 200.

Lisbon, 2
The centre-left party sweeps to power in Portuguese elections, on a platform of educational reform and a clampdown on crime.

Brighton, 2
Jack Straw, Labour's shadow home secretary, loses his seat on the party's National Executive.

Newcastle, 3
A secondary school gives its new intake of pupils alarm clocks to make sure they arrive on time.

Comoro Islands, 4
Bob Denard, leader of a coup in the Comoros seven days ago, surrenders to French forces in this former French colony.

Tokyo, 4
Japan's public television channel announces that Shoko Asahara, the leader of the Aum Supreme Truth cult, has confessed to the Tokyo gas attack.

New York, 4
The Pope arrives in Newark for a five-day visit to the eastern US.

London, 5
The Department of Health announces that last year saw a record number of deaths from the human equivalent of "mad cow" disease. (→ December 7)

Paris, 6
The public prosecutor's office confirms that it is to investigate corruption charges against the French prime minister, Alain Juppé, over the renting of a flat in Paris. (→ October 11)

London, 6
Eurotunnel announces losses of £465 million in the first six months of the year.

WINCHESTER, TUESDAY 3
Rosemary West murder trial starts

Rosemary West: charged with ten murders.

Rosemary West appeared in court here today at the beginning of her trial, charged with the murders of ten women and girls.

The case promises to be one of the most grisly heard in an English court this century, and is likely to involve accusations of sexual depravity. The alleged victims include Mrs. West's own daughter, and her husband's stepdaughter, who was only aged eight at the time of her death. The other victims were aged between 15 and 22.

Most of the bodies were uncovered by police in the basement and garden of 25 Cromwell Street, Gloucester, the house where Rosemary West and her husband, Fred, lived. Mrs. West's lawyers have claimed that the murders were carried out by Fred alone. He hanged himself in his prison cell at the beginning of the year. (→ October 12)

BRIGHTON, TUESDAY 3
Blair announces deal with BT

Tony Blair is tryng to extend the use of new information technology in the classroom.

Tony Blair stole a march over the government today at Labour's annual conference by announcing that the party had done a deal with the company that is the most cherished example of successful privatization. He told the delegates that British Telecom had agreed that in the event of Labour winning the next general election they would connect every school, college, library, and hospital to the Internet for free. In return Labour will overturn regulations that bar BT and its rival Mercury from entering into the cable market. Mr. Blair's vision of a new Britain wired up to the latest technology recalled Harold Wilson's 1964 promise to harness "the white heat of technology" in a new Labour government. Mr. Blair spoke of Labour leading a revitalized and confident country into the next century. However, all was not sweetness and light as the left wing reacted angrily to conference support for the NEC's rejection of a left-winger as a parliamentary candidate.

LONDON, THURSDAY 5
Lamont rejected

John Major's former Chancellor of the Exchequer, Norman Lamont, may be out of parliament at the next election for lack of a seat to contest. Boundary revisions have abolished his constituency, Kingston-upon-Thames. Tonight the party in the new constituency of Kingston and Surbiton nominated Richard Tracey, ex-sports minister, in preference to Mr. Lamont, who has had public disagreements with the Prime Minister.

Norman Lamont after his rejection.

BLACKPOOL, SATURDAY 7
Tory MP defects

Delegates starting to assemble in Blackpool for the Conservative Party conference are reeling from the news of the shock defection to the Labour Party of a former minister. Alan Howarth, MP for Stratford-upon-Avon, told his constituency party tonight that he was crossing the floor of the House because of what he considers to be the government's socially divisive policies, and its endorsement of growing inequality. He is not planning to stand down to allow a by-election.

Alan Howarth with Tony Blair.

LOS ANGELES, TUESDAY 3

Jury declares O. J. Simpson not guilty

The relief shows: O.J. Simpson with his chief defence counsel, Johnnie Cochran, to his right, after the verdict was announced.

The "trial of the century" came to its conclusion this morning, but the controversy continues. The jury of ten women and two men returned to the Los Angeles courtroom to give their verdict on the charge that O.J. Simpson had murdered his wife and her friend – America's most famous ex-football star was not guilty.

The trial lasted nine months, all of it under the full glare of national and international publicity, but the verdict was astonishingly swift. After retiring for less than four hours the jury announced yesterday to Judge Ito that they had reached their decision. The judge elected to wait until today to hear that verdict. As it was announced, O.J., visibly relaxed, smiled calmly.

The popular verdict, however, remains split. Questioned in the wake of the trial, most whites seem to be convinced that Simpson did commit the murders, persuaded by his record of wife beating and the prosecution accusations of jealousy. Blacks, on the other hand, welcomed his release, believing that he was set up by the Los Angeles Police Department, which they belived was revealed in the trial as being riddled with white supremacy. (→ October 11)

TAHITI, SUNDAY 1

Second nuclear-bomb test

Japanese protesting against the French tests.

Despite condemnation by Australia and New Zealand and the rioting in Tahiti that followed the first test, France tonight carried out the second of its series of nuclear-bomb tests. The explosion, on Fangataufa Atoll, was five times more powerful than the first test, on Mururoa Atoll. Greenpeace again said immediately that the test was outrageous and an affront to the people of the Pacific area, while the Japanese prime minister said that it was "extremely regrettable". The French government continues to argue strongly in the face of this censure that the tests are essential to its nuclear armaments programme. (→ October 29)

WASHINGTON DC, THURSDAY 5

US wins Bosnian cease-fire

American diplomacy has prevailed where the Europeans failed, obtaining a cease-fire in Bosnia that has a real chance of turning into a lasting peace. Assistant Secretary of State Richard Holbrooke, after weeks shuttling round the Balkans, has returned from Sarajevo with the signatures of all three warring parties to a 60-day truce and an agreement that they will come to the United States in two weeks time for further peace negotiations. The truce guarantees the restoration of gas and electricity to Sarajevo and an end to the Serb blockade of Gorazde. (→ October 13)

Manchester, Sunday 1. Eric Cantona returns to soccer after a ban imposed by the Football Association in February.

NEW YORK, SUNDAY 1

Blind Sheikh guilty of terrorism

An eight-month trial ended today with guilty verdicts against a blind Islamic cleric and nine followers on the charge of conspiracy to commit terrorist acts. Sheikh Omar Abdel Rahman, a 57-year-old Egyptian who came to the United States in 1990, and his accomplices had plotted to explode five bombs in New York in a single day, with the aim of destroying major targets such as the United Nations building, the main federal building in the city, the Lincoln and Holland tunnels, and the George Washington Bridge, which links Manhattan to New Jersey.

Stockholm, Thursday 5. Seamus Heaney, the 57-year-old Irish poet, wins the Nobel Prize for Literature.

O.J. Simpson and American race relations on trial

Judge Lance Ito, who heard the case.

The trial of former football star O.J. Simpson was one of the most controversial events America has seen this century. Simpson had been "every white man's favourite black man". His celebrity and the racial tensions exacerbated by the case made for gripping TV in the US and abroad.

Simpson was accused of murdering his former wife Nicole Brown Simpson and her friend Ronald Goldman on 12 June 1994. A glove found at the scene of the crime linked him to the murder. He agreed to appear at a hearing to face the charges but instead fled with police in pursuit. When he gave himself up, he had with him a false beard, a passport and $10,000.

After 1,000 jurors were vetted, the trial began in central LA. It had been moved there from Brentwood, where the crime was committed, because Brentwood is a white area and the jury would have been white. For political reasons, District Attorney Gil Garcetti switched venue.

The trial opened on January 24 1995 with the statement of Marcia Clark, the Deputy DA, for the prosecution. The court heard that DNA testing confirmed that blood belonging to Nicole was found on a pair of socks in Simpson's home. Detective Mark Fuhrman had also allegedly found a bloody glove linking Simpson to the crime in the O.J.'s garden.

The defence team, led by Johnnie Cochran, played the race card, and they were presented with a golden opportunity to come up trumps when it was revealed that Fuhrman was a virulent racist.

After that, the prosecution, despite strong forensic evidence, was fighting a losing battle. On October 3, the jury of eight blacks, three whites and one Hispanic, found O.J. Simpson not guilty of murder. One juror gave a black-power salute after the verdict was announced. Simpson was free but the US was more anxious than ever about its perennial racial problems. (→ October 11)

The not-guilty verdict is announced – O.J. Simpson (centre) visibly relaxes.

Chief prosecutor Marcia Clark.

The relatives of murder victim Ronald L. Goldman were distraught as they listened to the evidence.

Housekeeper Rosa Lopez gives evidence.

Margaret York, wife of Judge Ito.

Controversial detective Mark Fuhrman.

Murder victim Ronald Goldman.

O.J. and Nicole Simpson before their separation.

O.J. Simpson's attorneys Johnnie Cochran (left) and Robert Shapiro leave the courtroom on the second day of the trial.

Key moments, key evidence

Scene of the crime: the steps at Nicole's house.

Simpson flees on the freeway, filmed live on TV.

The body of Nicole Simpson is taken away.

The gloves that appeared to link O.J. Simpson to murder.

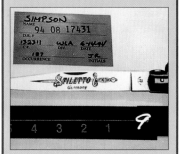

A single-edged knife was used to kill both victims.

S	M	T	W	T	F	S
1	2	3	4	5	6	7
8	9	10	11	12	13	14
15	16	17	18	19	20	21
22	23	24	25	26	27	28
29	30	31				

Phoenix, 9
Right-wing terrorists calling themselves the Sons of Gestapo are blamed for derailing a train in Arizona.

Liverpool, 10
Two policewomen are found guilty of keeping drugs in their flat and supplying them to friends.

Paris, 10
Five million public service workers go on strike across France, protesting against a government pay freeze and job cuts.

London, 11
News at Ten newsreader Trevor McDonald is appointed to head an official campaign to improve spoken English in schools.

Exmouth, 11
South Wales and West Railway increase fares by over 50% on overcrowded line to deter passengers.

Paris, 11
Court finds Prime Minister Juppé guilty of corrupt practice and orders him to vacate a flat owned by the city.

New York, 11
Prosecution tells court that boxing promoter Don King made huge fraudulent insurance claims.

Blackpool, 12
Businessman boasts to Conservative Party conference of employing juniors at £1 an hour.

Winchester, 12
The Rosemary West jurors hear that she often had casual sex in her home at Cromwell Street. (→ November 3)

Rome, 14
A judge orders former prime minister, Silvio Berlusconi, to stand trial on corruption charges.

Deaths
John Cairncross, the "fifth man" in Russia's post-war UK spy ring, aged 82, October 8.

Patric Walker, newspaper astrologer, aged 64, in London, October 8.

Alec Douglas-Home, Lord Home, Conservative Prime Minister in 1963-4 and twice Foreign Secretary, aged 92, October 9.

Over 60 die in Mexican earthquake

Rescuers hunt through the rubble for victims near the port of Manzanillo.

Over 60 people are believed to have died when an earthquake rocked west-central Mexico today. The worst-hit area is the Pacific coast, the epicentre being located off the coastal port of Manzanillo. The devastated area includes several resort towns, and in Manzanillo itself nine people are believed to have died when the eight-storey Hotel Costa Real collapsed. President Ernesto Zedillo has declared Manzanillo a disaster area.

The greatest fatalities are almost certainly in Cihuatlan where 26 people were killed. The school, bank, church, and gaol all collapsed. Shock waves were felt as far away as Mexico City, 843 km (524 miles) east of Manzanillo, but no damage occurred.

Retrial opens of brothers for parents' murder

Erik (left) and Lyle Menendez.

The opening statements were made today in the second trial of two brothers for the murder of their parents in Beverly Hills six years ago. Two juries were impanelled to hear the case; the first ruling last year was declared a mistrial after neither jury could reach a verdict. This time, only one jury has been appointed.

The two brothers, Erik, 24, and Lyle, 27, do not dispute that they killed their parents. They say that they shot them dead in self-defence after years of sexual and emotional abuse. Their plea made them popular heroes among some sectors of America's youth last year. The prosecution maintains that the killings were carried out because the brothers were frightened of being disinherited by their parents of their £10 million estate. David Conn, the deputy district attorney, said, "They shot their parents in the arms, legs, torso, and heads. Hundreds of shotgun pellets tore into the bodies of Jose and Kitty Menendez." He claimed the boys then shot them in the knees to make it look like a Mafia killing. The judge has barred TV coverage of the trial, which had a massive impact on the first trial.

Portillo delivers anti-European speech at Tory conference

Michael Portillo won himself the longest ovation of the first day of the Conservative Party conference, but also worried the moderates in the conference hall. In an impassioned and outspoken speech he rounded on the European Union, and stated that British soldiers should be commanded from London, not from Brussels. Conjuring up the spectre of a single European army, he said: "The European Court would probably want to stop our men fighting for more than 40 hours a week. They would send half of them home on paternity leave".

Although he won the plaudits of the right of the party, pro-Europeans privately condemned the speech, saying that Brussels has no pretensions to control Britain's defence policy. Mr. Portillo's sentiments seemed to have the support of the prime minister, however, who sat beside him on the rostrum and congratulated him fulsomely after the speech.

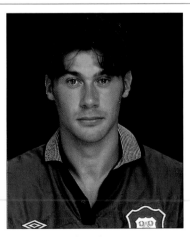

Glasgow, Wednesday 11. Duncan Ferguson is gaoled for assault.

GLASGOW, SATURDAY 14

Boxer near death after knockout and crowd violence

The referee beckons for help as James Murray collapses in the ring.

James Murray was tonight declared "clinically dead", a day after he was rushed unconscious from a fight in a Glasgow hotel. He had been haemorrhaging from his brain into his skull, and a two-hour operation by doctors to remove a clot from the brain has failed to save him.

Murray was fighting Drew Docherty for the British bantamweight title. In the twelfth round he collapsed and was taken to hospital on a stretcher. For most of the fight he had been ahead on points, but Docherty was closing the gap, and delivered a blow that had Murray counted out in the final round. Murray's supporters amongst the crowd then rioted, apparently unaware of the serious-

ness of the boxer's condition. Alcohol had been readily available during the evening at the Hospitality Inn, and the place was littered with empty bottles. Chairs and bottles were thrown by the crowd. "It was the most despicable scene I have ever witnessed at a boxing show," said John Morris, British Boxing Board of Control secretary, who was present at the fight.

Murray's family has been told that there is no hope for him, and his life-support machine will be turned off. The debate about whether boxing should be banned had already been triggered by the crowd violence and by Murray's injuries, and his death will be cited by those who support a complete ban. (→ October 15)

Stockholm, Friday 13. The Nobel Peace Prize is awarded to Joseph Rotblat, scientist and anti-nuclear campaigner.

NEW YORK, WEDNESDAY 11

O.J. pulls out of TV interview

Six hours before he was due to go on the air, O.J. Simpson pulled out of what was to be his first television interview since his acquittal last week. Lawyers advised him against being questioned on *Dateline NBC* because of some of the questions he was going to be asked. O.J. still faces civil suits from the families of his former wife and Ron Goldman, the other murder victim, and lawyers felt that he should avoid putting himself in a situation that might jeopardize his defence. (→ November 2)

BOSNIA, FRIDAY 13

Muslims and Croats besiege Banja Luka

Refugees have crowded into makeshift accommodation in Banja Luka.

Despite the recently announced cease-fire, fighting is still going on in Bosnia around the Serb stronghold of Banja Luka. Muslim and Croat forces are close to capturing the nearby town of Prijedor, from where over 40,000 people fled this afternoon.

The joint forces have made considerable advances into the area over the last three days. It is thought that the Muslims want to squeeze Banja Luka, which has largely escaped

direct action during the war, and is considered to be the cradle of the Serbian ethnic cleansing policy. In answer to criticisms for continuing to fight after the cease-fire, one Muslim commander said, "The international community does not understand the Serbs. Serbs only listen to military action and we cannot stop now."

UN observers have reported that fighting has all but ceased throughout the rest of Bosnia. (→ November 1)

Baghdad, Saturday 14. It is reported that Saddam Hussein has burned the cars of his errant son Uday (centre, bearded, at back).

October

S	M	T	W	T	F	S
1	2	3	4	5	6	7
8	9	10	11	12	13	14
15	16	17	18	19	20	21
22	23	24	25	26	27	28
29	30	31				

Tel Aviv, 15
Six Israeli soldiers are killed in an ambush by Hezbollah guerrillas.
(→ October 25)

Glasgow, 15
Boxer James Murray dies from a knockout blow sustained on Friday night after being in a coma all weekend.

Ankara, 15
Turkish prime minister, Tansu Ciller, resigns after parliament passes a vote of no confidence in her government.

Johannesburg, 15
Winnie Mandela is to contest divorce proceedings brought by her husband, South African president, Nelson Mandela.

Moscow, 15
A kidnapper dies when the Russian anti-terrorist squad successfully ends a siege of a tourist bus full of South Koreans.

London, 16
Sadler's Wells theatre is awarded £30 million from the National Lottery.

Paris, 17
A Frenchwoman, Jeanne Calment, reaches the age of 120 years and 238 days, to become the longest-living human on record.

Paris, 17
A terrorist bomb explodes on an underground train, injuring 26 people. (→ November 2)

Tripoli, 18
Libya announces that it intends to deport more than one million Africans.

London, 19
Home Secretary Michael Howard gives a confident performance in the Commons to defeat a Labour motion that he should resign after the report on the Prison Service.

Moscow, 19
President Yeltsin gives a speech saying that Russian troops in Bosnia would not take orders from NATO.

Moscow, 19
The Pushkin Museum unveils art treasures removed from Germany by Soviet troops at the end of World War II.

Aintree, Wednesday 18. Red Rum, three times Grand National winner, is buried.

LONDON, THURSDAY 19
Health scare over contraceptive pill

The Department of Health has been accused of causing unnecessary panic among women by releasing a report attributing new side-effects to the contraceptive pill. Around 1.5 million women were advised to contact their doctors after suggestions that women on certain brands of the pill were at greater risk of developing thrombosis than others.

The American scientists who compiled the report, *Oral Contraceptives and the Health of Young Women*, are now planning to fly to London to clarify matters after claiming that the Medicines Control Agency, which originally passed the warning on to the Department of Health, had been mistaken in its analysis of the original data. Its incorrect findings had then been given to GPs and the public. Brand manufacturers and independent analysts have also condemned the department's warnings.

LONDON, WEDNESDAY 18
Former director general of prisons sues for wrongful dismissal

Derek Lewis, who was sacked as director general of the Prison Service on Monday, has issued a writ claiming wrongful dismissal. He claims that Michael Howard, the Home Secretary, made his position untenable through constant interference in his work. Mr. Lewis has also released a series of letters that he hopes show that Mr. Howard sought to actively influence Mr Lewis' running of the Prison Service. The Home Secretary has always maintained that he is responsible for policy but not for the actual running of the Prison Service.

Mr. Lewis, director general for three years, was dismissed after a report on prisons in England and Wales concluded that the service was

Derek Lewis, ex-prison director general.

badly run due to a combination of poor security and alarming levels of bureaucracy. In response, Mr. Lewis wrote to the Home Secretary complaining of his lack of support. Labour has called for Mr. Howard to resign . (→ October 19)

BRUSSELS, FRIDAY 20
Belgian MPs send the head of NATO to trial

Willy Claes, the secretary general of NATO, has resigned after the Belgian parliament decided he should face trial. Claes will confront allegations of corruption over irregular payments made to the Flemish Socialist Party by foreign defence contractors. He will not be in court in the near future but the threat of court action would have put the NATO head in a very difficult situation, especially given the position in Bosnia.

SKYE, MONDAY 16
Skye bridge opens amid protests over toll

Scottish Secretary Michael Forsyth has opened the £24 million Skye bridge but the new construction has caused deep discontent among some locals. They complain that tolls on the bridge (£5.20 per car as soon as the toll booths were opened to the public) are inordinately expensive.

In protest, representatives of The Skye and Kyle Against Tolls organization drove past them without paying. Mr. Forsyth was the first to cross to Skye by car after he cut the ribbon to open the bridge.

In the afternoon, the last crossing of the ferry to Skye took place with over 200 people crowded on board.

Pipers lead the protests as the controversial Skye bridge opens.

Louis Farrakhan leads 400,000 black men on march on Washington DC

Nation of Islam representatives.

The biggest march by black people in the history of the US was led to Washington DC by Louis Farrakhan, the leader of the Nation of Islam. The man who had been denounced in some quarters as a purveyor of racism directed against Jews and whites, gave a speech that called on black men to scrutinize their own behaviour.

During his 150-minute speech, Farrakhan demanded of black men that they desist from violence unless it was in self-defence, that they do everything in their power to show respect towards black women, and that they also denounce rape and drugs. Mr. Farrakhan also launched virulent verbal attacks on the white founding fathers of the US and on President Clinton.

Crowds pack the Mall in Washington DC to hear black Muslim leader Louis Farrakhan.

Family of Briton show mercy to his killer

The family of a Briton who was killed by his Filipino maid have been thanked by her mother and father for preventing her execution. The convicted young woman, Sarah Balabagan, had claimed that she killed her employer in self-defence after he had attempted to rape her. However, she was found guilty of planning and carrying out the murder and sentenced to death. Balabagan was spared when the victim's family decided that they did not wish her to receive the death sentence.

New York, Tuesday 17. Actor Christopher Reeve appeared in public for the first time since being paralyzed.

London, Wednesday 18. Linda McCartney veggie burgers were recalled because of excess fat.

Saddam Hussein re-elected with "100 per cent" vote

Iraqi women show their support for Saddam Hussein.

Gunfire and the announcement of a one-day national holiday greeted the news that Saddam Hussein has been elected to rule Iraq for a further seven years. A minority of dissenters registered their disapproval of his dictatorship in today's elections but almost all of the seven million who voted opted to back the man who led their country into the Gulf War in 1991.

Although Iraqi government officials made noises about the poll having been an exercise in democracy, officials kept close watch on which way people were voting. Masses of propaganda surrounded the election in which voting centres were covered in pictures of Saddam Hussein.

October

S	M	T	W	T	F	S
1	2	3	4	5	6	7
8	9	10	11	12	13	14
15	16	17	18	19	20	21
22	23	24	25	26	27	28
29	30	31				

London, 22
The London Weather Centre confirms that the country is enjoying its warmest October since records began more than 300 years ago, with summer birds refusing to migrate and spring flowers already in bloom.

New York, 23
John Major and President Carlos Menem of Argentina meet at the UN in the first top-level contact between Britain and Argentina since the 1982 Falklands War, paving the way for a state visit to Britain by Mr. Menem.

Asia, 24
A total eclipse of the sun is witnessed from India to Vietnam.

West Bank, 25
Palestinian police officers arrive for the start of the process to end 27 years of Israeli military rule in most of the mainly Palestinian West Bank region. (→ November 4)

London, 25
The Court of Appeal lifts an order banning the naming of an 11-year-old leukaemia sufferer, formerly known as Child B and now identified as Jaymee Bowen. Money for further treatment can now be raised by selling her story.

Moscow, 26
President Yeltsin is rushed to hospital suffering from heart problems for the second time in three months, almost immediately after returning from the UN celebrations in the US.

Dayton, Ohio, 31
The three presidents at the centre of the Bosnian conflict, Alija Izetbegovic of Bosnia, Slobodan Milosevic of Serbia, and Franjo Tudjman of Croatia, arrive at a US air base for talks aimed at ending four years of war. (→ November 1)

Death
Gavin Ewart, one of Britain's funniest poets, aged 79, October 23.

Clinton and Yeltsin share a joke but make little progress

President Clinton laughs at Boris Yeltsin's remarks about the press.

Presidents Clinton and Yeltsin held a four-hour meeting at Hyde Park, in the Hudson valley, seeking a formula whereby Russian troops could be used as peacekeepers in Bosnia. They admitted to having made little progress, but confirmed that both were committed to finding a solution.

The main gain from the session was the obvious warmth between the two leaders, which concluded with the Russian's accusation that the press were predicting failure. "You're a disaster", he told the assembled journalists, to the surprised delight of President Clinton. (→ October 31)

Schumacher retains world motor-racing title

Michael Schumacher, driving for Benneton Renault, passed the chequered flag almost 15 seconds ahead of David Coulthard in the Pacific Grand Prix, to retain the world drivers' championship he first secured at Adelaide in 1994.

Schumacher had started the race in third place on the grid behind the Williams cars of Coulthard and Damon Hill. The latter, his main rival in the points table, took third place in this race. The familiar "war of words" between Schumacher and Hill continued afterwards, with the German accusing the British driver of pressing too hard and so letting through the Ferraris of Helmut Berger and Jean Alesi. Hill later dismissed this charge as "hypocrisy".

After eight victories Schumacher has opened up an unbridgeable gap in the drivers' table.

Major supports French tests

Prime Minister John Major confirmed his controversial support for France's right to carry out nuclear tests when the French president, Jacques Chirac, arrived at Chequers, the PM's Buckinghamshire residence, for a state reception and talks.

Hundreds of demonstrators from Greenpeace and the Campaign for Nuclear Disarmament clashed with police in the grounds of Chequers before President Chirac arrived, and 12 arrests were made.

London, Sunday 22. Sir Kingsley Amis dies in hospital, aged 73. He rose to fame in 1954 when his novel, *Lucky Jim*, captured perfectly the spirit of the times.

Queen hoaxed by Canadian DJ

The Queen was said to be "philosophical" following one of the most embarrassing incidents of her reign, when Canadian disc jockey Pierre Brassard conducted a 14-minute telephone conversation with her, posing as the prime minister of Canada, Jean Chretien.

The conversation, about the forthcoming referendum on Quebec's independence, was broadcast in an edited, seven-minute version on Montreal radio station CKOI-FM.

NEW YORK, SUNDAY 22

200 heads of state at UN's birthday party

World leaders assemble at the UN in New York for the organization's fiftieth birthday celebrations.

A mood for change was evident at the unprecedented gathering of world leaders in New York, celebrating the fiftieth birthday of the UN.

President Clinton, the first to address the assembly, spoke of the need to join in the fight against international terrorism, organized crime, drug smuggling, and the spread of nuclear and other massively destructive weapons. President Frederick Chiluba of Zambia warned that the major powers should not become "high priests to the rest of the globe", while President Boris Yeltsin of Russia suggested that in one of the most pressing of concerns – the future of Bosnia – the UN Security Council was being bypassed by NATO. The session was opened by the President of the General Assembly, Diego Freitas do Amaral of Portugal, and the speakers included Cuba's President Fidel Castro, who replaced his more customary battle fatigues with a formal suit in honour of the occasion.

NIGERIA, TUESDAY 31

Ken Saro-Wiwa sentenced to death

Nigerian writer Ken Saro-Wiwa

A court tribunal in Port Harcourt, Nigeria, has sentenced to death the political activist Ken Saro-Wiwa, one of the country's most distinguished writers, and three others. Five more were condemned on Monday.

The charges arose from the deaths of four leaders of the Ogoni people, killed during a protest rally. Mr. Saro-Wiwa, 54, has been convicted of murder, even though it is conceded that he did not kill the men himself.

Mr. Saro-Wiwa has been at the forefront of protests by the Ogonis that their land has been polluted by the oil companies operating there.

Nigeria is ruled by the ruthless military regime of General Sani Abacha, and human rights groups say that murders are carried out by troops to intimidate the people. (→ November 11)

MONTREAL, MONDAY 30

In close poll Quebec votes to stay in Canada

The people of Quebec have voted to maintain union with the rest of Canada, but only by the narrowest of margins, so leaving the long-term future of the province unresolved. With 50.6 per cent voting against secession, little more than 50,000 votes divided the sides.

The referendum in Quebec was held at the instigation of the hardline separatist Parti Québecois, which has governed the province since winning elections last year. Quebec's prime minister, Jacques Parizeau, blamed "money and the ethnic vote" for the defeat of his bid to make Quebec an independent state.

Under Canadian law, the referendum cannot be repeated during the current provincial government's term of office. Canadian prime minister, Jean Chretien, must now seek ways of mollifying the disaffected half of Quebec's electorate.

HOUSTON, TUESDAY 24

Fan convicted of killing singer

Fans mourn the death of their idol, Selena Quintanilla Perez.

A row over money is believed to be behind the murder of singer Selena, 23, shot in a motel room in her home town of Corpus Christi, Texas.

Yolanda Saldivar, 35, the founder and former president of Selena's fan club, faces life imprisonment after being found guilty of the murder. The defence claimed that the gun had gone off accidentally, and that Saldivar meant to commit suicide, while the prosecution asserted that the shooting occurred after Selena accused Saldivar of stealing money from her business account.

Selena Quintanilla Perez was a Grammy-winning singer of Tejano, a modern mixture of Mexican- and European-influenced musical styles, and was the genre's biggest star.

Massachusetts, Sunday 22. Maxene Andrews, the Andrews Sister who always appeared on the left, dies, aged 79.

	S	M	T	W	T	F	S
				1	2	3	4
	5	6	7	8	9	10	11
	12	13	14	15	16	17	18
	19	20	21	22	23	24	25
	26	27	28	29	30		

Dundee, 1
Stephen Fry, before being reinstalled as Rector of Dundee University, says he seriously considered killing himself when he walked out of the play *Cell Mates*.

Lille, 2
French police find a terrorist bomb-making factory, shortly after arresting an Arab on suspicion of organizing the bombing campaign.

London, 2
Conservative MPs from the right of the party force the government to abandon a bill giving greater protection to victims of domestic violence, on the grounds that it would undermine marriage.

London, 2
The Reverend Sun Myung Moon withdraws his application for a visa to visit Britain, despite a judge overthrowing the government's decision to ban him.

Winchester, 3
The court in the trial of Rosemary West hears a taped confession by Frederick West, telling how he killed and dismembered his daughter Heather. (→ November 22)

Bermuda, 3
Manchester is chosen as the site of the 2002 Commonwealth Games.

London, 3
Asprey, the royal jeweller's, is bought by the brother of the Sultan of Brunei after running into financial difficulties.

Washington DC, 3
Relatives of the victims of the Lockerbie bombing of Pan Am flight 103 boycott a memorial service in protest at what they see as American government inaction in the case.

Tripoli, 4
At the last minute Colonel Gaddafi withdraws permission for World War II veterans to enter Libya to visit Commonwealth war graves in Tobruk.

Deaths
Marti Caine, comedienne, dies of cancer in Oxford, aged 50, November 4.

Brian Lenihan, Irish former foreign minister, aged 64, November 1.

Washington DC, Friday 3. Pictures of Eagle Nebula from the Hubble Telescope show, for the first time, stars being created.

DAYTON, OHIO, WEDNESDAY 1
Bosnia talks begin in Dayton, Ohio

Presidents Slobodan Milosevic of Serbia, Alija Izetbegovic of Bosnia, and Franjo Tudjman of Croatia met today for the first time in four years at an American military airbase at Dayton, Ohio, to start talks aimed at ending the four-year civil war. The US government, coordinator of the talks, plans to keep the contents of the negotiations secret. (→ November 22)

LONDON, FRIDAY 3
Julia Somerville arrested over child photographs

Julia Somerville with her daughter.

ITN newsreader Julia Somerville was released from Charing Cross police station in the small hours of this morning after being arrested in connection with allegedly pornographic photographs of one of her children. Also detained was Jeremy Dixon, an architect, who lives with Ms. Somerville. The photographs had been handed in to the police by a branch of Boots, where they had been spotted by an assistant during developing.

Tonight Ms. Somerville forcibly asserted that she and Mr. Dixon had done nothing wrong. "I strenuously deny any allegation of wrong-doing. I am horrified that a wholly innocent family occasion has been completely misconstrued. I have given police a full explanation. I am deeply distressed that such an untrue allegation should have been made public when it is so likely to cause unhappiness to my children." (→ December 5)

NEW YORK, THURSDAY 2
O.J.'s girlfriend calls it off

Paula Barbieri and O.J. Simpson.

Despite having waited for him throughout the trial, O.J. Simpson's girlfriend has told American television viewers that their relationship is over. Model Paula Barbieri had been expected to marry O.J. once he had been cleared of the murder charges, and when the couple were seen in the Dominican Republic immediately after the trial it was thought they had gone there for a quick wedding. Citing her reasons Paula said, "It was a realization for me that he was going back to that lifestyle he used to have…I just want to work. I want to have children. I want to love."

SAN ANTONIO, FRIDAY 3
Scientists find a single gene is linked to nearly all breast cancers

Scientists from the University of Texas at San Antonio have announced a major breakthrough in their understanding of breast cancer. They have isolated a gene that seems to play a role in the formation of nearly all breast cancers.

The gene, called BRCA-1, was first implicated in breast cancers a year ago, but at the time it was thought responsible for only rare forms of the cancer that run in families. However, the latest research, which is published in today's *Science* journal, has found that the same gene also seems to be behind the more common forms of breast cancer. It has also been identified in some cases of ovarian cancer.

The gene triggers the manufacture of a particular protein, the BRCA-1 protein. In healthy people this protein works in the nucleus of cells. In the cases of familial cancer the BRCA-1 protein is defective. Now the researchers have found that in other forms of breast cancer, where the protein is not defective, it is found in the wrong part of the cell. The discovery does not have any practical implications for women who are already suffering from breast cancer, but in future it could help doctors in forecasting the onset of the disease and hence in treating it.

Geneva, Wednesday 1. The Aga Khan starts legal action to prevent his ex-wife selling her jewellery, citing an agreement that the jewels stay in his family.

JERUSALEM, SATURDAY 4

Rabin assassinated after call for peace

Israeli Prime Minister Yitzhak Rabin was shot dead tonight minutes after leaving a peace rally in Tel Aviv. A student has been arrested. He is believed to have acted alone.

Mr. Rabin had been addressing a rally, "Peace Yes Violence No", that had been called to counter a rising right-wing tide of resentment at the concessions made to Palestinians over self-rule. The organizers had called the rally to show that most Israelis were in favour of the peace accord, under which Palestinians have been given control of Gaza and Jericho and are shortly to take over more

towns in the West Bank. More than 100,000 people attended the rally.

Mr. Rabin was killed at 9.50 p.m. as he was leaving the speakers' platform in the Kings of Israel Square. The gunman pushed easily through the security men surrounding the Prime Minister and shot him twice from close range. Mr. Rabin was rushed to Ichilov Hospital for emergency surgery, but one hour later it was announced that he was dead.

The security forces seized the killer within seconds of the shooting. He was named as Yigal Amir, a 25-year-old law student at a religious

college. He had previously been involved in right-wing protests against the peace accord, including the setting up of illegal Jewish settlements in the West Bank. Amir told the police, "I acted alone on God's orders and I have no regrets." He had also intended to kill foreign minister Shimon Peres at the same time, but was thwarted when the two politicians left the rally separately. Amir said that he had been planning to kill Mr. Rabin for almost a year, and twice before had gone to sites where Mr. Rabin was due to appear. Mr. Peres has taken over as interim prime minister.

Yitzhak Rabin, who was a hero of the 1967 war, was killed for the cause with which he is most associated. It is very much his conviction and his ability to persuade the Israeli people that their security is not threatened by the concessions that have to be made to the Palestinians that have kept the peace process afloat, despite some fierce opposition and the bloody Arab extremist bombings. His last words spoken in public, at the end of his speech, were: "This rally must broadcast to the Israeli public and to many in the Western and outside world, that the people of Israel genuinely want peace, support peace. Thank you." (→ November 6)

Yitzhak Rabin.

Yigal Amir is hustled away by police.

Songs for peace at the rally. The spirit of forgiveness that characterized the gathering was soon shattered by gunfire.

Malan arrested for massacre

Malan, charged with apartheid murders.

South Africa's former defence minister General Magnus Malan and ten retired, high-ranking military officers have been arrested by police investigating violence and civil unrest in Natal during the final years of the whites-only government. They have been charged with the massacre of a priest, five women and seven children in a Natal township in January 1987.

It is thought that the men may have been responsible for a conspiracy to support the Zulu-based Inkatha movement at a time when its influence was waning, and thus provide opposition to Nelson Mandela's ANC. The whites-only government set up a training camp for Inkatha members who allegedly became members of hit squads that targeted ANC supporters.

LONDON, THURSDAY 2

"Raucous" Cliff Richard banned

Sir Cliff Richard's 37-year career in pop music took a most unlikely turn yesterday. Radio 2 decided that his latest single, "A Misunderstood Man", was "too raucous" to be included on the station's playlist – an unprecedented event for the 55-year-old, who is seen as being at the safe end of popular music. But today it is on the list after all, mysteriously having been played, despite the ruling, on *The John Dunn Show*.

November

S	M	T	W	T	F	S
			1	2	3	4
5	6	7	8	9	10	11
12	13	14	15	16	17	18
19	20	21	22	23	24	25
26	27	28	29	30		

Poland, 5
Voting in the Polish presidential election puts the current president, Lech Walesa, neck and neck with the former Communist Aleksander Kwasniewski (→ November 22).

Kazakhstan, 5
At least 28 people die in a gas explosion in a residential building.

Tokyo, 6
The Japanese government offers £16,000 to each of the 8,000 victims of a mass mercury poisoning that happened 40 years ago.

Bangladesh, 6
Thousands of anti-government protesters enforce a blockade of rail, road, and waterways, bringing the country to a standstill.

London, 9
Japanese investors buy 11,000 British Rail engines and carriages for £1.8 billion, representing one third of all trains running in Britain.

Athens, 9
Greek police posing as a television crew overpower an Ethiopian hijacker while he is holding an air stewardess hostage at knifepoint.

Budapest, 10
Hungary braces itself for a wave of strikes by civil service unions opposed to austerity measures.

Ireland, 10
Irish police find a bomb containing more than 450 kg (1,000 lb) of explosives in a stolen van just south of the Northern Ireland border. (→ November 24)

Sri Lanka, 10
The Tamil Tigers resume public executions of alleged Tamil traitors.

London, 10
Siamese twin boys joined from the breastbone to the navel are born to a Kuwaiti at a London hospital.

Madrid, 10
Two Spanish bankers try to blackmail King Juan Carlos in an attempt to get their fraud charges dropped.

LAGOS, SATURDAY 11
Nigeria executes Ken Saro-Wiwa

Ken Wiwa denounces his father's execution.

Nigeria's military dictatorship defied international appeals for clemency yesterday and went ahead with the execution of the dissident writer Ken Saro-Wiwa and eight other environmental campaigners. The nine had been convicted of murder at a special military tribunal.

The hangings prompted an outcry from Commonwealth leaders meeting in New Zealand, who are now likely to vote for Nigeria to be expelled. John Major said: "I don't see how Nigeria can stay in the Commonwealth without a return to democratic government."

Saro-Wiwa headed an environmental group that fought the exploitation of oil reserves in his native Ogoniland.(→ December 8)

Paris, Monday 6. The trial begins of Christian Didier, alleged assassin of Vichy police chief René Bousquet, who sent 12,000 Jews to their deaths.

TIBILISI, SUNDAY 5
Shevardnadze landslide in Georgia

Shevardnadze interviewed at the polls.

Eduard A. Shevardnadze, 67, the former Soviet Foreign Minister who returned to his native Georgia to become its leader three years ago, has won today's presidential election.

Shevardnadze, who was widely credited with helping to end the Cold War, ran as a moderate, a patriot and a crimefighter. Incomplete official results show he already has about 70 per cent of the vote. His centre-right Citizens Union Party also led in elections for the 250-seat parliament. His government will strengthen its fight against mafia-style crime and continue on a Western economic course.

JERUSALEM, MONDAY 6
World leaders mourn Rabin

Yitzhak Rabin was buried today before the greatest assembly of foreign leaders ever gathered in Israel, including the Arab heads of state King Hussein of Jordan, President Mubarak of Egypt, and representatives from Oman and Morocco.

He was eulogized by President Clinton, while King Hussein called him "a brother, a colleague, and a friend". John Major, Tony Blair, and Prince Charles were also among the 5,000 mourners of the 73-year-old Israeli prime minister, assassinated by a right-wing radical on Saturday.

President Clinton not only paid tribute to Rabin, but also highlighted the threat to the peace process. "Your prime minister was a martyr for peace, but he was a victim of hate," said Clinton. "If people cannot let go of the hatred of their enemies, they risk sowing the seed of hatred among themselves."

Scores of world leaders, including Jordan's King Hussein, attend Rabin's funeral.

Powell will not run for president in 1996

General Colin A. Powell, retired chairman of the Joint Chiefs of Staff and hero of the Gulf War, announced today at a packed news conference that he would not be a Republican contender in the 1996 US presidential election.

He explained that he had made his decision after looking deep into his soul, concluding that he lacked the kind of passionate commitment to politics that had sustained his bond of trust with the public across 35 years of army service. He said: "For me to pretend otherwise would not be honest to myself, it would not be honest to the American people, and I would break that bond of trust."

He ruled out any second thoughts as the campaign proceeds and said he would not consider serving as a candidate for vice-president. However, he left future candidacy open to speculation, saying: "The future is the future." He added that he believed he could "help the party of Lincoln move once again close to the spirit of Lincoln", in a clear reference to the issues of race, opportunity, and social welfare that have set him at odds with conservative Republican ideologues, who had threatened to put up fierce resistance to his candidacy.

Powell's decision has come as a great disappointment to the public, though it will be met with relief both by the Republican front-runner Bob Dole and by President Clinton.

Powell cites his lack of a calling as his reason for not entering the presidential race.

MPs to reveal outside earnings

Conservative MPs last night lost their battle to keep their outside earnings secret when the Commons voted overwhelmingly for the disclosure of payments for consultancies. The vote was a humiliation for John Major, who had put his personal authority behind the attempt to prevent compulsory disclosure.

Twenty-three Tories broke ranks and backed the Nolan Committee's call for the declaration of earnings to root out political sleaze, while 29 others abstained or were absent. The vote was 322 to 271. From next April, MPs are required to declare how much they earn for advising companies, pressure groups, and lobbyists.

MPs earlier approved, by 587 votes to 2, a complete ban on paid advocacy, such as cash payments for putting down questions, and backed the appointment of a new parliamentary commissioner for standards. Also approved was a Labour amendment preventing any MP with a paid interest from initiating or participating in a delegation to ministers.

The votes paved the way for the most stringent restrictions ever faced by MPs on their freedom to act as paid advisers on parliamentary affairs to outside bodies. However, MPs will not have to declare earnings from outside activities not connected with their work in Parliament.

Egypt, Sunday 5. The tomb of Queen Nefertari, the favourite wife of the Pharaoh Rameses II, is opened to visitors for the first time since its discovery in 1904. Some experts fear the opening could damage the fragile paintings that decorate the tomb at Luxor.

Death sentence for British serial killer

John Martin Scripps, 35, the British prison fugitive and convicted drug smuggler, was sentenced to hang in Singapore today, for murdering and dismembering a South African tourist. Scripps was convicted of murdering Gerard Lowe, 32, parts of whose body were found floating in bin liners in Singapore harbour.

He is already linked to three other killings. Thai police have charged him with murdering a Canadian mother and son, and he is the main suspect in the disappearance of a British tourist in Mexico. Scripps befriended his victims, then killed them for money.

London, Tuesday 7. Author Pat Barker wins the prestigious Booker Prize for her novel *The Ghost Road.*

S	M	T	W	T	F	S
			1	2	3	4
5	6	7	8	9	10	11
12	13	14	15	16	17	18
19	20	21	22	23	24	25
26	27	28	29	30		

Nepal, 12
At least 43 people die during the weekend in avalanches on trekking routes near Mount Everest.

Riyadh, Saudi Arabia, 13
Six people are killed and at least 60 injured in two explosions in the Saudi Arabian capital, at an American military establishment.

Wolverhampton, 14
Graham Taylor, former England soccer manager, resigns as manager of Wolverhampton Wanderers.

Baku, Azerbaijan, 14
International observers report that elections in this former Soviet republic have been openly rigged by government officials.

Exeter, 15
The Black Baron, whose real name is Christopher Pile, becomes the first Briton to be convicted and gaoled for creating and planting computer viruses.

Belfast, 15
Northern Ireland's football team beat Austria 5-3 in a European Championship qualifier. The Republic of Ireland and the Netherlands will meet to decide the last place in the 1996 European Championship. (→ December 13)

Paris, 15
Disneyland Paris (formerly known as Euro Disney), the troubled European version of Disneyland, announces its first annual profit.

Paris, 15
Prime Minister Alain Juppé wins massive support in the French parliament for welfare cuts.

London, 16
Today newspaper, launched by Eddie Shah in 1986 and latterly part of Rupert Murdoch's News International empire, produces its last edition, dated November 17.

Montreal, 18
Former Canadian prime minister, Brian Mulroney, denies receiving kickbacks over the 1988 sale of Swiss aircraft to Canada.

Death
Sir Robert Stephens, actor, in London, aged 64, November 12.

CHELMSFORD, ESSEX, THURSDAY 16

Leah Betts dies after taking Ecstasy

The parents of Leah Betts, the Essex teenager who went into a coma on Sunday after taking an Ecstasy tablet at her eighteenth birthday party, took the decision to switch off her life-support machine in the early hours of this morning. Leah was a patient at Broomfield Hospital, Chelmsford. In compliance with her known wishes, her parents donated her heart, kidneys, liver, lungs, and corneas for transplants.

The case had attracted huge publicity following Leah's parents' decision to talk to the press about her plight. Paul Betts is a former drugs squad officer with the Metropolitan Police and her stepmother is a drugs advice worker.

Leah was a student at Basildon College. The birthday party was held at the family home, with the parents in attendance to supervise the celebrations. Ecstasy is one of the most common drugs among the 15-25 age group. It was at first thought that Leah must have taken an adulterated tablet, but tests showed that this was not the case.

Leah's father, Paul Betts, and her stepmother, Janet, at an emotional press conference.

Paul Betts, in announcing his daughter's death, said: "Leah's ordeal is now over. One comforting thing is that she probably died in my arms on her eighteenth birthday party. It was purely the fact that Janet and I administered mouth-to-mouth resuscitation that kept her body functioning." Mrs. Betts had a message to young people: "I can lecture you like a mother until I am blue in the face but you are the only people who can prevent this happening again. Remember, the tablet Leah took was pure."

After four days of police enquiries 13 people had been taken in for questioning, including a 17-year-old arrested on the night of Leah's death.

WASHINGTON DC, FRIDAY 17

Deadlock over US budget

The operations of the US government were partially shut down today as the long-running financial feud between the Republican Congress and the White House reached a crisis.

President Bill Clinton is locked into a tough financial dispute with Congress.

With no agreement on the Federal budget deficit, President Clinton had attempted to extend the Federal debt limit to keep government running, but Republican amendments caused an impasse. As the cash dried up, "non-essential" government workers were sent home, including most Housing and Urban Development staff and all but 1 per cent of Education Department staff.

There was some comfort for the beleaguered President in the results of a national survey which indicated that 48 per cent of Americans blamed the Republican-dominated Congress for the situation, as opposed to 27 per cent who blamed Mr. Clinton.

Mr. Clinton accused Congress of pursuing "an explicit strategy" formulated by House Speaker, Newt Gingrich, to force through acceptance of Republican cost-cutting policies. (→ November 20)

Sun City, South Africa, Saturday 18. Miss Venezuela, Jacqueline Aguilera Marcano, 19, was crowned Miss World today. Miss Croatia, Anica Martinovic, came second.

LONDON, WEDNESDAY 15
The Queen opens Parliament

In the Queen's Speech, marking the state opening of Parliament, 16 bills were announced. These included proposals for reforms of the divorce laws, ending "quickie" divorces but allowing a no-fault divorce after a year's cooling-off period.

Other measures will include the introduction of vouchers for nursery education, allowing opt-out schools to borrow money for improvements, imposing tougher regulations on asylum-seekers, extending the remit of MI5 to include anti-drugs activities, and compelling the defence in court cases to disclose their arguments in advance.

Westminster, Wednesday 15. Brian Mawhinney, the Conservative Party chairman, is bombarded with flour and paint by demonstrators on College Green, following the state opening of Parliament. Three women, aged between 18 and 20, were eventually arrested by the police. They were protesting against the government's proposed tougher legislation on asylum and immigration.

JERUSALEM, WEDNESDAY 15
Peres appointed prime minister

Shimon Peres, new Israeli premier.

Shimon Peres received official confirmation today of his appointment as successor to the assassinated Israeli prime minister, Yitzhak Rabin. Peres had held the post on an interim basis since Rabin's death 11 days ago. On Monday he was chosen as the new leader of the ruling Labour Party.

A potential obstacle to his premiership was removed when the Likud Party announced that it would not obstruct the formation of a new Labour-led government, as to do so would mean that a murderer could affect political change.

Mr. Peres promised to "make every effort to boost understanding and peace with our neighbours."

ALGIERS, THURSDAY 16
Algerians defy threats to vote

In spite of threats by Islamic fundamentalists to kill anyone who voted, there has been an estimated 75 per cent turnout in the Algerian presidential elections held today. President Liamine Zeroual was re-elected by a landslide majority.

All four presidential candidates had pledged to bring to an end the bitter civil war that has claimed up to 50,000 lives since 1992, when elections were cancelled with a fundamentalist party, the Islamic Salvation Party, seemingly poised for victory.

Algerian women voted in huge numbers.

LONDON, THURSDAY 16
Queen Mother undergoes hip replacement operation

The Queen Mother's mobility has been restricted by a painful hip.

The Queen Mother was said to be making a good recovery after becoming, at 95, one of the world's oldest patients to undergo hip-replacement surgery. Pain from her right hip has meant that her mobility has been severely restricted, and she has become increasingly dependent on aids such as a wheelchair at home, a golf buggy for public appearances, and a pair of walking sticks. The operation was carried out at the King Edward VII Hospital for Officers in London.

New York, Tuesday 14. Radio City Music Hall saw the world premiere of the new action-packed James Bond film *GoldenEye*, which stars Pierce Brosnan as 007. One of his co-stars is the glamorous Izabella Scorupco (above).

November

S	M	T	W	T	F	S
			1	2	3	4
5	6	7	8	9	10	11
12	13	14	15	16	17	18
19	20	21	22	23	24	25
26	27	28	29	30		

Johannesburg, 20
Britain and Holland oppose a plan for a European Union oil embargo on Nigeria following the execution of writer Ken Saro-Wiwa and eight other environmental activists.

Argentina, 20
Erich Priebke, 82, an ex-SS captain, is extradicted to Italy to face trial for taking part in the massacre of 335 civilians at the Ardeatine Caves on March 24, 1944.

Washington DC, 20
US government employees return to work after President Clinton and Congress agree a budget compromise.

Lincoln, 21
The City School is closed as public health officials attempt to halt the meningitis outbreak that has killed five people in the city.

Dar es Salaam, 23
Benjamin Mkapa is sworn in as President of Tanzania following the country's first multi-party elections.

Moscow, 23
A radioactive parcel planted by Chechen rebels is discovered in the city's Izmailovsky Park.

Cairo, 23
An Egyptian military court jails 54 members of the fundamentalist Muslim Brotherhood and closes its offices in a pre-election purge.

London, 23
Stephen Lander, 48, is appointed director-general of MI5, Britain's security service.

London, 23
Attorney General Sir Nicholas Lyell threatens a ban on "cheque-book journalism" following payments to witnesses in the Rosemary West trial.

Rome, 24
Former Italian premier, Silvio Berlusconi, and four others are to stand trial for alleged embezzlement and false accounting over the 1988 purchase of an Italian film company.

Death
Peter Grant, former manager of Led Zeppelin, aged 60, November 21.

Bosnian peace plan agreed by three national leaders

US negotiator Richard C. Holbrooke scored a notable victory here today, when the three main national leaders involved in the Bosnian conflict accepted a peace agreement that may end the fighting in the troubled new nation. Slobodan Milosevic of Serbia, Franjo Tudjman of Croatia, and Alija Izetbegovic of Bosnia eventually all consented to a formula that ostensibly creates a unified Bosnia, but in fact divides the country along racial lines.

The muscle to make the agreement work will be provided by 60,000 NATO troops, who are to be sent into Bosnia before Christmas. Twenty thousand of the troops will be from the US and 13,000 from Britain.

The talks had been going on for 21 days before agreement was reached, and none of the leaders involved is totally satisfied with the outcome. There are four main points to the plan. The first is that there is to be a unified state called the Union of Bosnia-Herzegovina. This Union is to consist of two self-governing parts: a Muslim-Croat federation and a

From left: presidents Milosevic, Isetbegovic, and Tudjman applaud their agreement.

Bosnian Serb republic. The presidency of the Union will rotate between the Muslim, Croat, and Serb groups. And a single parliamentary authority will handle foreign affairs.

International monitors will oversee the first elections; refugees will be allowed to return home; human

rights are guaranteed and will be monitored; and war criminals will not be allowed to hold office.

The agreement is being presented as a triumph for President Clinton's diplomacy, but many Americans will oppose sending US troops into a foreign war zone. (→ November 29)

Ex-communist Polish president

Kwasniewski casts his vote.

Aleksander Kwasniewski, a former communist, today won Poland's presidential elections by a small majority. With 51.7 per cent of the vote in the decisive second round, he defeated the incumbent president, Lech Walesa. Kwasniewski joined the Communist Party when aged 23. Under the communist regime he ran a government-backed newspaper that urged Poles to reject Walesa's Solidarity. However, he has vowed there will be no return to the past.

Major and Bruton fail to agree

The prospects for any meaningful agreement between the UK government and the government of the Republic of Ireland were receding tonight. There was a third telephone conversation between John Major and the Irish premier, John Bruton, but nothing definite was decided about the conditions under which an international commission could oversee disarming paramilitary groups from either side.

The disagreement between London and Dublin centres on John Major's insistence that the IRA give up some weapons before the commission starts work – in other words, that an IRA surrender of some arms is a precondition for his agreement to the commission.

It was hoped that there could be some basic agreement between the two governments before President Clinton's visit to Britain and Ireland next week, but this now looks unlikely. (→ November 30)

Film director Louis Malle dies

Louis Malle receiving a BAFTA award.

Louis Malle, French film director, died today, aged 63. He will be remembered for French-language films such as *Zazie dans le Métro*, *Lacombe Lucien*, and *Au Revoir les Enfants*, as well as for English-language movies such as *Viva Maria!* and *Atlantic City*.

WINCHESTER, WEDNESDAY 22

Rosemary West jailed for the rest of her life

Rosemary West is escorted away. She has been found guilty of ten murders.

Mr. Justice Mantell today sentenced Rosemary West to imprisonment for the rest of her life for what he described as the "depraved" murder of ten young women and girls. The jury had pronounced her guilty on three of the charges yesterday and today the foreman gave the judge their guilty verdict on the remaining seven charges.

Giving testimony during the trial, Rosemary West had claimed her husband, Frederick West, was solely responsible for the killings. But witnesses described her involvement in abuse and sexual attacks on young women of the kind that, according to the prosecution, led to most of the murders.

The whole country has been shaken by the horrors recounted at the trial. Questions are being asked about why the young women, many of whom had previously been taken into care, were not missed when they disappeared. Frederick West told the police before his suicide that he had

Heather West, murder victim.

carried out 20 other killings. The police have said, however, that they have no plans at present to try to find more bodies.

Rosemary West will serve her life sentence in Durham gaol, alongside other high-security women prisoners, including "moors murderer" Myra Hindley.

DUBLIN, FRIDAY 24

Ireland votes yes to divorce

In a close-run referendum, the Republic of Ireland today voted in favour of legalizing divorce. The vote had been impossible to foretell, and, in the event, the majority was just 9,114, about six per cent of those voting. Earlier in the week, the Pope had advised voters to pray for "the welfare of marriage." The Irish government, however, backed the reform proposals.

New York, Tuesday 21. *The Beatles Anthology* **sells 450,000 copies on its first day of release.**

LONDON, MONDAY 20

Attacks and admissions from Di on TV

Tonight on the *Panorama* TV programme, the Princess of Wales gave a devastatingly candid interview. So frank were her confessions and pointed her attacks that she may not only have brought divorce from the Prince of Wales closer, but may also have driven a nail into the coffin of the monarchy itself.

The interview had been trailed beforehand: news of it had been leaked, seemingly to coincide with the birthday of her estranged husband Charles, the previous week. The subjects over which the Princess ranged included many areas that would normally have been strictly out of bounds to journalistic questions. She was asked about any extramarital love affairs, for example, and, when the name of James Hewitt was mentioned, admitted: "Yes, I adored him. Yes, I was in love with him." And she confessed she had been very hurt by Hewitt's book about their affair.

It was, however, her comments on the constitution and the Prince of

Princess Diana during her interview with Martin Bashir of the BBC.

Wales' entourage that may cause most damage. Obviously wishing to settle scores, she responded to a question as to whether her husband Charles should eventually become king with: "I don't think any of us know the answer to that." She made

no secret of the fact that she believed his advisors were "the enemy" who were trying to keep her out of public life. Princess Diana also said she believed that she would never be queen of Britain, but asserted "I would like to be queen of people's hearts."

BOSNIA, NOVEMBER

Europe's worst conflict since World War II

After four years of the worst fighting in Europe for half a century, the war in former Yugoslavia appeared over on November 21. The US-brokered cease-fire followed three weeks of negotiations at the Wright Patterson Air Force Base in Dayton, Ohio. A formal peace agreement is to be signed in Paris in December.

For over four years, Yugoslavia has been sliced apart by war. Around 200,000 people have lost their lives as tensions that had been simmering for decades boiled over into a vicious struggle for territorial domination.

Until 1990 the multinational state of Yugoslavia was held together by its communist rulers. But after democratic elections were held in the country's six constituent republics – Serbia, Croatia, Macedonia, Slovenia, Montenegro, and Bosnia – nationalism tore the country apart. In 1991, Slovenia declared its independence, as did Croatia. When Serb areas in eastern Croatia refused to become part of the new state, fighting began.

Bosnia, which borders both Croatia and Serbia, has a mixed population of Muslims, Serbs, and Croats. In 1992, the Muslims and Croats voted together to make Bosnia independent. The Bosnian Serbs rejected this decision and began to shell the Bosnian capital, Sarajevo. Despite the presence of UN peacekeepers, a dirty war of blockade and atrocities followed.

The conflict has been marked on all sides by "ethnic cleansing" – the forceable removal or even massacre of local populations to create ethnically unified zones. The Bosnian Serbs are regarded as the worst offenders. Both their political leader, Radovan Karadzic, and their military chief, General Mladic, are wanted by an International War Crimes Tribunal to stand trial as war criminals.

Under the cease-fire agreement, all armed groups in Bosnia are to disband, except authorized police. A 60,000-strong NATO force will be sent to Bosnia before Christmas, and it will take prompt action against any that do not comply. (→ November 29)

Sarajevo, the Bosnian capital, was devastated by Bosnian Serbs who besieged the city.

From the hills around Sarajevo, shells and mortars rained down on the population.

General Mladic addresses Bosnian Serbs.

UN peacekeepers endured harsh conditions.

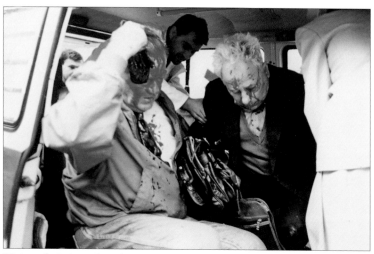

Victims of a Serb attack on the Croatian capital Zagreb.

Hundreds of thousands fled their homes, like these Serbian refugees in August 1995.

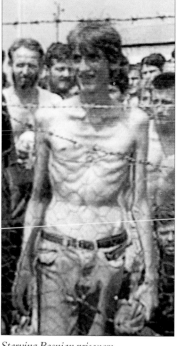

Starving Bosnian prisoners.

The first US military personnel arrive to prepare for NATO's presence in Bosnia.

The war leaders

Slobodan Milosevic, president of Serbia.

Alija Izetbegovic, the Bosnian Muslim president.

Radovan Karadzic, the Bosnian Serb leader.

President Franjo Tudjman, leader of Croatia.

November

S	M	T	W	T	F	S
			1	2	3	4
5	6	7	8	9	10	11
12	13	14	15	16	17	18
19	20	21	22	23	24	25
26	27	28	29	30		

Sarajevo, 26
Bosnian Serb leader Radovan Karadzic warns that the peace agreement could turn Sarajevo into a "new Beirut". (→ November 29)

London, 26
Rave priest Chris Brain admits to sexual misconduct.

Washington DC, 27
Newt Gingrich, Republican Speaker of the House of Representatives, announces that he will not run for president in 1996.

London, 27
Ernest Saunders and his three Guinness trial co-defendants lose their appeals against the convictions.

Moscow, 27
President Yeltsin leaves hospital after treatment for his heart condition but is immediately sent away on a rest cure. (→ December 18)

London, 27
Survey shows marked fall in reading abilities of 11-year-olds.

Yeovil, 27
Paddy Ashdown is attacked by a man armed with a flick-knife while touring his constituency in a bid to combat racism.

London, 28
A controversial video of clips shot with hidden cameras, including one of a couple making love in a lift, is withdrawn from sale.

London, 28
The government bans the sale of meat from cows' backbones in order to reduce the risk of cross-infection to humans of "mad cow disease".

Athens, 29
Greek President Andreas Papandreou is put on a kidney dialysis machine and a respirator.

London, 30
Lord Donaldson, former Master of the Rolls, accuses Home Secretary Michael Howard of making a "despotic" attack on the judiciary.

Beijing, 30
Fidel Castro starts his first official visit to China.

Paris, 30
Riot police use tear gas in Paris and Nantes against protesting students.

Clarke's Budget knocks a penny off income tax

Kenneth Clarke and his wife Gillian with the Chancellor's Red Box.

Chancellor of the Exchequer, Kenneth Clarke, has made a modest income tax cut, reducing the basic rate to 24p. Duty on spirits has been reduced by 4 per cent, which will, on average, knock 27p off a bottle of whisky – the first time that the duty has been reduced in 100 years. However, the taxpayer is required to find an extra 3.5p per litre for petrol and diesel, 15p for a packet of 20 cigarettes, and 8p a pint on strong cider.

Although analysts view such a cautious budget as having been prepared with the next general election in mind, it is assumed that Mr. Major is not planning to go to the country before spring 1997. Before then, it is expected another budget will be introduced that contains the big vote-winning tax cuts.

Rail chaos in France

Most of France ground to a halt again today as the railway workers already on strike were joined for a day by public service employees. All the public sector unions are angry at proposed changes in the social security system, which Prime Minister Alain Juppé claims are essential to restore health to the French economy, and to enable the French government to join the single European currency. The rail workers are further incensed by a new contract that they are being offered. Only a few inter-city trains ran across France, while in Paris there were no trains at all, most of the Metro was at a halt, and the bus service was skeletal. Cross-Channel ferries were turned away from Calais.

The unions are hoping that two million protestors will demonstrate, as the Prime Minister has said his government could not survive such a vast public protest. (→ December 7)

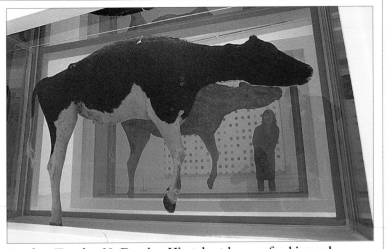

London, Tuesday 28. Damien Hirst, best known for his works comprising animal carcasses preserved in formaldehyde and displayed in glass cases, was given Britain's most prestigious art award, the Turner Prize, today.

Serbs protest at Bosnia plan

Serb protestors in Sarajevo's suburb, Ilidza.

Several thousand people turned out in a rally today in a Serb-held suburb of Sarajevo to protest against the peace plan, initialled on their behalf last week by Serbian president Milosevic. The Serbs are protesting at the prospect of having to live side by side with Muslims again: they swear that they will never give up the city. The organizers said that they would only use only peaceful means to force their case. About 40,000 Serbs live in Serb-held areas of Sarajevo.

Ulster visit triumph for Clinton

President Clinton turned on the Christmas lights in Belfast tonight. It was a gesture heavy in symbolism, appropriate to a historic day-long visit to Northern Ireland that seems to have brought more light to the Province than at any time since the peace process began 15 months ago.

Mr. Clinton is the first American president to visit Northern Ireland. He flew in shortly after 9 a.m. to begin a day that included a walk-about in the Protestant Shankhill Road, and then the nationalist Falls Road, where he met and shook hands with Sinn Fein leader, Gerry Adams. He visited a factory on the peace line, where he gave a carefully balanced speech that reiterated his support for the twin-track peace process and made it clear that he thought terrorism had no role to play. Later he travelled on to Londonderry, and, after his return to Belfast to turn on the lights, he had a 25-minute conversation with the Revd. Ian Paisley. He ended the day at a concert given by Van Morrison. He has been greeted everywhere by good-natured and cheering crowds from both sides of the political divide. The success of the visit in rekindling hope in the peace process was symbolized by two children who met the President while he was at the factory. One of them, a nine-year-old whose father had been killed in the Troubles, read Mr. Clinton a letter she had written him which summed up the day's feelings: "Now it is nice and peaceful... My Christmas wish is that we have peace and love and that it will last in Ireland forever."

Catherine Hamill, aged 9, reads her letter.

President Clinton turns on the Christmas lights in Belfast during his visit.

Anglo-Irish IRA deal

Irish premier John Bruton unexpectedly flew into London tonight for a lightning summit with John Major. Afterwards, at an 11 p.m. press conference, the two men announced an end to 12 weeks of sometimes bitter disagreement between them over the Northern Ireland peace talks. The meeting came after two telephone conversations earlier in the day between Mr. Major and Mr. Bruton, which in turn followed several weeks of talks on the issue between officials of the two governments and between the two leaders.

The two prime ministers told reporters that they had sorted out their differences over the twin-track proposals whereby an international commission will be set up to look at the issue of IRA arms. While the commission is at work, the two governments will open talks with all the political parties in Northern Ireland, including Sinn Fein, to lay the foundation for all-party talks. The three-man commission will be chaired by American George Mitchell, a former Democratic senator of Irish descent. However, one major area of contention remains between the British and Irish: whether the IRA will be allowed to participate in any all-party talks if the terrorist organization has not previously handed in its weapons. (→ November 30)

Cape Town, Sunday 26. Two boxers threw themselves out of the ring in mid-fight as gunmen opened fire in a botched attempt to steal the evening's takings. A security guard was killed, having been shot twice in the chest by the raiders.

Psychic "spies" used by Pentagon

It has emerged that the Pentagon employed psychics for 20 years in its intelligence-gathering operations. Six psychics were regularly called on to perform such tasks as identifying the exact whereabouts of Colonel Gaddafi, locating North Korean plutonium, and providing the layout of a building in Iran where American hostages were held. The use of psychics came to light when the CIA was asked to take over managing them in the summer. One CIA advisor has commented that it is doubtful that the psychics contributed anything of use, although they have claimed successes.

New York, Wednesday 29. Ivana Trump, former wife of property billionaire Donald Trump, marries an Italian businessman.

December

S	M	T	W	T	F	S
					1	2
3	4	5	6	7	8	9
10	11	12	13	14	15	16
17	18	19	20	21	22	23
24	25	26	27	28	29	30
31						

Oregon, 1
Two British women jailed for five years for plotting, while members of the Bhagwan Shree Rajneesh cult, to kill a lawyer acting for the state of Oregon.

Dublin, 1
President Clinton finishes his trip to Ireland with a day in Dublin.

London, 3
Princess Diana tells the *News of the World* that she frequently slips out at night to give comfort to the dying in London hospitals.

London, 4
The Queen Mother leaves hospital, supporting herself with two walking sticks, 18 days after having a hip-replacement operation.

Colombo, 5
Sri Lankan government forces recapture Jaffna, the rebel Tamil Tigers' capital for five years.

New York, 6
Jewellery belonging to the Duchess of York, reported missing 24 hours previously, is found in a garden shed in a New York suburb. A teenage baggage-handler is arrested.

London, 6
Snow and freezing conditions cause a 14-hour, 37-mile traffic jam on the southern stretch of the M25.

London, 8
Sales of beef drop by 10% and prices by 12% following another "mad cow disease" scare.

London, 8
Chancellor Kenneth Clarke announces the introduction of a £2 coin in two years' time.

London, 8
In a libel case brought by Tory MP David Ashby against the *Sunday Times* over allegations of homosexuality, his wife tells a court that she was relieved to discover that he apparently was gay. (→ December 19)

Death
Jimmy Jewel, comedian and actor, on the eve of his 83rd birthday, London, December 3.

Spaniard to be new secretary-general of NATO

Six weeks after the resignation of Willy Claes from the post of secretary-general of NATO, facing corruption charges in his native Belgium, a new secretary-general was announced today. He is Javier Solana, the foreign minister of Spain.

The appointment was greeted with some dismay in Britain by Tory Euro-sceptics, who pointed out that, as a socialist, Señor Solana campaigned in 1982 for Spain to withdraw from the NATO alliance. He also has a past record of having been an opponent of nuclear weapons. However, the socialist party of which he is a member reversed its policy when in power three years later, and called on the country to vote in favour of staying in NATO.

Solana is seen as a compromise candidate. Britain was in favour of European Commissioner Sir Leon Brittan, but did not press his case when soundings indicated little support from other countries. Ruud Lubbers of Holland looked the likely nominee until the Americans made it clear that they did not consider him suitably charismatic to handle the PR element of the job. The former Danish foreign minister Uffe Ellemann-Jensen fell foul of the French for having publicly criticized their nuclear testing programme.

It is believed that Germany was the main proponent of Señor Solana. He is also reported to be a good friend of Warren Christopher, the US secretary of state.

Javier Solana, NATO's new leader.

Close encounter with Jupiter

The first-ever close examination of Jupiter took place today when the Galileo space probe launched a capsule into the planet's atmosphere. Travelling at 170,000 kmph (106,000 mph) until slowed down by its parachutes, the capsule transmitted data for around 75 minutes, registering details of Jupiter's chemistry, temperature, and density. It was then burned up by the tremendous heat and crushed by the massive gravity of this planet 1,400 times larger than Earth.

The Galileo probe itself, which was launched in 1989, is expected to orbit Jupiter for two years, sending back further information about the planet and its moons.

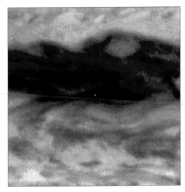

The probe's target area on Jupiter.

Head teacher stabbed to death by gang outside school

Murdered headteacher Philip Lawrence.

A dedicated and successful headteacher died early this morning in hospital after being stabbed by a gang of youths yesterday outside his school in London's Maida Vale. The head had gone to the assistance of one of his pupils from St. George's Roman Catholic school, who was being attacked with a machete by one of the gang members. The pupil himself ended up in hospital being treated for head injuries. The incident took place at 3 p.m.

One of the pupils later described what he had seen of the incident: "There was a massive scuffle. A gang outside the school was fighting with a boy. Then the headteacher suddenly ran out and tried to come between them. One of the gang lashed out with something looking like a baseball bat and then they grabbed the teacher and stabbed him."

Mr. Lawrence had been at the school for three years, and he had done much to stamp out unruly behaviour and to raise educational standards. He had been strong on discipline, having at one time expelled 25 pupils in a drive to crush troublesome elements. A school inspector's report praised his "strong leadership skills". The school draws on Kilburn, the Harrow Road, and Willesden for many of its pupils.

Gillian Shephard, Education and Employment Secretary, today called for a full review of security in schools throughout England and Wales in the aftermath of the murder. She said, however, that it was not desirable to have security guards patrolling inner-city schools. The Department for Education and Employment is due to issue fresh guidelines on security during the new year.

French strikes spread and bite

Comparisons are being made with the civil disturbances of 1968 in Paris as protests against the government spread. Today, as the national rail strike entered its fourteenth day, the Eurostar train service became a victim of industrial action for the first time. Parisians have been walking to work for two weeks, or else have been sitting in their cars in vast traffic queues, with the Metro and bus ser-

vices at a standstill. Schools have now closed as teachers have joined the strike, and striking mail workers have prevented all but a trickle of letters being delivered. Civil servants, electricity and telecommunications workers have all downed tools. Even employees of the Bank of France walked out today. And Paris has also seen vandalism and rioting on the streets. On Tuesday a huge march of

strikers, students, and disaffected workers braved freezing cold and snow to call for the resignation of Prime Minister Alain Juppé.

The government's lot worsened today, as talks to end the rail strike collapsed. However, Juppé can take some comfort from the fact that the shouting is not for revolution, but only against proposed social security changes. (→ December 15)

London, Sunday 3. Britain is trying to stop crowns of kings George I and George IV being bought by an American.

Union banners of railway, Metro, and telecommunications workers at the start of Thursday's demonstration in Paris.

Leeson gets six and a half years

Nick Leeson is reported to be shocked by the severity of the sentences handed down to him in court today. The 28-year-old trader held responsible for the collapse of Barings Bank was given six and a half years in gaol on two charges of fraud. The whole trial was over in a flash. Leeson faced 11 charges in total, but nine fraud and forgery charges were dropped as he pleaded guilty yesterday to the other two. Sentencing followed today. His term is nearly the longest permitted for the offences, and he had clearly been hoping for less after the prosecution said that they were not looking for an example to be made of him. With remission, he should be free in 1999.

Essex, Thursday 7. A Range Rover is removed from the site where it was discovered on a remote farm track. Inside were the bodies of three men who had been shot in the head. Police believe that the men were involved in drug dealing and were lured to the site.

French demand release of pilots

Two French pilots shot down during NATO raids in August are still being held by their Bosnian Serb captors. French officials at the peace talks at Lancaster House in London called today for their immediate release, implying that if it was not forthcoming the peace talks could be in jeopardy. Implementation of the peace agreement depends upon the involvement of NATO troops in three sectors, one of which will be under French command. Deployment is planned for ten days' time, but if the French are not satisfied it could be delayed until the New Year. (→ December 13)

Johannesburg, Monday 4. Mike Atherton's marathon 10 ¾ - hour innings saves England from defeat by South Africa.

December

S	M	T	W	T	F	S
					1	2
3	4	5	6	7	8	9
10	11	12	13	14	15	16
17	18	19	20	21	22	23
24	25	26	27	28	29	30
31						

South of England, 10
Freezing fog causes a 100-car pile-up on the M1 in Hertfordshire while more than 100 aircraft are diverted or seriously delayed, causing misery to thousands of passengers.

London, 10
A Gallup poll shows defence is the only election issue on which the Conservatives lead Labour.

London, 11
Labour leader Tony Blair says that if he is elected the country's leader at the next election he will revolutionize Prime Minister's Question Time and introduce powerful city mayors.

Madrid, 11
A huge car bomb explodes, killing six people and wounding 18. The attack is attributed to ETA, the Basque separatist group.

Paris, 12
Two French pilots held by the Bosnian Serbs since August 30 arrive safely back in Paris.

Nablus, 12
Israel hands over Nablus, the most important town on the West Bank, to the Palestinians. (→ December 21)

London, 12
Tory MP Sir David Lightbown dies of a heart attack, leaving Prime Minister John Major's government with a majority of just three.

New York, 13
Christmas trees in Grand Central Station are taken down because they might have offended Muslims.

London, 13
Two people who had threatened to release mice in Harrods food hall during the busy Christmas period are charged with blackmail.

Madrid, 15
European Community leaders decide on "Euro" as the name for the new single currency.

London, 15
The Court of Appeal rules that the sale of five of the first seven rail passenger franchises is illegal.

LONDON, WEDNESDAY 13
New riots in Brixton

For the third time in recent history Brixton in south London has been ripped apart by riots. The disturbances took place after a march to Brixton police station as part of organized protests about the death of a young black man, Wayne Douglas, while in police custody.

Petrol bombs were used and bottles and stones were thrown at riot police as the initially peaceful march disintegrated into mob violence. Several shops were looted and had their windows broken, while the 7-11 general store, beside Brixton underground station, was set alight. Cars from a showroom were overturned and set on fire. According to some reports, shots were also fired.

The demonstration had begun at 6.30 p.m. Agitators made impassioned speeches to the crowd, branding the police as "killers". In the scenes that followed, one police motorcycle rider came close to losing his life when a crowd dragged him from his bike and began kicking him viciously. He was saved by a member of the public driving into the crowd and dispersing his attackers.

Police sealed off the area, using helicopters with spotlights to pinpoint potential flashpoints.

Brixton in flames once again as some of the area's youths take to the streets for a confrontation with the police.

LONDON, MONDAY 11
Nuclear power stations scrapped

A £4.9 billion investment in two new nuclear power stations has been abandoned by British Energy. The company's chief executive, Robert Hawley, announced that the decision not to build the stations in Suffolk and Somerset was taken because of unstable energy prices. He went on to say that British Energy's major preoccupation was a successful privatization of the company in 1996. A government White Paper recently stated that nuclear power is unprofitable. Consequently, nuclear power's days as a source of energy in Britain now seem numbered.

PARIS, FRIDAY 15
France's national strike is almost over

Alain Juppé, the French prime minister.

After concessions by the French prime minister, Alain Juppé, transport in France was yesterday slowly getting back to normal. Services on the Paris Metro eased back into action yesterday on several lines, while the first trains to operate since November 24 went into action. The vast majority of postal workers and of public service employees also returned to work.

Juppé has conceded ground to the strikers by abandoning his plans to revolutionize French rail services and to reduce civil service pensions. However, he still intends to make very considerable changes to France's expensive welfare system.

PARIS, THURSDAY 14
Signing of Bosnian peace in Paris

The Bosnia-Herzegovina Peace Accord was signed today by the leaders of the three states that, over the past four years, have fought Europe's fiercest war since World War II.

President Milosevic of Serbia,

President Tudjman of Croatia, and President Izetbegovic of Bosnia signed the treaty. It was witnessed by President Bill Clinton, Prime Minister John Major, Germany's Chancellor Helmut Kohl, and

Russian Prime Minister Viktor Chernomyrdin, who attended in the absence of the sick Boris Yeltsin.

A major condition of the treaty, the details of which had been hammered out in Dayton, Ohio, in November, is that a 60,000-strong NATO peace-keeping force, due in Bosnia next week, will have the right to take retaliatory action against any group or individual in breach of the cease-fire.

"I feel like a man swallowing a bitter but useful medicine, but I can assure you we are signing this peace treaty with sincerity," commented President Izetbegovic. Serbia's President Milosevic said that the signing of the documents did not solve all the problems of Bosnia, but added: "I am sure a common language can be found." (→ December 26)

Presidents Milosevic, Tudjman, and Izetbegovic sign the Bosnian peace plan.

London, Saturday 16. Health supplement royal jelly should carry health warnings, say doctors, as it may harm asthmatics.

LONDON, TUESDAY 12
Safe alcohol level raised

A merrier Christmas than had been expected is in store for drinkers thanks to new government guidelines on sensible drinking. The new recommendations announced by the health secretary, Stephen Dorrell, raise the number of units of alcohol that men can safely drink from 21 to 28 per week, while women's consumption can safely go up from 14 to 21 units per week. A unit is defined as half a pint of beer, a glass of wine, or a single measure of spirits.

Some doctors now believe that moderate alcohol consumption can be beneficial to health. However, the British Medical Association described the new advice as confusing and unhelpful. Mr. Dorrell himself insisted that the new advice should not be seen as "a boozer's charter".

NEW YORK, MONDAY 11
Children are main war victims

The number of children who are victims of war is increasing at an alarming rate, according to a report issued by the United Nations Children's Fund (Unicef). *The State of the World's Children*, the organization's annual report, states that of all those who are caught up in war children are the most likely to be killed or exploited. Around 90 per cent of victims of modern warfare are civilians, as opposed to 50 per cent during the last century. In addition to being less able to defend themselves, children face being victims of horrific war crimes or being drafted into armies. Lightweight weapons make them effective as nimble foot-soldiers.

LONDON, MONDAY 11
Branson lottery allegations

Richard Branson.

The spectre of a dirty tricks campaign to obtain the national lottery concession has arisen with allegations made by Virgin chairman, Richard Branson. He claims that the chairman of GTech, a company that owns part of national lottery organizer Camelot, tried to bribe him before the concession was awarded to prevent him making a rival bid.

On this evening's BBC *Panorama* programme, Mr. Branson stated that at a lunch in September 1993, Guy Snowden, chairman of GTech, made him an open offer to stay out of the race for the lottery. Peter Davis, chairman of Oflot, the lottery regulator, denies that Mr. Branson told him of the bribe. (→ December 18)

Unicef says children are main war victims.

ROUEN, SUNDAY 10
Ukrainian ship captain gaoled for murder

A ship's captain and his second mate were gaoled for life for their part in one of the worst atrocities at sea in recent times. Other members of the Ukrainian crew who took part in the murders of eight African stowaways were also given heavy sentences.

Their merchant ship *Ruby* had docked in Ghana in October 1992. Eight Ghanaians made their way on board and hid in the hold, where they

found another African stowaway, a Cameroonian. The Africans were discovered six days later, when the ship was off the Portuguese coast. Wladimir Ilnitskiy, the captain, and his deputy, Valery Artemenko, ordered the crew to kill the stowaways. However, one Ghanaian, Kingsley Ofosu, managed to escape and hide. When the ship landed at Le Havre, he told the authorities of the murders.

London, Monday 11. Arthur Mullard, the archetypal Cockney comedian, has died at the age of 85.

S	M	T	W	T	F	S
					1	2
3	4	5	6	7	8	9
10	11	12	13	14	15	16
17	18	19	20	21	22	23
24	25	26	27	28	29	30
31						

Vienna, 17
Far-right Freedom Party of Jörg Haider gains over 22% in Austria's parliamentary elections, making it Europe's most successful extremist party.

London, 18
Article by Moors murderer Myra Hindley in the *Guardian* admits to her guilt and remorse.

Jerusalem, 18
An Israeli television station pays £260,000 for an amateur video of the assassination of Yitzhak Rabin.

London, 18
Virginia Bottomley discloses that lottery regulator Peter Davis accepted flights paid for by a company in the Camelot partnership, which runs the national lottery.

New York, 18
The Dow Jones index tumbles by 100 points, Wall Street's biggest one-day points fall for over four years.

London, 19
The first mainline rail service franchise is awarded to a bus company, Stagecoach.

London, 19
The government is defeated by two votes in a Commons motion on the European fisheries policy.

Sarajevo, 20
Nato officially takes over peace-keeping in Bosnia from the UN.

Warsaw, 21
The Polish prime minister, Jozef Oleksy, is accused by his own interior minister of having spied for Russia.

Grenoble, 23
The bodies of 16 members of the Solar Temple cult are found on an Alpine hillside. Fifty-three members of the same cult died in mysterious circumstances in October 1994.

Deaths
Economist and Nobel Prize winner Professor James Meade, in Cambridge, aged 88, December 22.

Communists triumphant in Russian poll

Gennardy Zyuganov, Communist leader.

With two fifths of the votes counted in Russia's parliamentary elections, the Communists have emerged as the dominant party in the next Duma. They are currently registering 22 per cent of the votes counted, a figure that is unlikely to be too different from the final result, and which should give them over 150 of the 450 seats. In some industrial regions, where production has dropped catastrophically under democracy, the Communist share has been as high as 63 per cent. The Communist leader, Gennardy Zyuganov, claimed that the result constituted "a complete rejection of the radical policy of so-called democratic reforms".

The results are a deliberate slap in the face for Boris Yeltsin. Of the reformist or moderate parties only Prime Minister Viktor Chernomyrdin's Our Home is Russia party has come close to 10 per cent of the vote. Nevertheless, President Yeltsin can take some consolation from the decline in support for Vladimir Zhirinovsky, whose extreme nationalist Liberal Democratic party has so far gained only 11 per cent of the vote, a half of the support that it won in the last Russian elections.

American Airlines jet crashes into Colombian mountainside killing 147

An American Airlines Boeing 757, on route from Miami to the town of Cali in southwest Colombia, crashed yesterday into a mountainside minutes before it would have reached its destination. The crash killed 147 of the mainly Colombian passengers. But to the amazement of rescuers who reached the wreckage earlier today, 17 people have been taken out alive. The plane was flying at 500 mph when it hit the mountainside.

The cause of the crash is unknown. The twin-engine 757 is one of the most up-to-date aircraft in regular use, and has an almost unblemished safety record. However, sabotage is not currently suspected.

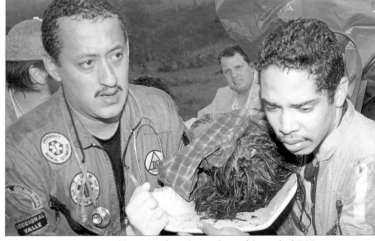

Rescuers carry a 14-year-old survivor from the wreckage of the crashed 757.

Washington, Tuesday 19. Oliver Stone's new film *Nixon,* starring Anthony Hopkins and Joan Allen (above), has been condemned by Richard Nixon's daughters as malicious "character assassination".

Hundreds die in school fire

Over 300 people are believed to have perished as fire swept through a temporary structure put up for a school prizegiving in the town of Dabwali in the north Indian state of Haryana. There were 1,300 people in the tent-like *shamiana* at the time, many of them children. Only two of the exits appear to have been left unlocked. As well as burns and smoke inhalation, deaths are attributable to injuries sustained in the stampede to escape.

LONDON, WEDNESDAY 20

Queen calls for royal divorce

The Queen has reacted angrily to the continuing public revelations about the failed marriage of Prince Charles and Princess Diana and has written to them urging them to divorce. A statement issued tonight by the Palace said: "After considering the present situation the Queen wrote to both the Prince and Princess earlier this week and gave them her view, supported by the Duke of Edinburgh, that an early divorce is desirable. The Prince of

Wales also takes this view and has made this known to the Princess of Wales since the letter." Princess Diana has not yet replied.

The Archbishop of Canterbury was consulted first. Divorce would not prevent Prince Charles from ascending the throne.

A family at war: from left to right, Prince Charles, the Queen and Prince Philip, and Princess Diana.

Conditions at Holloway found to be appalling

It was disclosed tonight that a team of prison inspectors was removed from Holloway, Britain's main gaol for women, before completing its survey because the conditions it found there were so bad. General Sir David Ramsbotham, the new Chief Inspector of Prisons, said that standards were unacceptably low and called for immediate improvements in the treatment of prisoners.

Inspectors found that some prisoners were locked up for 23 hours a day, that the gaol was filthy, bullying rife, and staff morale extremely low. The team had gone into the prison unannounced last Monday and was due to finish on Friday, but was pulled out on Thursday lunchtime, a day after Sir David joined them. He said: "Our early findings identified such shortfalls in the treatment of prisoners and in the conditions at Holloway that the proper course for us was to seek immediate improvements."

DUBLIN, THURSDAY 21

Charlton resigns as Ireland manager

Jack Charlton retired today as manager of Ireland's national football team, following their failure to qualify for next year's European championships. The former England player became a hero in Ireland after guiding the team to the final rounds of two successive World Cups. "Ten years is a long time in the job," he said. "They have been brilliant years. I have enjoyed every minute."

Jack Charlton, in a familiarly pensive mood.

Bethlehem, Thursday 21. Palestinian police are cheered by enthusiastic crowds as they enter the administrative buildings of the town after the withdrawal of Israeli troops. This will be the first Christmas to be celebrated at this holy site under Palestinian control.

LONDON, TUESDAY 19

MP loses "gay" libel action

Tory MP David Ashby leaves the court.

David Ashby, Conservative MP for Leicestershire North-West, today lost his libel action against the *Sunday Times* for an article that had called him a homosexual and a hypocrite. Mr. Ashby was ordered to pay costs totalling a likely £350,000, which could bankrupt him. The article said that he had shared a double bed with a male friend on holiday in India. Mr. Ashby denies he is a homosexual.

December

Sandringham, 25
In her Christmas broadcast, the Queen avoids mention of her family problems, concentrating instead on world peace.

Arles, France, 25
Solicitor André-François Raffray dies. In 1965 he began paying a monthly pension to Mme. Jeanne Calment in return for ownership of her apartment after her death. Mme. Calment, 120, survives.

London, 26
BBC Radio 4's *Today* programme announces that listeners have voted murdered headmaster Philip Lawrence personality of the year.

Vitoria, Spain, 26
Three suspected ETA Basque separatists are arrested and explosives seized in raids in the Basque capital.

Westminster, 26
It is revealed that the government has paid the legal costs of the families of the IRA terrorists who were killed in the "Death on the Rock" incident in Gibraltar. The case went to the European Court of Human Rights.

Moscow, 27
In defiance of American pressure, Russia pledges to continue nuclear and military assistance to Iran.

West Yorkshire, 28
Tracey Patterson, 11, and two men attempting to rescue her, Michael Mee and Jack Crawshaw, die in a frozen lake at Hemsworth Water Park.

South Africa, 28
Paul Adams, 18, the first South African Test cricketer from the black townships, takes his first Test wicket.

Worcester, 29
The body of missing French student, Celine Figard, is found in a lay-by.

London, 29
Government figures show that a record number of children are being refused admission to their first-choice state school.

Birmingham, 29
A man runs amok with three knives and stabs 10 people in a supermarket in Bordesley Green.

BOSNIA, TUESDAY 26
Serbs ask for more time

Admiral Leighton Smith shares an umbrella with Momcilo Krajisnik in Sarajevo.

The NATO commander in charge of implementing the Bosnian peace agreement, Admiral Leighton Smith, has been asked by the Bosnian Serbs to allow them an extra eight months before they have to hand over their areas of Sarajevo.

Under the terms of the Dayton peace accord, these areas are due to come under the supervision of French NATO troops on January 19 and Serb forces are to withdraw by February 3. However, Aleksa Buha, the Bosnian Serb foreign affairs spokesman, has asked that the Serbian pull-out be put back to the end of September at the earliest. Admiral Smith has replied that he is not empowered to renegotiate the peace agreement.

The population of the Serb areas of Sarajevo is around 70,000. The speaker of the Bosnian Serb assembly, Momcilo Krajisnik, warned that fear amongst the Serbs in the city had risen to such a point that they might be provoked into violent action if the deadline is not extended. Large numbers of Serbs are already quitting the city, even digging up the bones of relatives from the city's cemeteries to carry with them to Serbia.

Los Angeles, Monday 25. Dean Martin, straight man, film actor, singer and famous drinker, died today, aged 78.

WESTMINSTER, FRIDAY 29
Another Tory defection

Conservative MP Emma Nicholson, the member for Devon West and Torridge, today announced that she has joined the Liberal Democrats. This is a further blow to John Major's administration. Miss Nicholson criticised what she described as a move to the right within the Conservative Party. Her decision, she said, "is not so much a question of my leaving the party but the party leaving me."

BELFAST, WEDNESDAY 27
IRA blamed for shooting

A man was shot dead last night on a Catholic estate in West Belfast as he sat at home watching television with his family. His three-year-old son who was sitting next to him was injured in the hand by flying glass at the same time. No group has yet claimed responsibility, but the IRA is believed to be implicated.

The 30-year-old-man, who is known to the police as a petty criminal, may have been thought to be a drugs dealer. The killing follows two murders in the week before Christmas, and one earlier in the month, which were carried out by a group calling itself Direct Action Against Drugs, which many believe is a cover for the IRA.

Tusla, Bosnia, Monday 25. A Bosnian dressed as Santa Claus brings some traditional cheer by handing out gifts to American troops stationed at the NATO air base here. NATO troops taking up their positions in Bosnia were generally welcomed by local people.

Riot at Bondi Beach party

The annual open Christmas party at Bondi Beach ended tonight in a riot as thousands of young Australians fought with each other, and then turned on the police. A record 20,000 people turned up at the event that, although only a few years old, is now regarded as a tradition. So much alcohol was drunk that it took workers six hours to clear the bottles and cans.

Celebrating Christmas on Bondi beach.

Pope's address cut short through flu

The Pope caused alarm amongst the many thousands of Catholic faithful who gathered in St Peter's square today to hear his traditional Christmas message, and the many millions more watching on television. Looking ill and drawn he faltered and stumbled over his words, and then cut his address short, apologizing to the crowd and withdrawing from the balcony. After 15 minutes he reappeared to say that he was not well but was getting better.

The Pontiff was also unable to celebrate the Christmas mass in St Peter's Basilica. This is the first time he has missed the service in the 17 years of his papacy. Vatican officials said that he is suffering from a fever and a stomach upset. He is planning to rest entirely for two days, and is not scheduled to make any further public appearances until New Year's Eve.

The Pope is taken ill at the window of his room overlooking St Peter's square.

Flash flood kills hundreds

A severe flash flood has caused over 100 deaths in a black township in South Africa's KwaZulu/Natal province. Torrential rain late yesterday reached such a level that the Umsindusi River burst its banks and poured through the shanty town outside Pietermaritzburg. During one half-hour period 10 cm (4 in) of rain fell. So far 130 bodies have been recovered but hundreds more people are reported missing. The rain is still falling, hampering rescue efforts, and more is forecast.

Survivors search the wreckage by the river.

SPECIAL DOUBLE ISSUE   DECEMBER 25, 1995/JANUARY 1, 1996

TIME

MAN OF THE YEAR

NEWT GINGRICH

Big freeze hits the poor

The government announced yesterday that it is to make emergency cold weather payments to thousands of pensioners and people on income support as parts of Britain continue to suffer their coldest weather for many years.

Worst hit have been western Scotland and the Northern Isles. Glasgow recorded its coldest temperature ever as the mercury sank in the small hours of this morning to -18.6° C (-1.5° F), while near Fort William and at Altnaharra in Caithness it was even colder at -21° C (-5.8° F). The Shetland Islands continue to experience conditions not seen for 40 years. Blizzards first hit the islands on Christmas Eve. Drifting is up to 10 m (30 ft) deep in places, and on Tuesday the Shetland Islands Council declared a state of emergency.

Electricity cuts have been widespread across the islands, and some communities are now without electricity for their fifth day. As the cold weather moves south Whitby was cut off for much of yesterday and a thick blanket of snow covers Wales.

Some famous names among

Mohammed Siad Barre, **January 1**

Joe Slovo, **January 5**

Prince Souphanouvong, **January 10**

Gerald Durrell, **January 30**

Milovan Djilas, **April 20**

Jean Muir, **May 28**

Arturo Benedetti Michelangeli, **June 12**

Charlie Rich, **July 25**

January 1, Mohammed Siad Barre
Barre was president of Somalia from 1969, when, as commander of the armed forces, he seized power. He was overthrown in 1991. He ruled over one of the world's poorest countries, beset by civil war and starvation.

January 5, Joe Slovo
Slovo, chairman of the South African Communist Party, was one of the intellectual forces behind his country's rejection of apartheid. In 1985 he became the first white member of the national executive committee of the African National Congress.

January 7, Larry Grayson
Born Billy White, Larry Grayson became one of Britain's best-known comics, particularly for his catch phrases, "What a gay day" and "Shut that door". He achieved his greatest fame as host of *The Generation Game*, which he took over in 1978.

January 10, Prince Souphanouvong
Prince Souphanouvong, known as the "Red Prince" of Laos, led the Pathet Lao guerrillas against the right-wing government of his half-brother, Prince

Souvanna Phouma, for more than 20 years. He became president of Laos in 1975 when communism was established, serving until 1986.

January 30, Gerald Durrell
Animal conservationist Durrell was founder of Jersey Zoo, where he bred endangered species. Author of 37 books (notably *My Family and Other Animals*) and a dozen TV series, he used humour to popularize conservation.

February 5, Patricia Highsmith
American crime writer Highsmith spent most of her life in Europe, in particular England, France, and latterly Switzerland. In 1951 Alfred Hitchcock made a celebrated film of her first novel *Strangers on a Train*. Her most famous creation was the cultivated but amoral murderer Tom Ripley, whom she featured in a series of books.

February 9, J. William Fulbright
Arkansas Democrat, senator for three decades, and chairman of the Foreign Relations Committee for 15 years, Fulbright took a principled stand against the Vietnam War, which led, initially at least, to much criticism. He will also be

remembered for the international study fellowships he founded and which bear his name.

February 22, Robert Bolt
Dramatist and screenwriter Bolt won an Oscar for the film of his play *A Man For All Seasons* and for his screenplays *Lawrence of Arabia* and *Doctor Zhivago*. He directed his second wife Sarah Miles in the 1972 film *Lady Caroline Lamb*.

April 10, Maraji Desai
In 1977 Desai, a Brahman from western India, became prime minister in India's first non-Congress Party government, formed by his right-wing Janata Party. He was a veteran of the movement that led to India's independence from Britain in 1947, and a devout Hindu, renowned for his high moral standards.

April 20, Milovan Djilas
Former right-hand man to Tito and a fellow wartime partisan, politician, and writer, Djilas became an outspoken critic of the Yugoslav system in 1954, when he rejected communism in favour of British-influenced democratic socialism. He was an inspiration to other dissidents within communist regimes.

May 22, Les Aspin
A Democrat from Wisconsin, Aspin served for 11 months under President Clinton as Secretary of Defense. He was first elected to Congress in 1970 with an anti-Vietnam War stance, but in 1985 he became chairman of the House Armed Services Committee.

May 28, Jean Muir
Fashion designer Muir had a mathematical approach which she once described as "engineering with fabric". She showed her first collection in 1966, and in 1984 received the CBE for her contribution to the British fashion industry.

June 12, Arturo Benedetti Michelangeli
Reclusive and temperamental, Michelangeli was recognized as a supreme technical master of the piano. He often insisted that his own instrument be shipped to whichever concert hall he was due to appear in.

June 19, Peter Townsend
A hero of the Battle of Britain, who had the distinction of shooting down the first German aircraft over British soil in World War II, Townsend will be remem-

the many who died in 1995

Patricia Highsmith, **February 5**

J.William Fulbright, **February 9**

Robert Bolt, **February 22**

Maraji Desai, **April 10**

Ida Lupino, **August 3**

Phil Harris, **August 11**

Lord Home, **October 9**

Robertson Davies, **December 2**

bered less for his war record than for his famous love affair with Princess Margaret in the 1950s. Because he was divorced, the establishment deemed him an unsuitable match for the Princess, and she confirmed that they would not marry in a radio broadcast in 1955.

July 25, Charlie Rich
Pianist, songwriter, and singer, in the late 1950s Rich was session pianist on the Sun label, for which he made his first solo records. International stardom came in 1973 with the first of a series of hits, "Behind Closed Doors".

August 3, Ida Lupino
Screen actress Lupino specialized in "siren" roles in such films as *High Sierra* and *Dangerous Ground*. She made her film debut aged 15 – selected for the role for which her mother auditioned!

August 11, Phil Harris
A comedy partner of Jack Benny in the 1930s, Harris was also a singing band-leader – the fast-delivery vocalist on such hits as "Smoke, Smoke that Cigarette". Harris achieved fame again in 1967 as the voice of Baloo the Bear in Walt Disney's *Jungle Book*.

August 17, Howard Koch
Koch achieved notoriety in 1938 as the adaptor for radio of H. G. Wells's *The War of the Worlds*, produced by Orson Welles, which caused panic with its realistic newsflashes about a Martian invasion. His immortality was assured when he became one of the three writers of the movie *Casablanca*.

September 3, Sterling Morrison
Guitarist Morrison was a founder member of the hugely influential but, at the time, commercially unsuccessful 1960s rock group The Velvet Underground. When the band reformed in 1993 Morrison was working in Texas as a tug-boat skipper.

October 9, John Cairncross
Guy Burgess, Donald Maclean, Kim Philby, Anthony Blunt – and John Cairncross, the "fifth man" in the British spy ring who met at Cambridge University in the 1930s and subsequently worked for Soviet intelligence.

October 9, Lord Home
The last aristocratic leader of the Conservative Party, Home was prime minister for less than a year at the end

of the Tories' 13 years in government, before their defeat in the general election of 1964. He subsequently became a distinguished foreign secretary.

October 23, Gavin Ewart
The wit of the poet Gavin Ewart was exemplified in a poem claiming that he had buried all his best work in a tin box, to be dug up in 50 years' time "to confound the critics/ and teach every-body/ a valuable lesson". There was a 25-year gap (1939-64) between publication of his first and second collections, and he continued to publish sporadically.

November 1, Brian Lenihan
Fianna Fail politican Lenihan held more cabinet posts in the Irish Republic than anyone else, attaining deputy prime minister before being sacked by Charles Haughey in 1990. This sacking followed "Dublingate" – revelations that Lenihan had lied in denying phone calls eight years earlier seeking a delay in the dissolution of parliament.

November 12, Sir Robert Stephens
Sir Robert was a versatile actor who found his true greatness in the major classics. He was a Falstaff who showed

the sad complexity beneath the roister-ing surface, and a towering King Lear in his last major role. He also gave a famous performance as Sherlock Holmes on Broadway.

December 2, Robertson Davies
Novelist, journalist, and teacher, Robertson Davies won widespread acclaim outside his native Canada. His fiction deals with moral conflict, and he was heavily influenced by the theories of Carl Jung. As a newspaper editor, he displayed a wry cynicism.

December 6, James Reston
One of the most respected US journal-ists, James Reston became a newspaper columnist in 1953. He set out to describe the ways of Washington so that the average American could understand how government worked.

December 22, James Meade
Meade was one of the great economists of the century, noteable for his contri-bution to the ideas associated with John Maynard Keynes. He created a method of assessing national income. In 1957 he became Professor of Political Economy at the University of Cambridge.

General Index

Page numbers in roman refer to main stories. Those in *italics* refer to brief stories in chronology panels.

A
Abacha, Sani, 93
Abbott, George, *14*
Adams, Gerry, 26, 52, 80, 105
Afghanistan
Government forces attack last rebel stronghold, 25
Army re-enters Kabul after driving out Taliban Islamic movement, *28*
Tajikistan border guards fired on from, 34
Aga Khan, 94
Agassi, André, *10*, 24, 78
AIDS
Patients to receive bone marrow from baboons, *20*
Boy born with virus is cured, *30*
Kenny Everett dies of, 32
Drug AZT not effective in full-blown AIDS, *70*
Aitken, Jonathan, 22, *28*, 31, *34*, *52*
Alderton, Graeme, *58*
Algeria
Government forces step up campaign against rebels, *30*
Zeroual wins presidential elections despite disruption threats, 99
Allen, Joan, 110
Altman, Robert, 27
America's Cup, 24
Amir, Yigal, 95
Amis, Martin, *4*, *6*, *30*
Amrollahi, Reza, 73
Ancram, Michael, 44
Andreotti, Giulio, *22*
Andrew, Rob, 53
Angola
Unita rebels accept peace treaty, *18*
Angus, Sir Michael, 53
Antarctica
Ozone hole widens, 67
Arafat, Yasser, 83
Argentina
President's son killed in helicopter crash, *26*
Army admits killing and torture during 'Dirty War', *40*
Carlos Menem re-elected as president, *46*
Pilot reports encounter with UFO, 67
First top-level contact with Britain since the Falklands War, *92*
Ex-SS captain extradited to face war crime trial, *102*
Aristide, Jean-Bertrand, 31, *56*, 70
Arts and entertainment
Ancient cave paintings discovered in France, 8
Anonymous buyer pays £18 million for Picasso, *44*
Controversial video withdrawn from sale, *104*
Damien Hirst wins Turner Prize, 104
Arts and entertainment (cinema)
Forrest Gump Golden Globe award, *10*
Golden Globe awards, *10*
Donald Pleasance dies, 14
Shepperton Studios take-over, *14*
Doug McClure dies, 16
Karl Lagerfeld stops showing of *Prêt à Porter*, 27
Dianne West wins Oscar for *Bullets Over Broadway*, 30
Forrest Gump gains six Oscars, 30
Jessica Lange wins Oscar for *Blue Sky*, 30
Martin Landau wins Oscar for *Ed Wood*, 30
Pulp Fiction wins Best Screenplay Oscar, 30
Burl Ives dies, 34
British Film and Television Academy Awards, 41
Dancer and actress Ginger Rogers dies, 41
Four Weddings and a Funeral wins five BAFTAs, 41
Actor Sir Michael Hordern dies, 43
Superman star Christopher Reeve injured in fall, 49
Film critic Dilys Powell dies, *50*
Dole's wife sells shares in Disney over *Priest*, 51
Disney's *Pocahontas* opens, 54
Actress Lana Turner dies, 57
Hugh Grant arrested on prostitute charge, 57
Hugh Grant makes TV confession, 61
Filming of *Rapture* suspended, 64
Ida Lupino dies, *66*
Phil Harris dies, *68*
New president of Disney, 70
Screenwriter Howard Koch dies, *70*
Macaulay Culkin sacks father, 83
Christopher Reeve appears in public, 91
Premiere of new James Bond film *GoldenEye*, 99
Director Louis Malle dies, 102
Arts and entertainment (literature)
Martin Amis and publishing rights to next novel, *4*
Martin Amis signs book deal, *6*
Gerald Durrell dies, *10*
Novelist Patricia Highsmith dies, *16*
Martin Amis's *The Information* published, *30*
Thatcher's autobiography *The Path to Power* lambasts Major, 47
Book claims Jack the Ripper was an American, *62*
Stephen Spender dies, 62
Brigid Brophy dies, *68*
Colin Powell promotes autobiography, 76
Seamus Heaney wins Nobel Prize for Literature, 85
Poet Gavin Ewart dies, *92*
Pat Barker wins Booker Prize, 97
Arts and entertainment (music)
Conductor Sir Alexander Gibson dies, *8*
Giacomo Puccini's illegitimate daughter inherits, *14*
Roxette play in Beijing, 20
Grammy awards, 22
Vivian Stanshall dies, *24*
Beatles to record new songs, 26
Burl Ives dies, 34
Tessie O'Shea dies, 36
Cliff Richard knighted, 52
Concert pianist Michelangeli dies, *52*
Michael Jackson apologises for anti-semitic lyrics, *54*
Lottery grant for Royal Opera House, *62*
Singer and composer Charlie Rich dies, *64*
Father of Jimi Hendrix wins rights to son's music, 65
Grateful Dead leader Jerry Garcia dies, 68
Guitarist Sterling Morrison dies, *76*
Album to aid Bosnian war victims goes to Number 1, *78*
Sting accuses acountant of theft, 82
Fan convicted of murder of Selena Perez, 93
Former manager of Led Zeppelin dies, *102*
Arts and entertainment (radio and television)
Comedian Larry Grayson dies, *4*
Satirist and comedian Peter Cook dies, 6
Doug McClure dies, 16
Red Dwarf star cleared of rape, 23
John Humphrys quoted on interviewing politicians, *28*
Newsreader Peter Woods dies, *28*
Comedian Kenny Everett dies, 31
BBC television interview with Major banned in Scotland, 33
TV star Chris Evans as Radio 1 DJ, 41
Murdoch submits bid for Channel 5 in Britain, *42*
Bewitched star Elizabeth Montgomery dies, 47
Film critic Dilys Powell dies, *50*
First British radio station aimed at women, *58*
Hugh Grant makes TV confession, 61
BBC correspondent shot dead in Bosnia, *68*
Football results announcer Len Martin dies, *72*
Larry Hagman gets liver transplant, 73
Michael Barrymore wins three National TV Awards, 74
Janet Street-Porter quits *Live TV*, *78*
Candice Bergen wins Emmy Award for *Murphy Brown*, 79
Coronation Street's Julie Goodyear to leave, 81
O.J. Simpson pulls out of TV interview, 89
Comedienne Marti Caine dies, *94*
Radio 2 bans Cliff Richard single, 95
Comedian Arthur Mullard dies, 109
Arts and entertainment (theatre)
Dispute between Andrew Lloyd Webber and Faye Dunaway settled, *8*
Donald Pleasance dies, 14
George Abbott dies, *14*
Plaque to Oscar Wilde unveiled in Westminster Abbey, *18*
Playwright Robert Bolt dies, *20*
Stephen Fry disappears, 21
Stephen Fry returns, *28*
Burl Ives dies, 34
Tessie O'Shea dies, 36
Actor Sir Michael Hordern dies, 43
Memorial service for John Osborne, *50*
Sunset Boulevard wins Tony Awards, 51
Actor Jeremy Brett dies, *78*
Sadler's Wells awarded £30 million from lottery funds, *90*
Stephen Fry says he considered suicide, *94*
Actor Sir Robert Stephens dies, *98*
Comedian Jimmy Jewel dies, *106*
Asahara, Shoko, 46, *50*, *84*
Ashby, David, *106*, 111
Ashdown, Paddy, *104*
Astrology
13th sign of the Zodiac discovered, *8*
Atherton, Mike, 74, 107
Athletics
Nine seconds knocked off world 10,000m record, 50
Diane Modahl wins drugs appeal, 64
Linford Christie collapses in World Athletics Championship final, 68
Jonathan Edwards beats record for triple jump, 69
Bannister says black athletes are best, 78
Atlantis (space shuttle), *56*
Aung San Suu Kyi, Daw, *10*
Australia
Opposition leader resigns, 10
Austria
British Aerospace involved in corrupt deal, 10
Votes fund for victims of Nazis, 50
Automobiles
New MG sportscar, 19
US to threaten Japan with sanctions over automobile market, 35
Learner drivers to take written test in Britain, 48
US–Japan agreement on automotive trade, *56*
Azerbaijan
Elections rigged by government officials, *98*

B
Baker, James, *82*
Balbagan, Sarah, 91
Balladur, Edouard, *20*, 21, 41, 52
Bangladesh
Protesters use blockades to bring country to standstill, *96*
Bannister, *Sir* Roger, 78
Barbieri, Paula, 94
Bardot, Bridget, *18*
Barker, Pat, 97
Barker, Paul, 65, *66*
Barloon, William, 63
Barre, Siad, *4*
Barry, Marion, 5
Barrymore, Michael, 74
Baseball
Union strike over salary arbitration, *30*
Basketball
Michael Jordan stages comeback, 29
Battenbough, Karen, *42*
Beatles, The, 26
Becker, Boris, 60
Belgium
Severe flooding, 14
NATO chief denies receiving bribes over helicopter contract, *20*
MPs send NATO head to trial, 90
Benn, Nigel, *20*
Bergen, Candice, 79
Berger, Gerhard, 30
Berlusconi, Silvio, *44*, 47, *88*, *102*
Bermuda
People vote against independence from Britain, *70*
Bertin, Mireille Durocher, 31
Bethlehem, 111
Betts, Leah, 98
Birt, John, 33
Black Magic (yacht), *46*
Blair, Tony, 22, 40, 43, *54*, 63, 70, *78*, 84, *108*
Blandford, Marquess of, 33, *34*
Blunkett, David, 34
Boesak, Dr. Allan, *16*
Bolger, Jim, 61
Bolt, Robert, *20*
Borel, Eric, 82
Bose, Satyendra, 61
Bosnia
New cease-fire begins, *4*
Bosnian Serb forces will not withdraw from Sarajevo, 6
Fighting continues around Bihac, 6
Teenage girls killed in Bihac, *8*
US embassy shows dissent about talks with Bosnian Serbs, *10*
Cease-fire violations threaten peace plan, 17
Heavy fighting around Bihac, *18*
Signs pact with Croatia against the Serbs, *24*
UN threatens air strikes against Bosnian Serbs, *30*
Government forces attack Serbs around Tuzla, *32*
Airlifted girl Irma Hadzimuratovic dies, 33
Serb mortar attack kills nine in Sarajevo, *44*
UN troops taken hostage for NATO air strikes, 49
Most UN hostages released, 50
Downed American pilot rescued, 51
More UN hostages released, *52*
Serbs free the last UN hostages, *54*
Nine civilians killed in Sarajevo, *56*
Serbs bombard Srebrenica, 58
Serbs overrun Srebrenica, 60
US prepared to send helicopters to Gorazde, 62
Thousands of Muslim refugees flee from Serbs, 63
Karadjic and Mladic formerly charged with war crimes, *64*
War looks set to escalate, *64*
British troops head for Bosnia, 65
Croatians take Knin, 67
BBC correspondent Schofield shot dead, *68*
Photos indicate mass graves at Srebrenica, 69
NATO bombs Serbs, 75
NATO air strikes against Serbs are suspended, *76*
NATO halts Serb bombing raids in new peace hopes, 79
UN Secretary General calls for withdrawwl of UN troops, *80*
US wins cease-fire, 85
Muslims and Croats besiege Banja Luka, 89
Milosevich, Tudjman and Izetbegovic arrive in US for peace talks, *92*
Milosevich, Tudjman and Izetbegovic start peace talks, 94
Peace negotiations begin in Ohio, 94
Peace plan agreed by three national leaders, 102
Karadzic warns that peace treaty will turn Sarajevo into 'new Beirut', *104*
Serbs in Sarajevo protest against peace plan, 104
French call for immediate release of hostage pilots, 107
Peace treaty signed in Paris, 109
Bottomley, Virginia, 17, 33
Bousquet, René, 96
Bowe, Riddick, *26*
Bowen, Jaymee, *92*
Boxing
McClellan has operation to remove blood clot on brain, *20*
Riddick Bowe may challenge Mike Tyson, *26*
Mike Tyson released from jail, 29
Tyson wins comeback fight, 71
Bruno takes World Heavyweight title, *76*
Promoter Don King accused of fraudulent insurance claims, *88*
James Murray 'clinically dead' after knockout, 89
James Murray dies from knockout blow, *90*
Brain, Chris, 72, *104*
Brando, Cheyenne, 36
Brando, Marlon, 36, 64
Branson, Richard, 109
Brassard, Pierre, 92
Braun, Eva, 43
Brazil
New president inaugurated, *4*
Drug pushers shot by police in Novo Brasilia, *44*
People feared dead after explosions at weapons base, *62*
Brent Spar (oil platform), 49, *52*, 55, *76*
Brett, Jeremy, *78*
Britannia (Royal Yacht), 66
Brittan, Leon 106
Brophy, Brigid, *68*
Brosnan, Pierce, 99
Brown, Divine, 57, 61, *62*
Brown, Frederick, *58*
Brown, Gordon, 47
Bruno, Frank, *76*
Bruton, John, 14, 102, 105
Burma
Aung San Suu Kyi no deal on house arrest, *10*
Incursion into Thailand, *18*
Last Karen guerilla stronghold falls, 21
Bursford, Bruce, 73
Burundi
Hutu refugees flee for Tanzania, *30*
Hutus massacred, *32*

C
Caine, Marti, *94*
Cairncross, John, *88*
Calment, Jeanne, *90*
Campbell, Cheyenne Ben Nighthorse, *22*
Canada
Spanish gunboat to protect trawlers off coast of, 25
Spanish trawlers return to contested fishing grounds, *26*
British people support Canada in fishing dispute, 35
Agreement reached in fishing dispute with Spain, 36
Quebec votes to stay in Canada, 93
Mulroney denies receiving kickbacks over aircraft sale, *98*
Cantona, Eric, 11, 85
Cardosa, Fernando H., *4*
Carling, Julia, 82
Carling, Will, 43, *44*, 82
Castro, Fidel, 93, *104*
Catton, Trevor, *70*
Challenger (channel ferry), 81
Charles, Craig, 23
Charles, Prince of Wales, *10*, 111
Charlton, Jack, 111
Chechnya
Russians pound Grozny in new offensive, 4
Presidential Palace captured, *8*
Russia criticized for human rights abuses, *14*
Russians seal off roads to Grozny, *14*
Leader states that only discussion can end the war, *28*
Russians claim capture of last Chechen stronghold, 37
Russian troops resume offensive, *46*
Chechen rebels take hostages in Russian hospital, 53
Rebels return after using hostages as human shields, *54*
Chen Ziming, *50*
Chernomyrdin, Viktor, 61, 109
Childs, John, 60
Chiluba, Frederick, 93
China
Deng Xiaoping's health in decline, *6*
Criticized for human rights abuses in Tibet, *14*
President calls for re-unification with Taiwan, 14
Trade war with US looms, 15
Swedish group Roxette play in Beijing, 20
Economic boom brought inflation, corruption and crime, *24*
Five-day working week for government employees, *30*
Japanese premier pledges everlasting peace, *42*
Conducts underground nuclear test, *46*
Democracy leader calls for release of political prisoners, *50*
CIA assertion of missile sales to Iran and Pakistan, *54*
China moves to curb free discusssion at World Conference on Women, *76*
Demands made at World Conference on Women, 79
To send uranium to Iran, *80*
Fidel Castro makes first official visit, *104*
Chirac, Jacques, 41, 44, 52, 77, 78, 92
Christie, Linford, 68
Christo, 55
Christopher, Warren, *42*, 62, 106
Churchill, Winston, *40*
Ciller, Tansu, *80*, *90*
Claes, Willy, *20*, 79, 90, 106
Clapton, Jonathan, 64
Clark, Alan, 54
Clark, Marcia, 86
Clarke, Kenneth, 26, 28, 65, 104
Clayton, Lisa, 57, *66*, *74*
Clegg, Lee, *8*, 59
Clinton, Bill
Authorises plan for Mexican economy, *10*
State of the Union address, *10*
Plan to bail out Mexican peso blocked, 14
New budget criticized, *16*
Controversial choice of Surgeon General, *18*
To celebrate VE celebrations in Moscow, *24*
Meets Gerry Adams at White House, 26
To visit Haiti, 31
Backs call for IRA to give up arms, *32*
Attends VE Day celebrations in Moscow, *44*
Nomination for Surgeon General blocked by Senate, 55
Backs right to religion in schools, *60*
Holds talks with Yeltsin over peace in Bosnia, 92
Addresses UN birthday celebrations, 93
Pays tribute at funeral of Yitzhak Rabin, 96
In budget dispute with Congress, 98
Turns on Christmas lights in Belfast, 105
Ends trip to Ireland in Dublin, *106*
Witnesses signing of Bosnian peace treaty, 109
Close, Glen, 51
Cochran, Jonnie L. (Jr), 74, 86, 87
Coe, Sebastian, *48*
Coetzer, Amanda, 73
Cole, Michael, 33
Colombia
Earthquake, *16*
Bomb kills people at music festival, *52*
Most Cali drug barons in jail, *68*
Kidnapped British student found dead, *70*
People killed in armed raids, *70*
Comoros Islands
Ask for French help against coup, *82*
Coup leader surrenders to French forces, *84*
Concorde (aircraft), 70
Condon, *Sir* Paul, 58, *66*
Conn, David, 88
Cook, Peter, 6
Cork, Dominic, 56
Cornell, Eric, 61
Coulthard, David, 30
Crenshaw, Bob, *34*
Cricket
Illingworth to be England manager, 24
Pakistan cricketer Imram Khan marries Goldsmith heiress, 46
England victory over West Indies, 56
Lancashire beats Kent to take Benson and Hedges Cup, *60*
England draw Test series against in West Indies, 74
Warwickshire win NatWest trophy, *76*
Mike Atherton in marathon innings, 107
Croatia
Signs pact with Bosnia against the Serbs, *24*
Withdraws demand for UN forces to leave, *26*
Zagreb shelled in fresh fighting with Serbs, 42
War looks set to escalate, *64*
Croatians take Knin, 67
Leader arrives in US for peace talks, *92*
Tudjman starts peace talks with Serbia and Bosnia, 94
Tudjman signs peace plan, 102
Croft, Sally-Anne, *56*
Crow, Sheryl, 22
Culkin, Macaulay, 83
Cunningham, Jack, 31
Curtin, Maggie, 33
Cycling
World speed record on stationary bike, 73

D
Dalai Lama, *46*
Daliberti, David, 63
Davies, Chris, 64
Davies, Liz, *82*
Davis, Peter, 109
Delors, Jacques, 9
Denard, Bob, *84*
Deng Xiaoping, *6*, 14, *20*, 80
Denmark
UN World Summit on Social Development opens, *24*
Study claims alcohol in moderation helps longevity, *42*
Desai, Maraji, *34*
Diana, Princess of Wales, 82, *106*, 111
Dickens, Geoffrey, 64
Didier, Christian, 96
Dini, Lamberto, *6*
Disasters
South african miners crushed by runaway locomotive, *44*
Department store collapses in Seoul, 56
Disasters (air)
British U-2 pilot killed in crash, *74*
Disasters (floods)
Severe flooding in California, 6
Rivers burst dykes in Netherlands, *10*
Across European Low Countries, 14
Disasters (natural)
Storms in California, 6
Earthquake in Japan, 9
Earthquake kills people in Columbia, *16*
Thousands feared dead in Russian earthquake, 48
Hurricane devastates island of St. Maarten, 76
At least 64 killed in earthquake in Ankara, *84*
Over 60 die in Mexican earthquake, 88
People dead following avalanches in Nepal, *98*
Disasters (sea)
Channel Island ferry hits rocks, 37
Ferry runs aground at Calais, 81
Disasters (train)
Hundreds killed in Indian train crash, 73
Discovery (space shuttle), 16
Dixon, Jeremy, 94
Dixon, Pauline, 48
Djilas, Milovan, 36
Docherty, Drew, 89

Dole, Bob, 5, *6*, 14, 22, 51
Donahue, Thomas, 32
Donaldson, Lord, *104*
Douglas-Home, *Sir* Alec (Lord Home), 88
Downer, Alexander, 10
Dreyfus, Alfred, 78
Drollet, Dag, 36
Dudayev, Dzhokhar, 4, 37
Dunaway, Faye, *8*
Duncan, Alan, 33
Durrell, Gerald, *10*
Dykes, Hugh, 33

E

Economist, The (magazine), 29
Ecuador
Fresh offensive from Peru, 10
Fighting flares with Peru, *16*
Ends border fighting with Peru, 19
Edwards, Jonathan, 69
Edwards, Martin, 11
Egypt
Deaths in gun battles in Mallawi, *4*
Plot to kill President Mubarak, *16*
Largest Egyptian tomb yet discovered, *46*
Attempt on Mubarak's life, 57
Tomb of Queen Nefertari is opened for visitors, 97
Pre-election purge on fundamentalist Muslim brotherhood, *102*
Einstein, Albert, 61
Eisner, Michael D., 70
Elena, Princess, 27
Elizabeth II, Queen of Great Britain
Visit to South Africa, 29
Attends VE Day celebrations, 45
Hoaxed by Canadian DJ, 92
Opens parliament, 99
Urges Prince Charles and Princess Diana to divorce, 111
Elizabeth, The Queen Mother, 45, *62*, 67, 99, *106*
Ellemann-Jensen, Uffe, 106
Europe
Blocks US in peso crisis, 14
European Union (EU)
British Euro-rebels renew attack on Major, 9
Delors steps down as president of European Commission, 9
Border controls removed between seven members, 29
Successful negotiations with Canada over fishing dispute, 36
British Cabinet prepares for Inter-Governmental Conference, 47
Date for single European currency postponed, *54*
Signs trade pact with Russia, *62*
Britain and Holland oppose oil embargo on Nigeria, *102*
Decides on 'Euro' as name for new currency, *108*
Evans, Chris, 41
Evans, Stewart, *62*
Evening Standard (newspaper), *70*
Everett, Kenny, 32
Ewart, Gavin, *92*

F

Fairburn, Sir Nicholas, *18*
Fangio, Juan Manuel, 63
Farrakhan, Louis, 91
Farrell, Mairead, 83
Farrkhan, Louis, *6*
Fashanu, John, 27, *64*
Faulkner, Gordon, *66*
Faulkner, Sharon, 71
Fayed, Ali, 22
Fayed, Mohammed, 22
Ferguson, Colin, *18*, *28*
Ferguson, Duncan, 88
Fishburn, Dudley, *64*
Fleiss, Heidi, 69
Fletcher, Keith, 24
Foot, Michael, *58*
Football (American)
San Francisco 49ers beat San Diego Chargers in Super Bowl, *10*
Football (European)
Cantona attacks fan, 11
Chelsea captain guilty of assault, *16*
Riot at England-Ireland match, 18
Arsenal manager Graham sacked, 21
Manchester United beat Ipswich Town 9–0, *22*
Dennis Wise sentenced to jail for assaulting taxi driver, *26*
Grobbelaar, Segers and Fashanu arrested on match-fixing allegations, 27
Liverpool beat Bolton to win Coca-Cola Cup, *32*
Man killed in mass brawl before FA Cup semi-final, *34*
Blackburn Rovers win Premier League Championship, *46*
Everton win FA Cup, 47
Three premiership players charged with fixing matches, *64*
BBC results announcer Len Martin dies, *72*
Cantona returns after ban, 85
Duncan Ferguson gaoled for assault, 88
Graham Taylor resigns as manager, *98*
Northern Ireland win in European Championship, *98*
Jack Charlton resigns as manager of Republic of Ireland team, 111
Forsyth, Michael, 90
Fortier, Michael, 69
Foster, Henry W. (Jnr), *18*, 55
France
Ancient cave paintings discovered, 8
Fall in road deaths, *14*
Severe flooding in northeast, 14
Discovery that early man used coal, 16
Eiffel Tower repainting, 17
Senior policeman resigns over wire-tapping, *20*
US citizens expelled for industrial espionage, 21
Transport strike brings chaos, *30*
Lyons mayor guilty of embezzlement, 36
Socialist presidential candidate Jospin wins first round, 41
Chirac elected president on second ballot, 44
To resume nuclear tests in Pacific, 52
National Front win three municipal elections, *54*
Four killed by Paris Metro bomb, 64
Concorde beats round-the-world speed record, 70
Paris nail bomb explodes, 71
Muslims arrested in police raids, 74
Commandos capture Greenpeace ships before nuclear tests, *76*
Greenpeace protest at nuclear tests is broken up, *76*
Runaway boy spends thousands at EuroDisney, 76
Carries out underground nuclear test in Pacific, 77
Army guarding Channel Tunnel entrance, *78*
Army officially absolves Dreyfus, 78
Nuclear tests to continue, 78
Ferry runs aground at Calais, 81
Boy shoots family and villagers before suicide, 82
Prepares to aid Comoros Islands in suppressing coup, *82*
Corruption charges levelled at Prime Minister Juppé, *84*
Conducts second nuclear bomb test, 85
Prime Minister Juppé found guilty of corruption, *88*
Public service workers go on strike across country, *88*
Longest-living human record beaten, *90*
Terrorist bomb explodes on underground train, *90*
Terrorist bomb-making factory discovered and Arab arrested, *94*
Trial of alleged assassin of René Bousquet starts, 96
Beaujolais wine goes on marketing exercise, *98*
Juppé wins support in National Assembly for welfare cuts, *98*
Public service workers join strike, 104
Riot police use tear gas against student protest, *104*
Talks to end rail strike collapse, 107
Pilots released by Bosnian Serbs arrive in Paris, *108*
Strikers return to work following concessions by prime minister, 108
Franquet, Jacques, *20*
Freeman, Bryan and David, 23
Fry, Stephen, 21, *28*, *94*
Fuhrman, Mark, 11, 26, 65, 74, 76, 86, 87
Fujimori, Alberto, 35

G

Gaddafi, Muammar, 11, *94*, 105
Galileo (space probe), 106
Garcia, Jerry, 68
Gardiner, Mark, 53
Gardner, Joy, *52*
Gaza Strip (see Palestinian Occupied Territories)
Gebresilasie, Haile, 50
Gee, Robert, 65, *66*
Georgia
Shevardnadze survives car-bomb assassination attack, 75
Shevardnadze wins presidential elections, 96
Germany
Man who stabbed Monica Seles goes on trial, *4*
Lockerbie bombing suspect freed, *8*
Severe flooding in northwest, 14
Metal workers preparing to strike, 17
Herzog makes reconciliation speech in Dresden, 19
Kohl accuses US over pollution at environment conference, 32
50th anniversary of Allied forces entering Belsen, 34
New evidence on Hitler's death, 43
Court ruling on East German spymasters, *48*
Shell petrol stations boycotted over Brent Spar plan, *52*
Artist and wife wrap Reichstag, 55
Forces to support UN peacekeepers in Balkans, *56*
IRA woman found guilty of bombing but released, *56*
Steffi Graf may quit Germany after tax raids on her home, *62*
Motor racing's Schumacher weds, *66*
Generals tried for 'shoot to kill' policy on Berlin Wall, *72*
Ruling on crucifixes in every Bavarian classroom, *72*
Ghali, Boutros Boutros, *80*
Ghalmi, Lamine, 76
Gibson
Sir Alexander, *8*
Giles, Carl, *74*
Gingrich, Marianne, *68*
Gingrich, Newt, 5, *8*, 14, *80*, 104
Goldman, Ronald, 11, 86, 87
Goldsmith, James, 46
Goldsmith, Jemima, 46
Golf
Crenshaw wins US Masters, *34*
Corey Pavin wins US Open, 55
Palmer plays last-ever round in British Open, 63
Europeans win Ryder Cup, 83
González, Felipe, 6, 32, *52*
Gonzalez, Pancho, 58
Goodyear, Julie, 81
Gould, Bryan, 70
Grade, Michael, *64*
Graf, Peter, 58, 66
Graf, Steffi, 58, *62*, 66
Graham, Billy, 38
Graham, George, 21
Grant, Bernie, 58
Grant, Hugh, *10*, 41, 57, 61, *62*
Grant, Peter, *102*
Grayson, Larry, *4*
Great Britain
Breakout from Parkhurst prison, 4
13th sign of the Zodiac discovered, *8*
Animal rights protesters arrested, *8*
Lord Kagan dies, *8*
Missing body in Lockerbie disaster, *14*
Tennis champion Fred Perry dies, 14
Animal rights protester killed by lorry carrying calves, 15
Funeral of animal rights protester Jill Phipps, *18*
Plaque to Oscar Wilde unveiled in Westminster Abbey, *18*
Man survives in snow-hole in Scotland, *20*
Three climbers found dead in Highlands, 24
Deputy governor of Bank of England resigns over affair, 29
Gummer reiterates policy on pollution control, 32
Unexploded German bomb is defused, *32*
British-born killer Nicky Ingram executed in US, 33
50th anniversary of Allied forces entering Belsen, 34
New national phone codes, 36
One of world's biggest diamonds to go on sale, 36
Child Support Agency reform cuts support payments, 37
Police raid uncovers £18 million in counterfeit, *40*
Winston Churchill archives bought with £12 million of lottery money, *40*
Dangerous smog levels in heatwave, 43
Metropolitan police to have body armour and CS gas, *44*
Murdoch apologizes for newspaper story about Earl and Countess Spencer, *44*
Sunday horse racing introduced, *44*
50th anniversary of VE Day celebrations, 45
Germaine Greer launches personal attack on *Guardian* writer, 46
Islington council censured over child abuse investigations, *48*
Greenpeace activists on Brent Spar oil rig brought ashore, 49
Church of England report rejects idea of people 'living in sin', *50*
Cornish fisherman claims Spanish trawler cut nets, 50
Scrabble player sues tournament officials, *50*
Asians riot in Bradford for two nights, 51
Police find US gold and silver deposit certificates, *52*
Record lottery winner unpopular, 53
Shell abandons plan to sink Brent Spar, 55
Suicide boy rescued from Beachy Head, 55
Effects of heatwave in Scotland, 57
Lisa Clayton sails round world, 57
Condon says most muggers are black, 58
Foxhunters injured by letter bomb, *58*
Man reburied after relatives battle over words on headstone, *58*
Photojournalist Bert Hardy dies, *58*
House sales hit new low, 60
Heatwave continues, 63
Three children murdered, 65
Egon Ronay criticizes service-station food, 66
Lottery millionaire to go to jail, 66
Man accused of supermarket 'trolley rage', *66*
Police operation to cut London street crime, *66*
Woman and daughter killed as motorist has heart attack, *66*
Countryside fire alert, 67
Yorkshire Water company seeks measures to conserve water, 69
British woman dies climbing K2, 71
Celebrations to mark VJ Day, 71
First drought order this year sanctioned, *72*
Notting Hill Carnival gets under way, *72*
Cartoonist Carl Giles dies, *74*
Stamps bought at car boot sale sold for thousands, *74*
Greenpeace apologizes to Shell over Brent Spar, *76*
Gummer moves to avert water cuts in Yorkshire, *76*
Red Arrows sponsorship agreement, *76*
Scotland Yard accused of allowing Yardie gangster to enter country, *78*
Yorkshire population urged restraint in using water, 81
Three IRA members shot in Gibraltar condemned by European Court, 83
Water restrictions to end of year possible, *84*
Astrologer Patric Walker dies, *88*
Spy John Cairncross dies, *88*
Home secretary defeats Labour motion that he should resign over Prison Service, *90*
Sadler's Wells awarded £30 million from lottery funds, *90*
Warmest October for 300 years, *92*
Manchester chosen for 2002 Commonwealth Games, *94*
Leah Betts dies after taking Ecstasy, 98
New Director-General of MI5, *102*
Headmaster killed by gang outside his school, 106
Ecstasy dealers found dead, 107
Riots in Brixton, 108
Great Britain (arts and entertainment)
Actor Donald Pleasance dies, 14
Shepperton Studios take-over, *14*
Stephen Fry disappears, 21
Beatles to record new songs, 26
Stephen Fry returns, *28*
Kenny Everett dies, 32
BBC television interview with Major banned in Scotland, 33
British Film and Television Academy Awards, 41
Four Weddings and a Funeral wins five BAFTAs, 41
TV star Chris Evans as Radio 1 DJ, 41
Murdoch submits bid for Channel 5, *42*
Actor Sir Michael Hordern dies, 43
Memorial service for John Osborne, *50*
Cliff Richard knighted, 52
First British radio station aimed at women, *58*
Covent Garden Opera House to receive grant from lottery, *62*
Stephen Spender dies, 62
Coronation Street's Julie Goodyear to leave, 81
Sting accuses acountant of theft, 82
Stephen Fry says he considered suicide, *94*
Radio 2 bans Cliff Richard single, 95
Great Britain (disasters)
Channel Island ferry hits rocks, 37
Great Britain (economy and industry)
Saatchi forced out of his advertising agency, 5
Rumbelows closes, *16*
Boardroom pay rockets for PowerGen bosses, 17
Barings' office revealed it warned bank HQ of Leeson's trading, *22*
Dillons bookshops go into receivership, *22*
Tiny Rowland forced out of Lonrho, *22*
Retail sales have slowed, *36*
National Grid chairman gets share windfall, 47
Electricity Board chief receives pay award, *48*
British Airways board members get huge salary package, 53
National strike by train drivers, *60*
Six Co-op executives gaoled for fraud, *66*
Electricity-water merger talks, 77
Eurotunnel's banks freeze interest payments on loans, *78*
Nuclear Electric fined over safety procedures, *78*
Building society accused of depressing housing market, *80*
Vast dividend entitlements for National Grid directors, 82
Leading book publishers to cease setting minimum prices, 83
Eurotunnel announces six-monthly losses, *84*
Businessman boasts to Tory Conference of paying £1 an hour, *88*
Linda McCartney veggie burgers recalled, 91
Asprey the royal jeweller's is bought, *94*
Japanese investors buy one third of British trains, *96*
Vauxhall workers to strike for better pay offer, *102*
British Energy abandons plans to build nuclear power stations, 108
Richard Branson alleges dirty tricks in bids for National Lottery, 109
Great Britain (education)
Oxford University drops entrance exam, *14*
David Blunkett jostled at NUT conference, 34
Many teachers have poor grasp of three Rs, *42*
First head girl for Rugby School, *52*
Millions to be spent reviving sport in schools, *60*
College head suspended for sexual harrassment, 74
Man goes back to school posing as schoolboy, 81
School gives pupils alarm clocks, *84*
Newsreader heads campaign to improve English in schools, *88*
Survey shows fall in reading ability of 11-year-olds, *104*
Gillian Shephard calls for review of security in schools following fatal stabbing of headmaster, 106
Great Britain (finance)
Barings Bank collapses: Leeson disappears, 21
Barings' Singapore office warned of Leeson's trading, *22*
Dutch Bank ING to buy Barings for £1, *24*
Lloyd's names win right to £500 million, *40*
Former chairman and deputy of Barings both resign, *32*
Endowment mortgages more risky and expensive than repayment mortgages, *40*
Legal aid budget to be capped, *46*
Plans for tax on share options to be dropped, 65
Bank awards damages for lending money before housing market collapse, *76*
British workers in Germany claim dole in Britain, *78*
Clarke announces new £2 coin, *106*
Great Britain (foreign policies)
US intelligence that Iran paid for Lockerbie, 11
Aitken denies 'arms to Iran' contract, 31
Calls for Britain to back Spain in fishing dispute, *32*
Cornwall supports Canada in fishing dispute with Spain, 35
Heseltine orders enquiry into Iranian arms deals, *52*
Accusation made to government over 'arms to Iraq', 54
British troops head for Bosnia, 65
Top-level contact with Argentina at UN, *92*
Britain and Holland oppose plan for oil embargo on Nigeria, *102*
Great Britain (health)
Nurses reject pay offer, *18*
Injured man flown from London to Leeds, 25
Boy born with AIDS virus is cured, *30*
Parents should have been informed that artery operations were dangerous, 32
Airlifted Bosnian girl Irma Hadzimuratovic dies in London, 33
Cancer victim spent nine hours on trolley, 33
51-year-old woman has test-tube baby, *34*
Woman in coma has caesarean section, *42*
Nurses vote to end no-strike rule, *46*
Surgeon saves passenger's life on flight, 48
Baby dies after being taken to four hospitals in eight hours, *52*
Parents to sue over wire left in baby, 64
Pigs' hearts to be used in transplants, 79
Record deaths in 1994 from human equivalent of 'mad cow disease', *84*
Health scare over contraceptive pill, 90
Banning order lifted on naming child leukaemia sufferer, *92*
Siamese twins born in London, *96*
School in Lincoln closed due to meningitis outbreak, *102*
Government bans sale of beef from cows' backbone, *104*
Beef sales drop after 'mad cow disease' scare, *106*
Doctors warn that royal jelly health supplements may harm asthmatics, 109
Safe drinking levels are raised, 109
Great Britain (justice)
Alleged serial killer Frederick West hangs himself, 5
Parkhurst jailbreakers caught, 7
Private Lee Clegg has appeal rejected, *8*
Police officers at Hillsborough disaster to receive compensation, *14*
Virginia Bottomley receives summons to appear in court, 17
Woman charged with abducting Lydia Owens in Prestatyn, *18*
Ronnie Kray dies, 27
Girls found guilty of mugging Liz Hurley, 29
Fixed rate of compensation for victims of violence illegal, *32*
Blandford held on drugs charges, 33
Aitken to sue *The Guardian* newspaper for libel, *34*
Blandford gaoled for drug theft, *34*
Hillsborough Disaster police officers have claims dismissed, *34*
Suicidal overworked junior doctor gets compensation, *40*
Scotland Yard clerical officer jailed for stealing funds, *46*
Couple jailed for lying about minor traffic accident, 47
Robert Maxwell's sons on trial for fraud, *48*
High Court judge upholds ban on homosexuals in armed forces, *50*
Kevin Maxwell does not think father committed suicide, *50*
Police acquitted of manslaughter of Joy Gardner, *52*
Man sentenced for killing his children in a house fire, *58*
Paranoid schizophrenic receives life sentences, *58*
Woman freed after conviction changed to manslaughter of boyfriend, *58*
Man charged with murder of two boys, *66*
Woman charged with murdering student near RAF base, *78*
Rosemary West murder trial starts, 84
Duncan Ferguson gaoled for assault, 88
Policewomen found guilty of drugs charges, *88*
Rosemary West often had casual sex in her home, *88*
Former director general of prisons sues for wrongful dismissal, 90
Julia Sommerville arrested over child photograph, *94*
Rosemary West trial hears taped confession from Frederick West, *94*
Man jailed for planting computer viruses, *98*
Ban threatened on 'cheque-book journalism' following Rosemary West trial, *102*
Guinness trial defendants lose appeal, *104*
Police charge Harrods blackmailers, *108*
Great Britain (literature)
Martin Amis and publishing rights to next novel, *4*
Martin Amis signs book deal, *6*

Gerald Durrell dies, *10*
Martin Amis's *The Information* published, *30*
Thatcher's autobiography *The Path to Power* out next month, 47
Great Britain (politics)
Euro-rebels attack Major, 9
Plans for joint North-South Irish authority causes alarm, *10*
Banning orders excluding Irish Republicans begin to be lifted, *18*
Sir Nicholas Fairburn dies, *18*
Framework peace document for N. Ireland approved, *20*
Lilley admits crime may be linked to poverty and unemployment, *20*
Lamont supports Labour in Commons vote, 22
Minister resigns over affair, 24
Kenneth Clarke makes gaffe on radio, 26
Major refusing to enter into talks with Sinn Fein, 26
Kenneth Clarke accused of undermining Major, 28
Clinton and Major call on IRA to give up arms, *32*
Two 'Cash for questions' Tories suspended, 36
Blair wins vote to rewrite Clause 4 of party constitution, 40
Letter bombs sent to William Waldegrave and Tom King, *40*
Party whip restored to Euro rebels, 41
Labour has huge gains in local elections, 43
Ministers in first Sinn Fein meeting for 23 years, 44
Nolan report recommends stringent controls for MPs, 44
Nolan committee barred from examining party donations, 46
Thatcher's autobiography criticizes Major over Europe, 47
Former Prime Minister Lord Harold Wilson dies, 48
MP apologizes for putting down a motion in Sebastian Coe's name, *48*
Scottish National Party wins by-election, *48*
Waldegrave accused of lies to Parliament, *50*
Gerry Adams pulls Sinn Fein from peace talks, 52
Heseltine orders enquiry into Iranian arms deals, *52*
Blair suspends Scottish Labour group, *54*
Douglas Hurd to stand down as foreign secretary, *54*
Major resigns as Conservative leader, 54
Major challenged by Redwood for Tory leadership, 56
Michael Foot receives damages for suggestions that he was a KGB agent, *58*
Heseltine becomes deputy prime minister, 59
Major wins leadership election, 59
Tory MPs vote against revealing outside earnings, *62*
Blair makes pro-competition speech, 63
Liberal Democrats win by-election, 64
MP to resign after finding job too demanding, *64*
Newspaper prints wrong anti-Blair story, 70
Blair at TUC conference, *78*
Leaked document about shortage of funds for education, *78*
Government to recompense MPs for night work, *80*
Downing Street cat returns after being presumed dead, *82*
Prospective Labour candidate rejected for being too left wing, *82*
Blair announces deal with British Telecom, 84
Jack Straw loses seat on National Executive, *84*
Lamont rejected for new constituency, 84
Tory MP Howarth defects to Labour, 84
Former Prime Minister Lord Home dies, *88*
Portillo makes anti-European speech at Tory conference, 88
Bill protecting victims of domestic violence abandoned, *94*
MPs to reveal outside earnings, 97
MP Mawhinney pelted by demonstrators, 99
Modern designs for Ludlow supermarket turned down, *102*
Chancellor makes modest tax cuts in budget, 104
Howard attacked by former Master of the Rolls, *104*
Poll reveals defence is only issue on which Conservatives lead Labour, *108*
Sale of five rail franchises declared illegal, *108*
Death of Tory MP leaves Government majority of three, *108*
Great Britain (radio and television)
Larry Grayson dies, *4*
John Humphries quoted on politicians, *28*
Newsreader Peter Woods dies, *28*
Great Britain (religion)
Dean of Lincoln cleared of adultery, 62
Rave priest suspended, 72
Sun Myung Moon withdraws application for a visa, *94*
Rave priest admits sexual misconduct, *104*
Great Britain (Royal Family)
Camilla Parker Bowles to divorce, 7
Prince of Wales to sue former housekeeper, *10*
Queen to visit South Africa, 29
Present at British VE Day celebrations, 45
Group Captain Peter Townsend dies, *54*
Queen Mother recovering after cataract operation, *62*
Royal Yacht Britannia to go on sale, 66
Queen Mother's 95th birthday, 67
Prince Philip makes outspoken comment in Oban, *68*
Media reminded to respect Prince William's privacy at Eton, *72*
Princess Diana blamed for Carling's split with wife, 82
Queen hoaxed by Canadian DJ, 92
Queen Mother undergoes hip replacement operation, 99
Queen opens parliament, 99
Princess Diana tells of hospital trips to comfort the dying, *106*
Queen Mother leaves hospital, *106*
Baggage-handler arrested for stealing Duchess of York's jewellery, *106*
Crowns belonging to George I and George IV face export threat, 107
Queen urges Prince Charles and Princess Diana to divorce, 111
Great Britain (science and technology)
Arctic flowering plants prove global warming, *28*
Scientists closer to cure for baldness, *62*
Ozone hole over Antarctica widens, 67
Great Britain (sports) see each individual sport
Great Britain (transport)
New MG sportscar, 19
Plans for 14-lane M25 scrapped, 31
Anti-motorway protesters in tree-top battle, 42
West Highland sleeper train service is saved, *44*
Learner drivers to take written test, 48
First sponsored London Underground train, *54*
Eight die in coach crash, *58*
Tank driver guilty of careless driving in streets, *72*
Variable speed limits for part of M25, *74*
Railtrack has to correct train timetables, *82*
Over 50 per cent fare increase on overcrowded railway line, *88*
Skye bridge opens, 90
Freezing fog causes 100-car pile-up on M1, *108*
Greece
Traffic ban in part of Athens, *35*
Two killed in terrorist bomb blast in Athens, 36
Newspaper prints nude pictures of Papandreou's wife, *82*
Police overpower air hijacker, *96*
Greenpeace, 49, 61, *76*
Greenspan, Alan, 14
Greer, Germaine, 46
Griffiths, Nigel, 77
Grobbelaar, Bruce, 27, *64*
***Guardian**, The* (newspaper), 22, *34*, 46
Gucci
Maurizio, 31
Gummer, John, 32, *72*, *76*, *102*

H

Hadzimuratovic, Irma, 33
Hagan, Susan, *56*
Hagman, Larry, 73
Haiti
Presidential opponent assassinated, 31
Elections questionable as President hails them a success, 56
Elections take place, 70
Hall, *Sir* Peter, 50
Hallowes, Odette, *26*
Hanks, Tom, *10*, 30
Hardy, Bert, *58*
Hargreaves, Alison, 71
Harriman, Pamela, 21
Harris, Phil, *68*
Hatfield, Mark, 22
Hawley, Robert, 108
Health
New way to destroy cancer, *6*
AIDS patients to be given marrow from baboons, *20*
New cancer gun, 29
Boy born with AIDS virus is cured, *30*
Parents should have been told that artery operations were dangerous, 32
British cancer victim spent nine hours on trolley, 33
51-year-old woman has test-tube baby, *34*
Alcohol in moderation helps longevity, *42*
Woman in coma has caesarean section, *42*
Ebola virus outbreak in Zaire, 44
British nurses vote to end no-strike rule, *46*
More Ebola virus deaths, *48*
Surgeon saves passenger's life on flight, 48
Propensity to smoke could be genetic, 51
Polio vaccine discoverer Jonas Salk dies, *54*
US doctor suspended for cutting off patient's toe, *62*
British parents to sue over wire left in baby, 64
Pigs' hearts to be used in transplants, 79
Nancy talks of Ronald Reagan's Alzheimer's, 83
Record deaths in 1994 from human equivalent of 'mad cow disease', *84*
Scare over contraceptive pill, 90
Breast cancer gene found, 94
Siamese twins born in London, *96*
School in Lincoln closed due to meningitis outbreak, *102*
Government bans sale of beef from cows' backbone, *104*
Beef sales drop after 'mad cow disease' scare, *106*
Doctors warn that royal jelly health supplements may harm asthmatics, 109
Safe drinking levels are raised, 109
Heaney, Seamus, 85
Heaney, Steven, *66*
Hendrix, Al, 65
Herro, David, 5
Herzog, Roman, 19
Heseltine, Michael, *52*, 59
Hickson, Paul, *82*
Hide, Herbie, *26*
Highsmith, Patricia, *16*
Hill, Damon, 23, 30, 92
Hinchcliffe, Martin, 55
Hirst, Damien, 104
Hitler, Adolf, 43
Holbrooke, Richard, 79, 85, 102
Home, Lord, *88*
Hong Kong
Companies suspend trading on Stock Exchange after chairman arrested, *20*
Vietnamese boat people riot against repatriation, 50
Pro-democracy candidates win victory in elections, 80
Call rejected for British passport holders to be allowed into Britain, *82*
Hook, Sophie, 65
Hope, Dr. David, *34*
Hopkins, Anthony, 110
Hordern, Sir Michael, 43
Horse Racing
Sunday racing introduced in Britain, *44*
Red Rum is buried, 90
Howard, John, 10
Howard, Michael, *32*, *82*, 90, *90*, *104*
Howarth, Alan, 84
Hughes, Robert, *24*
Humphreys, Emma, *58*
Humphrys, John, *28*
Hungary
Prepares for civil service strikes, *96*
Hurd, Douglas, *54*
Hurley, Elizabeth, 29, 61
Hussein
King of Jordan, *30*
Hussein, Saddam, *8*, 63, *68*, 89, 91
Hussein, Uday, 89
Hutchings, Donald, 60

I

Illingworth, Ray, 24
India
Ruling Congress party faces defeat in Maharastra, *16*
Former prime minister Maraji Desai dies, *34*
Guerilla seige ended at Islamic shrine in Kashmir, 44
People die in violent protests against government, *48*
People die in hottest weather this century, *54*
Tigers protected in 'tiger state', *56*
Hostages taken by Kashmiri rebels, 58
American hostage escapes Kashmiri rebels, 60
Kashmiri separatists kill Norwegian hostage, *70*
Hundreds killed in train crash, 73
School fire kills 300, 110
Ingram, Nicky, 33
Iran
Secret deal to free Lockerbie bombing suspect, *8*
US intelligence claims Iran paid for Lockerbie bombing, 11
Oilfield deal with Conoco blocked in US, *26*
Britain's Aitken denies 'arms to Iran' contract, 31
Bans satellite TV dishes, 36
Accused of trying to develop nuclear weapons, *42*
Britain orders enquiry into arms to Iran, *52*
CIA assertion of Chinese missile sales to, *54*
Men charged with embezzlement from banks, *66*
To get nuclear reactors from Russia, 73
To get uranium from China, *80*
Iraq
Air Force officers executed, *8*
UN to maintain sanctions against, *26*
Americans who strayed into Iraq sentenced for spying, *28*
Turkey withdraws troops, *40*
Further Turkish troop withdrawal, *42*
Releases two Americans who strayed into Iraq, 63
Hussein's daughters flee to Jordan with their husbands, *68*
US sends equipment to Gulf in case of invasions by, *70*
Planned to invade Saudi Arabia after Kuwait, *82*
Saddam Hussein burns son's cars, 89
Saddam Hussein re-elected, 91
Ireland, Republic of
Cash robbery from security depot, *10*
Riot at England-Ireland football match, 18
Former foreign minister Brian Lenihan dies, *94*
Police discover bomb south of border, *96*
Major and Bruton fail to agree talks, 102
Clinton visit, *106*
Isles, Donald, 31
Israel
Israelis accidentally kill three Palestinian policemen, *4*
Suicide bomb attacks by Islamic Jihad, 10
Security forces shoot three Hamas fighters in Hebron, 36
250 Palestinian prisoners to be freed, 44
Retreats on Jerusalem land annexation, 49
Arabs killed in protest over Palestinian prisoners, *56*
To seek extradition of leading Hamas member from US, *64*
Settlers clash with police on West Bank, 66
Bus bombing in Jerusalem, 72
To give Palestinians autonomy in the West Bank, 83
Six soldiers killed by Hezbollah guerillas, *90*
Start of process to end Israeli military rule in Palestinian West Bank, *92*
Rabin assassinated after call for peace, 95
Funeral of Yitzhak Rabin, 96
Peres appointed prime minister, 99
Italy
Lamberto Dini agrees to be new prime minister, *6*
Mafia's first 'godmother' arrested, *16*
Mummified man in Alps to go on display, *18*
Former prime minister charged with belonging to Mafia, *22*
Maurizio Gucci shot dead, 31
Freedom Front Party suffer in local elections, *44*
Prosecutors apply to bring Berlusconi to trial, 47
Former prime minister Berlusconi to stand on corruption charges, *88*
Berlusconi to stand trial for embezzlement and false accounting, *102*
Ito, Lance A. (Judge), 11, *42*, *70*, 74, 87
Ives, Burl, 34
Izetbegovic, Alija, *92*, 94, 102, 109

J

Jackson, Jesse, *80*
Jackson, Michael, *54*
Jaganjac, Eno, 33
James, Gerald, 31
Japan
Earthquake devastates Kobe, 9
Arguments over whether to apologize for World War II, *24*
Gangsters arrested for profiteering from Kobe earthquake, 27
Nerve gas attack on Tokyo subway, 28
Tokyo and Mitsubishi Banks to merge, *30*
Top policeman shot follwing warnings, *30*
Sect threatens Tokyo disaster, 34
Voters choose TV personalities for city governorships, *34*
US sanctions over automobile market, 35
Aum cult suspected of further gas attack in Japan, 36
'Justice minister' of Aum cult arrested in connection with gas attacks, *42*
Premier pledges everlasting peace on Chinese visit, *42*
Aum cult man confesses to making nerve gas, *44*
Sect leader arrested on suspicion of organizing gas attack, 46
Cult charged with Tokyo gas attack, *50*
Expresses remorse over World War II, 50
Police storm airliner hijacked by Aum sect member, 55
Reaches agreement with US on automotive trade, *56*
Renewed spate of gas attacks, 58
Hiroshima remembers the A-bomb, 68
Reiterates remorse on VJ Day, 71
Largest credit union collapses, 75
Leader of Aum cult confesses to Tokyo gas attack, *84*
Compensation offered to victims of mass mercury poisoning, *96*
Jefferies, David, 47, 82
Jewel, Jimmy, *106*
Jiang Zemin, 14
John Paul II, Pope, 4, 7, 37, *60*, *84*, 113
Johnson, David T., 69
Jones, Sir Gordon, *76*
Jordan
King requests US Congress write off Jordan's national debt, *30*
Jospin, Lionel, 41, 44
Juan Carlos, King of Spain, 27, *52*, *96*
Juppé, Alain, *84*, *98*, 104, 108

K

Kagan, Lord, 8
Karadzic, Radovan, *40*, *64*, 79, *104*
Katzenberg, Jeffrey, 70
Kazakhstan
At least 28 killed in gas explosion, *96*
Kennedy, Mr. Justice, 47
Kennedy, Rose, 10
Kerry, Peter, 20
Khaddafi (Gaddafi), Muammar, 11, *94*
Khan, Imran, 46
King, Don, *88*
King, Tom, *40*
Kissinger, Henry, *52*
Koch, Howard, *70*
Kohl, Helmut, 32, 109
Kraft, Hermann, 10
Krajisnik, Momcilo, 112
Kray, Ronnie, 27
Kreuger, Robert, *32*
Kulikov, Anatoly, 37
Kuwait
Possible invasion by Iraq, *70*
Kwasniewski, Aleksander, *96*, 102

L

Lagerfeld, Karl, 27
Lamont, Norman, 22, 84
Landau, Martin, 30
Lander, Stephen, *102*
Lange, Jessica, 30
Laos
Prince Souphanouvong dies, *6*
Lawrence, Philip, 106
Le Pen, Jean-Marie, 41
Lean, Rachel, *78*
Lee, Brandon, 81
Leeson, Nick, 21, *22*, *32*, 107
Lenihan, Brian, *94*
Lewis, Derek, 90
Li Peng, *24*
Libai, David, 44
Liberia
Peace celebrations in the streets, *74*
Libya
Claims reasserted that Libya involved with Lockerbie bombing, 11
To deport over a million Africans, *90*
Permission for World War II veterans to enter Libya withdrawn, *94*
Lightbown, Sir David, *108*
Lilley, Peter, *20*
Listyev, Vladislav, *22*
Livingstone, Ken, 33
Lloyd Webber, Sir Andrew, *8*, 51
Lomu, Jonah, 55
Lopez, Rosa, *18*, 87
Lubbers, Ruud, 106
Lunn, David, 72
Lupino, Ida, *66*
Luxembourg
Date for single European currency postponed, *54*
Lyell, Sir Nicholas, *102*
Lynn, Vera, 45

M

McCall, Oliver, 76
McCann, Daniel, 83
McCartney, Linda, 91
McCartney, Paul, 26
McClellan, Gerald, *20*
McClure, Doug, 16
McDonald, Trevor, *88*
MacDonell, Herbert, 65
Mackay, Lord, *46*
MacKinnon, Brian, 81
McNamara, Robert, *34*
McNaughton, William, 31
McNeeley, Peter, 71
McVeigh, Timothy J., 38, 40, *60*, 69, *70*
Maguire, Donna, *56*
Major, John
Vows to resist erosion of sovereignty in Europe, 9
Makes TV plea to people of Ulster, 14
Reported Mohammed Fayed to DPP, 22
Refusing to enter into talks with Sinn Fein, 26
Call for IRA to give up arms, *32*
BBC television interview banned in Scotland, 33
Restores party whip to Euro rebels, 41
Street riots on visit to Londonderry, 42
Authority questioned after Labour gain in local elections, 43
Attends VE Day celebrations in Moscow, *44*
Prevents Nolan committee examining party donations, 46
Criticized over Europe in Thatcher's autobiography, 47
Pays tribute to Harold Wilson, 48
Resigns as Conservative leader, 54
Supports Shell over Brent Spar, 55
Challenged by Redwood for Tory leadership, 56
Wins leadership election, 59
New Ulster Unionist leader poses new threat to, 77
Has top-level contact with Argentinian president, *92*
Supports French nuclear tests, 92
Fails to agree with Ireland over peace process, 102
Meets Irish PM to end disagreements over Northern Ireland peace talks, 105
Witnesses signing of Bosnian peace treaty, 109
Malaysia
Runaway London boy found, 20
Malcolm X, *6*
Malle, Louis, 102
Mandela, Nelson, 8, 18, 22, 31, 52, 56
Mandela, Winnie, 18, 22, 31, *90*
Mangan, Keith, 60
Manning, Anne, *68*
Marcano, Jacqueline Aguilera, 98
Marcos, Imelda, 30
Margaret, Princess, 45, *54*
Marizzi, Peter, 10
Marshall, *Sir* Colin, 53
Martin, Dean, 112
Martin, Janet and Jasmina, *66*
Martin, Len, *72*
Marzook, Mousa Mohamed Abu, *64*
Mawhinney, Brian, 31, 99
Maxwell, Ian (son of Robert), *48*
Maxwell, Kevin (son of Robert), *48*, *50*
Maxwell, Robert, *48*, *50*
Mayhew, Sir Patrick, 52, *72*
Menem, Carlos Facundo, *26*, 46, *92*
Menendez, Erik and Lyle, 88
Mexico
Peso unstable threatening trade links with US, *4*
Riots against financial crisis, *6*
Financial markets fall after US fails to support peso, *8*
Clinton authorises rescue plan for economy, *10*
Europe blocks US in peso crisis, 14
New austerity measures from government, 25
Ex-president Salinas denies exile, *26*
Plans for new round of privatization, 51
Smog not caused by car exhaust, 70
Over 60 die in earthquake, 88

Michelangeli, Arturo Benedetti, *52*
Milosevic, Slobodan, 17, 50, *92*, 94, 102, 104, 109
Mir (space station), 16, *56*
Mitchell, George, 105
Mitchell, Jason, *58*
Mitterand, François, 52
Mkapa, Benjamin, *102*
Mladic, Ratko, 6, *40*, 49, *64*, 79
Modahl, Diane, 64
Modjeski, Leland William, 49
Molyneaux, James, *74*
Montgomery, Elizabeth, 47
Moore, Keith, 82
Moore, Suzanne, 46
Moore, Vicki, *62*
Morris, John, 89
Morrison, Sterling, *76*
Morrison, Van, 105
Motor Racing
Damon Hill banned for speeding, 23
Schumacher disqualified after winning Brazilian Grand Prix, 30
Juan Manuel Fangio dies, 63
Schumacher weds, *66*
Schumacher retains world title in Pacific Grand Prix, 92
Mountaineering
British woman climber dies on K2, 71
Mubarak, Hosni, *16*, 57
Mugniyeh, Imad, *36*
Muir, Jean, *48*
Mullard, Arthur, 109
Mulroney, Brian, *98*
Murayama, Tomiichi, *42*
Murdoch, Rupert, *8*, *42*, *44*, *54*, 63, *80*
Murray, Gilbert, 41
Murray, James, 89, *90*
Murray, Malcolm, 25

N

Nadir, Asil, 46
NATO (North Atlantic Treaty Organization)
NATO chief denies receiving bribes over helicopter contract, *20*
Air strikes against Bosnian Serbs, 49
Serbs release UN hostages captured following NATO airstrikes, 50
NATO planes destroy Serb tanks attacking Srebrenica, 60
NATO bombs Bosnian Serbs, 75
Air strikes against Serbs suspended, *76*
Bombing raids halt Serbs in new peace hopes, 79
Belgian MPs send NATO head to trial, 90
NATO troops to oversee Bosnian peace plan, 102
Spanish foreign minister to be new Secretary-General, 106
Nefertari
Queen, 97
Nemtsov, Boris, 55
Nepal
People dead following avalanches, *98*
Netherlands, The
Rising rivers burst dykes, *10*
State of emergency due to floods, 14
Tribunal names Karadzic and Mladic as war crimes suspects, *40*
Karadic and Mladic charged with war crimes, *64*
New York Times (newspaper), 41, 81
New Zealand
Wins America's Cup, *46*
French seize Rainbow Warrior II, 61
Newell, Mike, 41
News of the World (newspaper), *44*
Newton, Trevor, 81
Nichols, James D. and Terry, 40
Nichols, Terry, 38, 69, *70*
Nidal, Abu, 11
Nigeria
Report that government killing Ogoni people, *28*
Ken Saro-Wiwa sentenced to death, 93
Ken Saro-Wiwa executed, 96
Britain and Holland oppose EU oil embargo plan, *102*
Nixon, Paul, *34*
Noir, Michael, 36
Nolan, Lord, 44, 46
Norris, Steven, 48
North Korea
US sanctions lifted and trade pact agreed, *8*
Northern Ireland
End of daylight patrols in Belfast, 6
Plans for joint North-South Irish authority causes alarm, *10*
John Major makes TV plea to people of Ulster, 14
UK begins to lift banning orders excluding Irish Republicans, *18*
House of Commons approves framework peace document, *20*
Street riots as Major visits Londonderry, 42
Ministers in first Sinn Fein meeting for 23 years, 44
Gerry Adams pulls Sinn Fein from peace talks, 52
IRA woman found guilty of bombing in Germany but released, *56*
Riots after paratrooper Lee Clegg is released, 59
Protestant march ends in violence, 60
Troubles flare on anniversary of cease-fire, *68*
Troop withdrawals promised, *72*
Ulster Unionist Molyneaux to retire, *74*
First anniversary of cease-fire, 75
New Ulster Unionist leader, 77
Adams warns peace process is doomed, 80
IRA refuse to hand over weapons, *82*
Shooting of three IRA members in Gibraltar condemned by European Court, 83
Bill Clinton turns on Christmas lights in Belfast, 105
Former US senator to chair international commission, 105

O

O'Grady, Scott, 51
O.J. Simpson trial
Trial opens, 11
Key witness quits the country, *18*
O.J. Simpson's book a bestseller, 18
Detective to be quizzed on racism, 26
Prosecution witness ruled 'hostile', *30*
Juror excused, *42*
Results of DNA tests, *44*
Simpson struggles to fit incriminating gloves, 52
Lawyers argue that sock and glove were part of frame-up, 65
Calls for Judge to withdraw so his wife can give evidence, *70*
Judge rules on Fuhrman tapes, 74
Detective Fuhrman pleads the Fifth Amendment, 76
O.J. will not testify in own defence, *80*
Final summing up, 82
Tape played of O.J.'s wife calling police for help, *82*
Jury declares O.J. not guilty, 85
An overview, 86–7
O.J. pulls out of TV interview, 89
O.J.'s girlfriend calls it off, 94
Olechowski, Andrzej, *6*
oneAustralia (yacht), *24*
Orejuela, Miguel Rodriguez, *68*
Ortiz, Guillermo, 25
Osborne, John, *50*
O'Shea, Tessie, 36
Ovitz, Michael, 70
Owens, Lydia, *18*

P

Paisley, Ian, 105
Pakistan
Sectarian fighting and deaths in Karachi, *18*
Blasphemy charges against boy and uncle are dropped, *20*
People killed by car bomb during fighting between Muslims, *24*
Cricketer Imran Khan marries Goldsmith heiress, 46
CIA assertion of Chinese missile sales to, *54*
Palestinian Occupied Territories
Accidental bomb explosion kills eight in Gaza, 32
Suicide bombers kill seven in Gaza Strip, 35
Muslim militants arrested in Gaza, *74*
Israel to give Palestinians autonomy in the West Bank, 83
Start of process to end Israeli military rule in West Bank, *92*
Bethlehem celebrates first Christmas under Palestinian rule, 111
Palmer, Arnold, 63
Panorama (television program), 33
Papandreou, Andreas, *82*, *104*
Parachini, Allan, 23
Parche, Günther, *4*
Parizeau, Jacques, 93
Parker Bowles, Camilla, 7
Patten, Chris, *82*
Pavin, Corey, 55
Pennant-Rea, Rupert, 29
Penthouse (magazine), 81
Peploe, John, 23
Peres, Shimon, 99
Pérez de Cuéllar, Javier, 35
Perez, Selena Quintanilla, 93
Perry, Fred, 14
Peru
New attack on Ecuador, 10
Fighting flares with Ecuador, *16*
Ends border fighting with Ecuador, 19
Fujimori re-elected as president, 35
Philip, Prince (Duke of Edinburgh), *68*
Philippines
Papal visit to go ahead, *4*
Successful papal visit, 7
Vietnamese boat people threatening suicide rather than undergo deportation, *26*
Imelda Marcos seeks election to Congress, 30
World Trade Center bombing suspects arrested, 32
Phipps, Jill, 15, *18*
Picasso, Pablo, *44*, *48*
Picture Post (magazine), *58*
Pile, Christopher, *98*
Playboy (magazine), 25
Pleasance, Donald, 14
Polanco, Jorge, 67
Poland
Foreign minister resigns, *6*
Ceremonies commemorate the liberation of Auswitz, 12–13
Voting puts Walesa and Kwasniewski neck and neck, *96*
Ex-communist Kwasniewski is new president, 102
Portillo, Michael, 28, 54, 88
Portugal
Centre-left party wins elections, *84*
Powell, Colin, 76, *80*, 97
Powell, Dilys, *50*
Priebke, Erich, *102*
Puccini, Giacomo, *14*

Q

Qatar
Crown prince forces father to leave country, *56*
Quayle, Dan, *16*
Québecois, Parti, 93

R

Rabin, Yitzhak, 35, 49, 66, 83, 95, 96
Rahman, Omar Abdel, 85
Rainbow Warrior II (ship), 61
Raman, Atiq, 32
Reagan, Nancy, 83
Reagan, Ronald, 83
Redwood, John, 56, 59
Reeve, Christopher, 49, 91
Reilly, Karen, 59
Religion
Pope to visit the Philippines, *4*
Pope has successful tour in the Philippines, 7
Married Anglican clergy can become Catholic priests, *14*
US Catholic priests sacked after child sexual abuse, *16*
Dr. David Hope appointed Archbishop of York, *34*
Pope's Easter message, 37
Dalai Lama names child as reincarnation of the Pachen Lama, *46*
Church of England report rejects idea of people 'living in sin', *50*
Clinton backs right for children to have religion in schools, *60*
Pope apologizes to women for Church's past discrimination, *60*
Dean of Lincoln cleared of adultery, 62
British rave priest suspended, 72
Ruling on crucifixes in every Bavarian classroom, *72*
Hindu idols in milk-drinking 'miracles', 80
Pope arrives on visit to US, *84*
Rich, Charlie, *64*
Richard, Sir Cliff, 45, 95
Richardson, Bill, 63
Riddick, Graham, 36
Riskin, Shlomo, 66
Rogers, Ginger, 41
Rolling Stones, The, 22, 72
Romania
Airbus crash kills all on board, 31
Ronay, Egon, 66
Rose, General, 6
Rotblat, Joseph, 89
Rowland, Tiny, *22*
Roxette, 20
Rugby
England beat France in Five Nations Championship, *14*
England beat Scotland in rugby Grand Slam, *26*
Will Carling sacked as England captain, 43
Will Carling reinstated as captain after apologising, *44*
First match of World Cup, *48*
England beat Australia in World Cup semi-final, 53
Rupert Murdoch signs deal, *54*
South Africa wins World Cup, 55
Rugby Union can become professional, *74*
Carling to separate from his wife, 82
Russell, Jack, 107
Russia
Russians pound Grozny in new offensive, 4
Russian forces capture Presidential Palace in Grozny, *8*
Criticized for human rights abuses in Chechnya, *14*
Roads to Grozny sealed off, *14*
Moscow politician in 'Mafia' shooting, 15
Discovery rendezvous with *Mir*, 16
Funeral of TV joualist murdered by Mafia, *22*
Commander forcasts long war with Chechnya, *28*
Forces claim capture of last Chechen stronghold, 37
Troops resume offensive in Chechnya, *46*
Thousands feared dead in earthquake, 48
Chechen rebels take hostages in hospital, 53
Chechen rebels return after using hostages as human shields, *54*
Zhirinovsky in TV orange-juice brawl, 55
Atlantis docks with *Mir* space station, *56*
Yeltsin taken to hospital with heart condition, 61
Signs trade pact with European Union, *62*
Yeltsin leaves hospital, *64*
Yeltsin returns to work, *68*
Demonstrations outside KGB headquarters, *70*
3,000-year-old Siberian preserved in ice, 72
To supply Iran with nuclear reactors, 73
Zhirinovsky assaults female MP in Russian Parliament, *78*
Kidnapper dies after bus seige ends, *90*
Treasures removed from Germany after World War II on show, *90*
Radioactive parcel planted by Chechen rebels found in park, *102*
Rwanda
Aid workers pull out of refugee camps, 18
Hutus killed as Rwandans close refugee camp, 37
Estimated 2,000 Hutus massacred, *40*
Zairean troops expel Rwandan refugees, 72

S

Saatchi, Maurice, 5
Sadat, Anwar, 57
Sailing
Australia's America's Cup contender sinks, *24*
New Zealand yacht win America's Cup, *46*
Lisa Clayton sails round world, 57
Lisa Clayton asked to substantiate record claim, *66*
Lisa Clayton's round the world record confirmed, *74*
St. Maarten
Hurricane devastates island, 76
Saldivar, Yolanda, 93
Salinas, Carlos, *26*
Salk, Jonas, *54*
Sampras, Pete, *10*, 24, 60, 78
Sanchez, Rolando, *62*
Santer, Jacques, 9
Saro-Wiwa, Ken, 93, 96
Saudi Arabia
Failure to co-operate with US in catching terrorist, 36
Possible invasion by Iraq, *70*
Iraq had plans to invade after taking Kuwait, *82*
Explosion at military establishment kills six, *98*
Saunders, Ernest, *104*
Savage, Sean, 83
Schofield, John, *68*
Schumacher, Michael, 30, 92
Science and Technology (see also Space)
New galaxy discovered, 5
Early man used coal, 16
Mummified man in Alps to go on display, *18*
'Top quark' sub-proton particle discovered, *22*
Film of dolphins attacking and killing porpoises, 25
Official status sought for Munchkin cat, 28
Senate committee wants to outlaw Internet pornography, *28*
Spread of flowering plants in Arctic, *28*
Largest Egyptian tomb yet discovered, *46*
'Super atom' predicted by Einstein is created, 61
Scientists closer to cure for baldness, *62*
Footprints of primitive man found in South Africa, *64*
Ozone hole over Antarctica widens, 67
Evidence of primitive humans found, 68
Smog in Mexico City not caused by car exhaust, 70
3,000-year-old Siberian preserved in ice, 72
Southeast Asian tigers face extinction, 78
Internet usage is 50 per cent porn, 79
Rotblat awarded Nobel Peace Prize, 89
Total eclipse of the sun visible in Asia, *92*
Breast cancer gene found, 94
Briton jailed for planting computer viruses, *98*
Scorupco, Izabella, 99
Scott, Ridley and Tony, *14*
Scripps, John Martin, 97
Secombe, Sir Harry, 45
Segers, Hans, 27, *64*
Selena, 92
Seles, Monica, *4*, 73
Serbia
Moves military supplies to Bosnia, 17
Milosevich arrives in US for peace talks, *92*
Milosevich starts peace talks with Croatia and Bosnia, 94
Signs peace plan with Croatia and Bosnia, 102
Shabazz, Quibilah Bahiya, *6*
Shapiro, Robert, 87
Shaya-Castro, Carol, 25
Shevardnadze, Eduard A., 75, 96
Shumacher, Michael, *66*
Sierra Leone
Britons held hostage by rebels are released, 36
Rebel troops surround capital, *42*
Starvation warning, *82*
Simpson, Nicole, 11, 52, *82*, 86, 87
Simpson, O.J., 11, 18, 52, *80*, 85, 86–7, 94 (see also O.J. Simpson trial)
Singapore
Barings Bank collapses: Leeson disappears, 21
Barings' office revealed it warned bank HQ of Leeson's trading, *22*
Trial of British serial killer begins, 36
Death sentence for British serial killer, 97
Leeson sentenced to six and a half years, 107
Skorochkin, Sergei, 15
Slovo, Joe, *4*, 8
Smith, Admiral Leighton, 112
Smith, Susan, 8, *60*, *62*, *64*
Snowden, Guy, 109
Solana, Javier, 106
Somalia
Former president Siad Barre dies, *4*
Marines land to oversee UN troop withdrawal, *20*
US Marines withdraw from Somalia, *22*
Somerville, Julia, 94
Souphanouvong, Prince, *6*
South Africa
Joe Slovo dies, *4*
Top police chief to stand down, *6*
State funeral of Joe Slovo, 8
Boesak embezzled funds during apartheid years, *16*
Mandela tells wife Winnie to apologize or resign, 18
Winnie Mandela's house raided for evidence of fraud and corruption, *22*
Queen to visit, 29
Winnie defiant after dismissal from government, 31
Miners crushed by runaway locomotive, *44*
Truth Commission to expose human rights abuses, *56*
Footprints of primitive man found, *64*
Man killed in clash between blacks and whites, *76*
Winnie Mandela to contest divorce proceedings, *90*
Malan arrested for massacre, 95
Venezuela wins Miss World contest, 98
Armed robbers attempt to raid boxing match, 105
Severe flooding, 113
South Korea
Over 100 killed by gas explosion, 40
Department store collapses in Seoul, *56*
Man rescued from collapsed department store after nine days, 61
Space
New galaxy discovered, 5
Discovery rendezvous with *Mir*, 16
Water in liquid form found on Mars, 32
Woodpeckers delay launch of space shuttle, 50
Atlantis docks with *Mir*, *56*
Astronomers warn of asteroid crash, *80*
Pictures of Eagle Nebula show stars being created, 94
Galileo space probe sends back information about Jupiter, 106
Spain
Prime minister denies allgations of 'dirty war' against Basques, 6
Sends gunboat to protect trawlers off coast of Canada, 25
Returns trawlers to fishing grounds off Canada, *26*
Princess Elena marries, 27
Calls for Britain to back Spain in fishing dispute, 32
British people support Canada in fishing dispute, 35
Agreement reached in Canadian fishing dispute, 36
Genuine Picassos found in flea market, *48*
Prime minister in row over phone tapping, *52*
British animal rights campaigner gored by bull is to fly home, *62*
Evidence of primitive humans found, 68
Two bankers try to blackmail King Juan Carlos, *96*
Six killed by car bomb, *108*
Spectator (magazine), 46
Spencer
Earl and Countess, *44*
Spender, Sir Stephen, 62
Spirit of Birmingham (yacht), 57
Springsteen, Bruce, 22
Sri Lanka
Tamil Tigers agree a cease-fire, *4*
People killed in Tamil attacks, *56*
Government sends troops against Tamil Tigers, *60*
Suspected Tamil suicide bomber causes explosion, *68*
Tamil Tigers resume public executions, *96*
Government forces recapture Tamil Tigers' stronghold, *106*
Stanshall, Vivian, *24*
Stephens, Sir Robert, *98*
Stevens, Derek, 53
Stone, Oliver, 110
Straw, Jack, *84*
Street-Porter, Janet, *78*
Sun Myung Moon, *94*
Sunday Times, The (newspaper), *58*
Swimming
Former Olympic coach jailed for indecent assault, *82*
Switzerland
Aga Khan to prevent wife from selling jewellery, 94

T

Tahiti
Brando's daughter commits suicide, 36
French commandos capture Greenpeace ships before nuclear tests, *76*
Taiwan
China calls for re-unification with Taiwan, 14
Tajikistan
Appeals for help after border guards fired on by Afghanistan, *34*
Tanzania
Hutu refugees flee from Burundi, *30*
Mkapa president after first multi-party elections, *102*
Tarango, Jeff, *58*
Tarantino, Quentin, 30
Taylor, Graham, *98*
Taylor-Ryan, Lee, 66
Tejada, Jaime de Marichalar Saez de, 27
Television (see also Arts and entertainment)
Red Dwarf star cleared of rape, 23
Iran bans satellite TV dishes, 36
Channel 4 gives Grade 20 per cent salary increase, *64*
Larry Hagman gets liver transplant, 73
O.J. Simpson pulls out of TV interview, 89
Tennis
Agassi beats Sampras in Australian Open, *10*
Fred Perry dies, 14
Sampras and Agassi play tennis in San Francisco street, *24*
Jeff Tarango accuses Wimbledon official of corruption, *58*
Pancho Gonzalez dies, 58
Steffi Graf wins Wimbledon ladies' singles, 58
Sampras wins third consecutive Wimbledon title, 60
Steffi Graf considering leaving Germany, *62*
Steffi Graf's father on tax charges, 66
Seles wins in comeback match, 73
Sampras beats Agassi to win US Open, 78
Teriipia, Tarita, 36
Terrorism
Trial of World Trade Center bomb-

ing suspects, *6*
Lockerbie bombing suspect freed, *8*
Suicide bomb attacks by Islamic Jihad in Israel, 10
Report claims Iran paid for terrorist activities, 11
US intelligence that Iran paid for Lockerbie, 11
Missing body in Lockerbie disaster, *14*
World Trade Center terrorist admits plot to kill President Mubarak, *16*
Japanese top policeman shot, *30*
Clinton and Major call for IRA to give up arms, *32*
World Trade Center bombing suspects arrested, 32
Suicide bombers kill seven in Gaza strip, 35
Israeli security forces shoot three Hamas fighters, 36
Saudi failure to co-operate with US in catching terrorist, *36*
Two killed in Athens bomb blast, *36*
Bomb devastates building in Oklahoma City, 38–9
US serial bomber describes motives, 41
People killed by bomb at Colombian festival, 52
Moscow fears terrorist attacks from Chechnya, 53
IRA woman found guilty of bombing but released, *56*
Four killed by Paris Metro bomb, 64
Oklahoma bombing men indicted by Grand Jury, 69
Men plead not guilty to Oklahoma bombing, *70*
Paris nail bomb explodes, 71
Hamas carries out bus bombing in Jerusalem, 72
Muslims arrested in police raids in France, 74
Shevardnadze survives car-bomb assassination attack, 75
French army guarding Channel Tunnel entrance, *78*
Unabomber manifesto published, 81
Three IRA members shot in Gibraltar condemned by European Court, 83
Sheikh Rahman guilty of terrorism in US, 85
'Sons of Gestapo' derail train in Arizona, *88*
Bomb explodes on French underground train, *90*
Bomb-making factory discovered and Arab arrested in France, *94*
Thailand
Incursion by Burmese forces, *18*
Burmese Karen guerrillas flee into, 21
Thani, Hamad Bin Khalifa al-, 56
Thatcher, Margaret, 47
Thimbleby, Harold, 79
Thomas, Kristin Scott, 41
Tibet
Tibetan Buddhism: Dalai Lama names child as reincarnation of the Pachen Lama, *46*
Tierney, Michael, *66*
Towes, Sharon, 17
Townsend, Peter, *54*
Tracey, Richard, 84
Travolta, John, 41
Tredinnick, David, 36
Trefgarne, Lord, 54
Trimble, David, 77
Trump, Ivana, 105
Tsuchiya, Masami, 44
Tudjman, Franjo, 17, *26*, *92*, 94, 102
Turkey
Rioting by Islamic Alawite sect kills four, *26*
Troops enter Iraq looking for Kurdish separatists, *28*
Pulls troops out of Northern Iraq, *40*
Troops withdraw from northern Iraq, *42*
PM resigns as coalition government falls apart, *80*
At least 64 killed by earthquake, *84*
Prime minister resigns after vote of no confidence, *90*
Turner, Lana, 57
Turner, Ted, *80*
Tyson, Mike, 19, *26*, 29, 71

U

Ukraine
Locust plague destroying crops, *62*
Ukrainian ship captain jailed for murdering stowaways, 109
Unabomber, 41, 81
United Arab Emirates
Family of Briton shows mercy to his killer, 91
United Nations
Dole wants Congressional assent for forces sent on UN peacekeeping, *6*
Croatian president requests UN troops to leave, 17
UN troop withdrawal from Somalia, 20
World Summit on Social Development opens, *24*
Wants to arrange peaceful transfer of power in Afghanistan, 25
Croatia withdraws demand for UN forces to leave, *26*
Security Council votes to maintain sanctions against Iraq, *26*
Threatens air strikes against Bosnian Serbs, *30*
UN troops taken hostage by Bosnian Serbs, 49
Most UN hostages released by Serbs, 50
More UN hostages released by Serbs, *52*
Serbs free the last UN hostages, *54*
Peacekeepers in Srebrenica threatened by Serbs, 63
Rapid Reaction Force deployed in Bosnia, 65
World Conference on Women ends, *76*, 79
Troops should withdraw from Bosnia, *80*
World leaders meet for 50th birthday of UN, 93
Reports that children are main victims of war, 109
United States
Prisoners in Florida attempt gaol break, *4*
'Pro-life' campaigner shoots people at abortion clinics, 4
Grey wolves reintroduced, 9
Rose Kennedy dies, 10
Claims that languages will die out due to spread of English, *20*
US citizens expelled from France for spying, 21
Policewoman dismissed for posing in *Playboy*, 25
Senate committee wants to outlaw Internet pornography, *28*
'VJ' Day not to be replaced by 'VP' Day, *28*
Kohl accuses US over pollution at environment conference, 32
Smoking ban in New York restaurants, 34
Bomb devastates building in Oklahoma City, 38–9
Serial bomber describes motives, 41
Search abandoned for Oklahoma bombing victims, *42*
Anonymous buyer pays £18 million for Picasso, *44*
New Zealand yacht win America's Cup, *46*
Federal building ruins in Oklahoma demolished, *48*
Gunman shot and wounded in White House grounds, 49
Dole's wife to sell shares in Disney over *Priest*, 51
Kissinger to receive honorary knighthood, *52*
Corey Pavin wins US Open golf tournament, 55
Senate blocks Clinton's nomination for Surgeon General, 55
Murder rate in New York drops to new low level, *60*
Seventh Avenue flooded, *60*
First female military academy candidate unable to take oath, 71
Unabomber manifesto published, 81
Terrorists derail train in Arizona, *88*
Farrakhan leads black men on march to Washington DC, 91
Lockerbie memorial service is boycotted by relatives, *94*
Pentagon used psychics in intelligence-gathering operations, 105
United States (disasters)
Storms and flooding in California, 6
Heatwave kills twelve in Chicago, *60*
Hundreds die in Chicago heatwave, 62
American Airline jet crash kills 147 passengers, 110
United States (economy and industry)
Threatens Japan with sanctions over automobile market, 35
Reaches agreement with Japan on automotive trade, *56*
New president of Disney, *70*
Launch of Microsoft Windows 95, 72
Turner Broadcasting System sold to Time Warner, *80*
United States (education)
Clinton backs right for children to have religion in schools, *60*
United States (finance)
Trade links with Mexico threatened, *4*
US not to support peso, *8*
Clinton authorises rescue plan for Mexican economy, *10*
Europe blocks US in peso crisis, 14
New budget criticized, *16*
Democrats halt budget measure, 22
Record trade deficit, *28*
International decline in dollar gone far enough, *40*
Dollar soars, *70*
Clinton in budget dispute with Congress, 98
United States (foreign policies)
Dole wants Congressional assent for forces sent on UN peacekeeping, *6*
Lifts sanctions and makes trade pact with North Korea, *8*
US embassy shows dissent about talks with Bosnian Serbs, *10*
Intelligence that Iran paid for Lockerbie, 11
Human rights abuses by China and Russia criticized, *14*
Trade war with China looms, 15
Clinton meets Gerry Adams at White House, 26
White House blocks Conoco oilfield deal with Iran, *26*
King asks Congress to write off Jordan's national debt, *30*
Clinton and Major call for IRA to give up arms, *32*
Vietnam War strategist admits he was wrong, 34
Sanctions to Japan threatened over automobile market, 35
Iran accused of trying to develop nuclear weapons, *42*
Kissinger to receive honorary knighthood, *52*
Diplomatic relations with Vietnam to be restored, *60*
US prepared to send helicopters to Gorazde, 62
Equipment sent to Gulf after warnings of possible invasions by Iraq, *70*
US wins Bosnia cease-fire, 85
United States (health)
New way to destroy cancer, *6*
Clinton's controversial choice of Surgeon General, *18*
Judge rejects tobacco companies' 'free will' plea, *20*
Patients to be injected with bone marrow from baboons, *20*
New cancer gun, 29
Doctor suspended for cutting off patient's toe, *62*
Drug AZT not effective in full-blown AIDS, *70*
New York municipal hospital system should be abolished, *70*
United States (justice)
Trial of O.J. Simpson (see O.J. Simpson trial)
Malcolm X's daughter arrested for hiring hitman, *6*
Trial of World Trade Centre bombing suspects, *6*
Mother accused of drowning sons, 8
World Trade Center terrorist pleads guilty to plot to kill President Mubarak, *16*
Colin Ferguson guilty of Long Island Railroad shootings, *18*
Mike Tyson has release date, 19
Judge rejects tobacco companies' 'free will' plea, *20*
Man gets 25 years for stealing pizza, 23
Neo-Nazis charged with murder of parents and brother, 23
Long Island Rail Road murderer sentenced, *28*
Mike Tyson released from jail, 29
World Trade Center bombing suspects arrested in Philippines, 32
Killer Nicky Ingram executed, 33
Brothers accused of conspiring with Oklahoma bomb suspect, 40
Sixteen Bronx policemen arrested, *42*
British women on trial for conspiring to murder attorney, *56*
Death penalty sought for man accused of Oklahoma bombing, *60*
Woman who drowned sons competent to stand trial, *60*
Prostitute found with Hugh Grant seeks a trial, *62*
Woman found guilty of drowning sons, *62*
Mother who drowned sons gets life sentence, *64*
Heidi Fleiss guilty of tax evasion and money laundering, 69
Oklahoma bombing men indicted by Grand Jury, 69
Men plea not guilty to Oklahoma bombing, *70*
Police chief files lawsuit against Los Angeles, *80*
Sheikh Rahman guilty of terrorism, 85
Retrial of Menendez brothers for parents' murder, 88
Fan convicted of murder of singer Selena Perez, 93
British women jailed for plotting to kill US Attorney for Oregon, *106*
United States (politics)
Marion Barry's political comeback, 5
New Congress dominated by Republicans, 5
Newt Gingrich attacked for agreeing book deal, *8*
Clinton's State of the Union address, *10*
Quayle drops out of 1996 presidential race, *16*
Native American senator switches to Republicans, *22*
Clinton meets Gerry Adams at White House, 26
Gingrich's wife does not want him to be president, *68*
Woman admits affair with Gingrich, *68*
Colin Powell undecided whether to run for presidency, 76
Gingrich to be investigated over book deal, *80*
Jesse Jackson leads attacks against Colin Powell, *80*
Nancy talks of Ronald Reagan's Alzheimer's, 83
Colin Powell will not run for president, 97
United States (religion)
Catholic priests sacked after child sexual abuse, *16*
Clinton backs right for religion in schools, *60*
Pope arrives on 5-day visit, *84*
United States (science and technology)
'Top quark' sub-proton particle discovered, *22*
Fast foods cause more pollution than buses in Los Angeles, 24
'Super atom' predicted by Einstein is created, 61
United States (space)
New galaxy discovered, 5
Discovery rendezvous with *Mir*, 16
Water in liquid form found on Mars, 32
Woodpeckers delay launch of space shuttle, 50
Atlantis docks with *Mir*, *56*
US astronomers warn of asteroid crash, *80*
Pictures of Eagle Nebula show stars being created, 94
United States (sports) see each individual sport

V

van Hille, Phil, 25
Vatican City
Announcement on papal visit to Philippines, *4*
Venezuela
Miss Venezuela wins Miss World contest, 98
Verity, Anthony, 74
Vietnam
Repatriation of boat people, *20*
Boat people in Philippines threatening suicide rather than return, *26*
US Vietnam War strategist admits he was wrong, *34*
Boat people in Hong Kong riot against repatriation, 50
Diplomatic relations with US to be restored, *60*

W

Wakeham, Lord, *72*
Waldegrave, William, *40*, *50*, 54
Walesa, Lech, *96*, 102
Walker, Mr. Justice, *34*
Walker, Patric, *88*
Wallace, Angus, 48
Walton, Philip, 83
Washington Post (newspaper), 81
Wells, Paul, 60
West, Frederick, 5, *94*
West, Rosemary, 84, *88*, *94*
White, David, 79
Whitehead, Patricia and David, 47
Wieman, Carl, 61
Wiesel, Elie, 12
Wiest, Dianne, 30
Wiggins, Jerry, *48*
Wilde, Oscar, *18*
William, Prince, *72*
Williams, Anthony, *46*
Williams, Jerry Dewayne, 23
Williams, Willy, *80*
Wilson, Andrew, *20*
Wilson, Harold (Lord Wilson), 48
Wise, Dennis, *16*, *26*
Woods, Peter, *28*
Woolley, David and Josh, *58*
World Conference on Women (China), *76*, 79
World Trade Center, *6*, *16*, 32
Wylie, Andrew, *4*

Y

Yeltsin, Boris
Aims to bring peace to Chechnya, 4
Taken to hospital with heart condition, 61
Leaves hospital, *64*
Returns to work, *68*
Says Russian troops will not take orders from NATO, *90*
Holds talks with Clinton over peace in Bosnia, 92
Rushed to hospital with heart problems, *92*
Addresses UN birthday celebrations, 93
Leaves hospital for rest cure, *104*
Dealt blow by communist success in poll, 110
York, Margaret, 70, 87
Young America (yacht), *46*
Yousef, Ramzi Ahmed, 32
Yugoslavia (former)
Those responsible for ethnic cleansing, *24*
Dissident Milovan Djilas dies, *36*
Tribunal names Karadzic and Mladic as war crimes suspects, *40*

Z

Zaire
Ebola virus outbreak, 44
Ebola virus deaths rise, *48*
Troops expel Rwandan refugees, 72
Zedillo, Ernesto, 88
Zeroual, Liamine, 99
Zhirinovsky, Vladimir, 55, *78*
Zyuganov, Genardy, 110

PICTURE CREDITS

b= bottom, c= centre, l= left, r= right, t= top

ALLSPORT:
89t

ASSOCIATED PRESS:
83tr, 88t, 89cl, 91cr, 95c, 95b, 99tr, 104br, 105c, 106tr, 106bl, 107c, 107br, 110c, 110b, 111bc, 112tl, 112b, 113tl, 113bl, 113tr, 114bl, 114bcr, 114tcr, 115bcl, 115br, 115tr

COLORIFIC:
115tcl

COLORSPORT:
47br, 53b, 56c,

HULTON DEUTSCH/REUTER
S: 6b, 8cr, 11, 14b, 18br, 21tl, 21cr, 24br, 27bl, 31, 36t, 50cl, 55tr, 71bl, 74br, 84cr, 85tr, 114tcl

FRANK LANE PICTURE AGENCY: 78bl, 109tr

LONDON FEATURES INTERNATIONAL:
47cr, 65tl, 65tcl, 90b, 97br, 104tl, 105cl, 111bl, 111br, 111cr

REX FEATURES:
6t, 7tl, 7tr, 7c, 7cr, 12, 12/3, 13, 15t, 15c, 17c, 18c, 19br, 22, 23t, 23bl, 24t, 25t, 25cr, 25bl, 26t, 27cl, 27br, 28br, 29tl, 29tr, 29br, 30, 32tr, 32bc, 33, 34, 35t, 35bl, 36br, 36bc, 37t, 37cr, 38, 38/9, 39, 40bc, 40br, 41, 42t, 42b, 43, 44t, 45, 46, 47tr, 47tl, 47cl, 48cr, 48bl, 49cr, 49bl, 50cr, 51tr, 51c, 51br, 52t, 52c, 54t, 54cr, 55tc, 55bl, 55br, 56t, 56br, 57, 58, 59tr, 59tl, 61cr, 61b, 62b, 63tl, 63tr, 65tr, 65br, 65bl, 66c, 66b, 67tr, 67cr, 68c, 68bl, 68br, 69tl, 69tr, 71br, 72, 73tl, 73cr, 73bl, 74bl, 75cl, 75br, 76tl, 76br, 77, 78br, 79cl, 79cr, 80, 81tl, 81cr, 82tl, 82cr, 83cl, 83cr, 84tl, 84br, 85tl, 85bc, 86tr, 86cr, 86b, 87tl, 87tcl, 87cl, 87c, 87b, 87tr, 87crt, 87cr, 87crb, 87br, 88br, 89bl, 90tl, 91tl, 91tc, 91bl, 92c, 92b, 93tr, 93br, 94tc, 94br, 95cl, 95tr, 96tr, 96tl, 96br, 97bl, 98, 99tc, 99c, 99bl, 100t, 100b, 100/1t, 100/1b, 101tl, 101c, 101bc, 101tr, 101crt, 101crb, 101br, 102, 103, 104bl, 105bl, 105br, 106c, 107tr, 107bl, 112tr, 114tl, 114tr, 114bcl, 115tl, 115tcr, 115tcb

FRANK SPOONER PICTURES/GAMMA:
1l, 1tr, 3, 4, 5, 7br, 8t, 8br, 9, 10, 14tr, 15cr, 16, 17tr, 17tl, 17bl, 18tr, 19tl, 20, 21bl, 23br, 25cl, 26br, 27tr, 28t, 29cl, 35cr, 37cl, 40tr, 42cr, 44b, 48t, 49t, 50tl, 51tl, 52b, 53t, 54bl, 59br, 60, 61t, 62t, 63b, 64, 66t, 67tl, 68t, 69br, 70, 71c, 73br, 74tl, 75tr, 76tr, 76cl, 78tl, 78tr, 79t, 81tr, 81bl, 82br, 83tl, 84cl, 85br, 86cl, 87tcr, 88cl, 89cr, 91bc, 92t, 93tl, 93c, 94tl, 94cl, 96cl, 97t, 99br, 100/1c, 110t, 111tl, 111tr

TRH PICTURES:
19bl, 32cr

Dorling Kindersley would like to thank the following for editorial assistance:
Fran Baines, Philippa Baker, Edda Bohnsack, Claire Calman, Luci Collings, Maggie Crowley, Miranda Fellows, Sue George, Maxine Lewis, Sue Leonard, Lorrie Mack, Anna Milner, Christine Murdock, Flora Pereira